Compromise Formations

For Bob—
with affection
Nina

Compromise Formations

Current Directions
in Psychoanalytic Criticism

---

edited by Vera J. Camden
for the Center for Literature and Psychoanalysis
Department of English, Kent State University

KENT STATE UNIVERSITY PRESS
Kent, Ohio, and London, England

Library of Congress Catalog Card Number 88-28464
ISBN 0-87338-380-X (cloth)
ISBN 0-87338-381-8 (paper)
Manufactured in the United States of America

Published by The Kent State University Press in association with the Center for
Literature and Psychoanalysis, Department of English, Kent State University

"Redefining the Revenant: Guilt and Sibling Loss in Guntrip and Freud" by
Peter L. Rudnytsky has been reprinted with permission of *The Psychoanalytic
Study of the Child,* copyright 1988 by Yale University Press.

"Gastro-exorcism: J.-K. Huysmans and the Anatomy of Conversion" by Carol
A. Mossman has been reprinted with permission of the *Romanic Review,* copyright 1988 by the Trustees of Columbia University.

Library of Congress Cataloging-in-Publication Data

Compromise formations : current directions in psychoanalytic criticism
  / edited by Vera J. Camden for the Center for Literature and
Psychoanalysis, Department of English, Kent State University.
      p.   cm.
   Papers selected from the Fourth International Conference on
Literature and Psychology at Kent State University, Aug. 7-9, 1987.
   Includes bibliographies and index.
   ISBN 0-87338-380-X (alk. paper). ISBN 0-87338-381-8 (pbk. : alk. paper) ∞
   1. Psychoanalysis and literature—Congresses.   2. Literature—19th
century—History and criticism—Congresses.   3. Literature—20th
century—History and criticism—Congresses.   4. Literature—
Psychology—Congresses.   5. Symbolism in literature—Congresses.
6. Criticism—History—20th century—Congresses.   I. Camden, Vera
J.   II. International Conference on Literature and Psychology (4th :
1987 : Kent State University)   III. Kent State University. Center
for Literature and Psychoanalysis.
PN56.P92C66   1989
801'.92—dc19   88-28464
                                                                      CIP

British Cataloging-in-Publication data are available.

Contents

Acknowledgments

This volume, the conference from which it sprang, and the Center for Literature and Psychoanalysis at Kent State University all owe their conception to the vision of Dr. Robert Bamberg, Director of the Center, to whom I extend my sincere gratitude. I also wish to thank Dr. Peter Rudnytsky for his generous and experienced editorial assistance. Appreciation is due to Dr. Connie Doyle for typing and making sense of the manuscript and to Dr. Mark Bracher for helpful comments. Special thanks also to Dr. Jeanne West and Julia Morton of the Kent State University Press for their diligent overseeing of this project, and to Dr. John Hubbell, Director of the Press, for his support. Finally, I wish to thank Drs. Norman Holland, David Willbern, and Catherine Portuges, each of whom helped to bring the Fourth International Conference on Literature and Psychology (August 7-9, 1987) to Kent State, for which we remain very grateful.

Introduction

Vera J. Camden

It is a pleasure to introduce this volume of selected papers from the Fourth International Conference on Literature and Psychology (August 7-9, 1987) hosted at Kent State University, as it commemorates an important gathering of psychoanalytic thinkers from around the world and attempts to capture some of the tremendous interest and energy engendered by the conference. It is doubly gratifying to present this collection because it is the first volume to spring from the varied conferences being hosted by the Center for Literature and Psychoanalysis in the Department of English at Kent State, under the generous support of an Academic Challenge Grant from the State of Ohio. With its unique integration of training in psychoanalytic practice with on-going research in literary criticism and critical theory, the center's program unfolds, in its design and implementation, the growing rapprochement between psychoanalysis and the university.

In drawing these papers together, I have not attempted, however, to enforce a synthesis within a field which takes as its operating premise the critic's, and the clinician's, role as analyst. Indeed, if there is one thing psychoanalysis has taught us, it is that our attempts at unifying the productions of the human mind often disguise strategies of control. What this collection achieves, at best, is a "compromise formation." I use the phrase to invoke its origins in Freudian symptomatology because it strikes me that the psychoanalytic notion of the neurotic symptom as a compromise which expresses drive and defense simultaneously provides a felicitous formulation of the critical enterprise.

The symptom simultaneously disguises and reveals unconscious desire. Even as it exposes some truth of the unconscious, it displaces that truth onto a false representation. The critic, like the analyst, attempts to employ "technical methods of filling up the gaps in the phenomena of our consciousness, . . . [to] infer a number of processes which are themselves 'unknowable' and interpolate them in those that are conscious to us" (Freud 23:196–97). Our attempts to recover and interpret the unconscious material gaping within conscious discourse are themselves riddled with "unaccountable" holes, the traces of unconscious intention (Forrester 5). Conscious discourse, language itself, becomes "symptomatic" of the "compromises between the conscious and the unconscious" (Freud 9:86, 87), expressing both drive and defense. It is the compromised and compromising character of human language which I take as the starting point for this collection. If we are positioned between conscious and unconscious knowledge of ourselves, it is our language which both denies and discloses this state to us.

The essays collected here attempt to describe, analyze, and in some way resolve the experience of the gaps in our consciousness created by this in-between state. Psychoanalysis and literature teach us to tolerate the separation in our being by the production of meaning in the language which in its structure both enforces our alienation and affords us our only link to ourselves, others, and the world. It is in this sense that all of our productions within language are compromise formations: symptoms which constitute our existence in language and which bring at least the illusion of integration, recovery, and understanding of our condition through an analysis of its representations.

Each of the writers in this volume is, accordingly, concerned with the place of the unconscious in the determination of the human subject and its representations. Whether the approach is primarily clinical or literary, each identifies and analyzes the anguish of the incomplete self—a self which looks to construct, identify, regain, or even deny meaning. A crucial difference emerges, however, among these authors as to how the experience of human alienation and the quest for identity is to be analyzed, interpreted, and treated. Some would suggest, after Jacques Lacan, that the task of analysis is to recognize the illusion of the unitary self and to reconcile the individual to that state. Others contend that the task of analysis should be to recover, by the transference relationship, the lost unity missing in childhood and reflected in adult object-relations. The essays here offer not so much a resolution to opposing positions as a fuller articulation of the space they occupy. In doing so, they traverse pathways which at times lead to meaningful convergences. Bringing representative readings from Lacanian and object-relations theory into a compromise formation permits, at least in this volume, the fluidity of discussion which has characterized the discoveries of psychoanalysis since Freud's earliest experiments. The collected essays are not, therefore, grouped according to strict methodology but rather along a chain of association linking one essay into the next. Such an ordering preserves, I hope, the dynamic of exchange which directed the conference from which these papers are taken and which continues to direct the on-going research, teaching, conferences, and psychoanalytic projects sponsored by the Center for Literature and Psychoanalysis at Kent State University.

Robert Silhol's essay clarifies, from a Lacanian perspective, the paradox of language: that the fundamental separation between word and thing, signifier and signified in language itself signifies the fundamental split between the subject and the object world. Yet the human subject in language as in the world *must* forge a link, however illusory, in order to attain "meaning" in existence. Silhol's essay offers a foundation— indeed, a rationale—for our preoccupation with the self in both literature and psychoanalysis. In our predicament as speaking subjects, we sense "with Lacan, after Freud, how fundamentally unacceptable this notion of gap, of disruption, is for us." Our language as critics, artists, and psychoanalysts rushes in to fill the gaps even as we recognize that our attempts to forge meaningful links—identifications—ultimately accent the impossibility of fulfillment. Language, by its very structure (the word does not equal the thing; the sign does not equal the idea), expresses the human being's incomplete status as a subject and his or her separation from the world. At the same time, language paradoxically enables the subject to know, to describe, in short to constitute a meaningful subjectivity in the world. Psychoanalysis is at once the subject and the object of its own discourse. Like language, it rushes in to fill the lack left by our lost, fantasmatic memory of unity while it acknowledges and describes the illusions we create in order to recover that lack.

The literal recovery of a lost, primordial memory becomes the basis— both narrative and theoretical—of Peter Rudnytsky's account of Harry Guntrip's analysis with D. W. Winnicott. In line with the object-relational theorists he espouses, Rudnytsky's recognition of the gap exposed in the compromises of our language is finally more developmental than ontological. Feelings of anguished separation do not so much signal a fundamental lack in our being as recall infantile experiences of deprivation and abandonment. The therapeutic actions of the transference aim at the reconstruction of an integrated self. The psychoanalytical cure is not, as Silhol suggested, in the recognition of the lack, the fragmentation at the core of our being—or non-being (our "self" constituted in the Other)—but in the overcoming of lack. Winnicott's interpretation of Guntrip's bleak memories of his mother witnesses the power of the transference: "The gap is not you forgetting mother, but mother forgetting you, and now you've relived it with me." However, Guntrip's memory of vacancy, of the "faceless depersonalized mother" symptomatically re-covers the real gap in his memory: the amnesia over the death of his brother, Percy. For in dream memory Percy emerges as a double of the patient, Harry Guntrip himself. Rudnytsky takes Guntrip's dream of standing "with a double of myself" as a kind of final filling of the gap in memory. It is in Guntrip's grieving over the ghosts of the past and, crucially, in the breaking down of distinctions between self and other, or "between interpsychic and intrapsychic relations," that he becomes reconciled to all his ghosts and doubles.

The psychoanalytical cure through the transference love so dramatically recounted in Guntrip's narrative receives contrasting consideration by Frederick Wyatt and Jan Ackerman. Each takes up the question of literature in psychoanalysis: Wyatt in the contemporary context of his own analytical practice, and Ackerman in the historical reconstruction of Jung's "religious crush" on Freud—a transference performed in part through their correspondence about Jensen's *Gradiva*. The literature which stands at the origins of Freud's paradigmatic discoveries in psychoanalysis can, in the analytic encounter, fill the space between analysand and analyst.

Wyatt's example of a young man's radical isolation—broken through an identification with Milton's Satan—points to the power of poetic language as a shared "third voice" in the analytic transference. The poem accomplishes what a well-reasoned, singular interpretation may not. It speaks from within a shared cultural discourse into which both speakers are born and by which both are "read." Literature helps express and resolve a classical transference. In contrast, Ackerman finds in the passionate exchange between Freud and Jung about Jensen's *Gradiva* Freud's remarkable inability to analyze his own implication in the language of transference love. In Freud's evasion of the uncanny and fantastic reappearance of Gradiva in the real woman Zoe, Ackerman sees an inability to acknowledge fully that love is always fantasy: an imaginary substitution for a real lack. Freud's need to retain scientific mastery over the material brought to him by analysis finally overran his capacity to recognize the truth of the fantasy of "Gradiva *redivivia*."

For Ellie Ragland-Sullivan, it is in fact the "language of *fantasm*" in the prose of James Joyce which constructs nothing less than the artist's very subjectivity. In her essay on the "singularity" of Joyce's language, Ragland-Sullivan introduces the crucial distinction between the classical Freudian notion of the symptom as the manifest "substitute" for the unconscious sexual drive and the Lacanian rethinking of that definition. Lacan redefines Freud's notion of the symptom as a compromise formation, a compromise between the signifier and the signified. It is language of the symptom, verbally uttered or enacted in the body, which "slips" beneath the conscious discourse of the subject, disguising and revealing her or his anguished "lack of being." For Joyce, however, the language of the symptom neither symbolizes unconscious desire nor mediates between self and Other so much as it functions as a kind of ritual refabrication of the self; the symptom *becomes* the self. Joyce's writing, notably in *Finnegans Wake,* reveals, in Lacan's terminology, an ego structure which has all but lost its ability to create meaningful substitutions between signifiers and which is desperately trying to stave off its unmediated gaze into the gap—the "hole in the Other"—by the production of a seemingly infinite metonymy. Far from the symptom slipping *under* Joyce's discourse, here, as Ragland-Sullivan stresses, Joyce *is* the symptom: he is his language. Joyce's prose partakes of what Lacan identifies as the obsessive's need to erect language as a border or fortress against the Other and against the encroaching "sterility of psychotic speech where there is no distance," while at the same time, his symptom is, like the hysteric's (and the mystic's), writ large in the blindness of his flesh.

Such Lacanian linking of metaphor with corporal experience finds enactment in Diane Richard-Allerdyce's analysis of the peculiarly feminine subjectivity of the *Diary of Anaïs Nin.* In Nin's metaphor for creativity in the act of childbirth, Richard-Allerdyce argues, the feminine subject's awareness of lack and her inextricable tie to the Other in some ways privilege her over the male subject. She is less prone to the fantasy of an ego unity or "wholeness" which the masculine identification with the phallus perpetuates and projects. Richard-Allerdyce shows that for Nin the striving after sexual union provides a metaphorical tie with the

Other and a reaching through the Other—beyond the body to a knowledge of the "Real." The feminine subject, like Lacan's mystic, reaches
"something of One"—in experience if not knowledge. Without the en-
cumbering identification with the symbolic phallus, she recognizes lack
and uncovers the *jouissance* which *goes beyond.* Nin forcefully posits
the woman's creative position: "I do not delude myself as man does, that
I create in proud isolation. . . . Woman is not deluded. . . . She must
create that unity which man first destroyed by his proud consciousness."

In Virginia Blum's analysis of L. P. Hartley's *The Go-Between,* the
child becomes not the metaphorical creation of woman's peculiar *jouissance* but instead represents—rather as Nin's proud male progenitor—
the phallic bridge between the gap in the sexual relation. Here, the child
"joins in the conversation" to bespeak the impossibility of sexual relation based, as all language, on the male position. The child who should
be the fruit of sexual union instead "reveals the very space of difference it
is bound to mystify. . . . [I]ts unifying function belies the insuperable
gap it traverses." Leo, the child of Hartley's novel, embraces his role as
sexual liaison—"I volunteered to fill the gap"—but his function as
"phallus," the linking agent, is ultimately as self-negating as Lacan's
symbolic phallus which finally "comes" to represent lack. For Blum the
child is no metaphor for *beyond* but is illustrative of a universal predicament; he is the messenger of a language into which he is inextricably
webbed and of which he is a master. He is caught between.

It is not the space between the sexes but that between matter, mind,
and spirit which controls the religious fantasies of J.-K. Huysmans. According to Carol Mossman, the very orifices of the human body take on a
threatening function for Huysmans, inviting an incubuslike visitation
and impregnation in his "anatomy of conversion" from *A rebours.*
Huysmans's fantastic constructs reach a remarkable if nearly psychotic
apprehension of the correlation between the "fissures" in the mind,
body, and soul. His obsessions with bodily apertures and alimentary
processes make it easy to diagnose his pre-Oedipal fixations and castration anxiety. But it is in Huysmans's fantastic deconstruction of the
body in the very language of his illness in *A rebours* that his text becomes
an instancing of the inextricable bonding of the flesh in metaphoric
elaborations. It almost seems as if Huysmans's text is designated to stage
Lacan's metaphor of castration as signifying a lack in being. The dread
of "puncture and penetration translates into a discourse which is riddled
with holes, scars, orifices, and wounds being sutured up." It is through

these gaps—as Freud's Dr. Schreber feared—that the divine and the demonic enter. Penetration is both courted and feared.

From her work with contemporary psychotics in a clinical setting,
Nancy Blake demonstrates that the loss of boundaries and the experience
of "depersonalization" by which the self is "evacuated" can engender a
language which does approach an articulation of what Lacan saw as the
"hole in the Other." Blake recognizes an overlap between the language
of the clinic and the language of creativity in modern poetics. The unmasking of the unitary self so central to modern poetry (notably Wallace
Stevens) has all along, she argues, been the "truth" of the psychosis. The
truth of poetry—like that of the symptom—lies not in language itself
but in the subject's separation from the world. Quoting William
Faulkner, Blake observes that the word "is just a shape to fill a lack."
The "I speak" of modern poetry, like the psychotic symptom, affirms a
temporary presence in language while unmasking absence in the world.
Blake identifies in the feminine subject in Stevens's "The Idea of Order
at Key West" a kind of creativity which understands the absence at the
heart of all representation. In this poem, the "substitution of a feminine
persona for the father of mankind [Adam]" in the act of creating proposes a type of creation that is not unilateral but reciprocal. "If the singer creates, . . . she is created by her world." Like Richard-Allerdyce,
Blake observes that the feminine figure experiences and knows the desire
of the Other in her desire; her creativity is always already contingent.
Here is no fantasy of self-sufficiency.

In a similar gesture of unmasking the fragile construction of the self,
Elise Miller's analysis of Maxine Hong Kingston's *The Woman Warrior*
uses the central insights of object relations to understand the dispersal of
the author in the autobiographical "relation." Turning like Blake and
Richard-Allerdyce to the figure of the feminine creator, Miller employs
the metaphor of birthing and mothering to figure the creation of the
autobiographical self. But this is, once again, "more" than the construction which emerges from traditional castration anxiety. Metaphors for
human creativity posit in language a relation to the mother, a relation
which acknowledges separation and lack in the construction of the self
from amongst the fragments of the past. Miller turns to the pre-Oedipal
configurations of object-relation theorists to provide insight into the
"selves" of Kingston's chronicle of a California childhood. Kingston's
narrative self is constructed through telling the stories of "m/Others."
The central dilemma of her text is the dilemma of infancy: "the longing

for symbiotic union as it competes with a desire for an independent, separate self." Like Rudnytsky, Miller understands our separation from the self and Other as rooted in developmental disturbances. But she points out that Kingston's narrative is infused with the fragility of that self. Integration is the goal of narrative as autobiographical reconstruction, yet the "I" is no less transitory and unstable for all of its aspiring to a secure center. Indeed, the terms of Kingston's narrative explorations of the self are reminiscent of Huysmans. The processes of internalizing—of eating and expelling, of merging and identification, separation and annihilation—all conjure the primitive, complex anxieties of finding a fusion for the fragmented self. And like Huysmans, Kingston's preoccupations thinly disguise how the language of her narrative must "establish a relationship with" or a border against madness. Brave Orchid's story of the child without an anus, who can take in but cannot expel, partakes of the same terrifying fantasies of "suture" in *A rebours* in which the attempt to close up the spaces in the body only encase within it diabolical filth.

Scenes of infantile abandonment and annihilation provide Jeffrey Berman with the textual "crevices" through which to interpret an unconscious structure of repetition compulsion in Hardy's *Jude the Obscure.* The scenes of infanticide and suicide, usually avoided by critics in this novel, offer a figure of childhood terror which captures the despair of Hardy's characterization. Little Father Time, the enigmatic, wizened child at the boundaries of the novel, becomes not just the allegorical figure ignored by critics but takes on a crucial reality when viewed in terms of early object relations; his "real self show[s] through the crevices" of his presentation in the novel. Morbid and obsessive, he recognizes the despair of human existence in nature. The self of Father Time is, like Guntrip's doppelgänger, the "lost object" of his parents' own psychic past. The absence of his real mother and the deprivation inflicted by his stepmother, Sue Bridehead, swamp this strange creature into acting out his despair in the double murder of his half-brother and sister, and in his own self-murder. His violent end is a final grasp at a fusion, achieved only in death.

Berman takes this scene as an entry into the repetition compulsion enacted through generations of bad parenting. Neither Jude nor Sue can nurture their children any more than they can truly care for their own needs. Cycles of moral and psychological masochism and sadism drive Hardy's novel even as they define his fictional world. Sue and Jude "seem to be one person split in two." They play out both sides of the "pain-inducing/pain-suffering object relationship." The intrapsychic conflict is projected onto the interpsychic conflict and can only result in a struggle, to the death, within and without the self.

It is through a similar collapse of character into "intrapsychic constructs" that David Willbern sees Shakespeare's *Rape of Lucrece* as not so much a "narrative of rape" as a "fantasy of violation." Precisely by extending the allegorical tradition of the *psychomachia* against which the dramatic poem was written, Willbern analyzes the poem's actions and characters as a "circulating flux of desire." Like Jude and Sue, who are caught in the sadomasochistic compulsion of their psychological legacy, Lucrece and Tarquin become, under Willbern's scheme, inseparable aspects of a trajectory of desire. But that trajectory is broken precisely at the point of consummation. The act of rape which is missing from the narrative of the poem becomes the gap in the text which points, like Blum's "insuperable gap" between the sexes, to the impossibility of sexual union. The poem is not, according to Willbern's scheme, "about" rape but about "the before-and-after" design. Between that before and after, the absent present becomes a "fecund interval," a space which separates yet connects desire and gratification in the illusory present of *writing* character.

By their examinations of contemporary film, Andrew Gordon and Terrence Holt bring psychoanalysis out of writing into an examination of twentieth-century popular culture. I conclude this collection with these two essays because they provide, as contrasting analyses of popular media, a sense of the kinds of insights yielded by object-relations and Lacanian theory as psychoanalysis looks at image production in culture.

Andrew Gordon's analysis of the paranoid fantasies dramatized in Steven Spielberg's *Duel* draws from object-relations theories of pre-Oedipal development to highlight how the intrapsychic conflict of the hero, David Mann, is projected onto the nightmare landscape of his world. Mann's rear-end torment (while he is sealed in his Plymouth sedan) by a menacing truck, displays the persecuting imagoes of both parents. Gordon sees a universal challenge in Mann's struggle against this projection of the split-off and ultimately repudiated introjects of his psyche. "Man" must expel the intrusive tormentors, the "personal demons," of his humanity by the kind of stark confrontation and duel to the death visualizd by David Mann's ordeal. It is man's self, preserved and victorious, which emerges from this *psychomachia* enacted along the American highway.

Like Gordon, Terrence Holt identifies the unconscious fantasies of anal penetration—both dreaded and courted—in current films of anxious heroism. Holt's paper on science fiction stories of alien invasion is indebted to Lacan for its unfolding of the unconscious structure which directs overt political strategies. His paper is doubly suggestive, however, for its determination to set psychoanalysis in conversation with current political discourse, and, conversely, to accept the challenge to psychoanalysis by the political conscious. Holt's critique of current political debate offers areas for future psychoanalytic criticism of culture and cultural productions. He demonstrates that beneath the overt indictments of exploitation and colonialism of the alien invasion story there frequently lies a repressed structure of sexual anxiety which subverts conscious narrative strategy and reinscribes archaic systems of Oedipal hierarchy. Explicit political stances—such as those suggested in the companion films *Alien* and *Aliens*—finally resolve themselves into anxieties over the female Other who must always remain monstrously vacant in a world constructed around the fantasy of phallic sufficiency. Here behind the political futurism of the science fiction tale lurks a consoling yet totalizing nostalgia.

By highlighting the unconscious in the political position, Holt is not abandoning the political "agenda" in the current critical scene. His critique of the peculiar amalgamation in, for instance, the figure of Warrant Officer Ripley (*Alien* and *Aliens*), of popular "women's liberation" and masculinist fantasies of heroic competency leads to one major point: the protection of phallic armor (the massive forklift which literally encases her) conferred on Ripley to supplement her lack is an "apotropaic response to the insufficiency of the subject." This response is of a piece, as it were, with the political stance which attempts to use totalizing systems to "scare away" the influence of the body and to master narratives of history. Such systems, unconscious of their own psychic structure, are all too readily reinscribed in the most archaic Oedipal hierarchies and condemn us, finally, to a prolonged duel for mastery.

Norman Holland's "Brainy Afterword" proposes a kind of radical breakthrough in the contemporary history of psychoanalysis and is important in its "futuristic" divergence from some of the terms of discussions so far. Yet Holland offers a final compromise to the present volume. Hoping to cut through the debate reflected in the essays introduced above, into the scientific calm of a "fourth" phase in psychoanalysis, Holland incorporates new research into the physiology of the brain into psychoanalytic theories of development. Crucial to the point Holland makes about the relation of current brain research to literary criticism is the conviction that theories of language and culture must take into account the direct environmental influences on brain development in both the child and the adult. Holland's call to literary critics and psychoanalysts is in many ways an echo of Freud's early research in "A Project for a Scientific Psychology," which proposed an understanding of the psychological through a dissection of the somatic. "We will," Holland argues, "be able to trace psychological concepts as physiological things: anxiety or aggression as neurotransmitters; repetition compulsion as the sum of our well-worn neural pathways; cultural codes and identity as structures in the brain." Holland heralds an unprecedented confluence of all the sciences of the mind which may yield, through psychoanalysis, a unique compromise between the "hard" sciences and art.

Psychoanalysis *is* the sublimate science of the mind. It promises some relief from the symptom yet becomes, in all of its history, schools, applications, divisions, and distortions, as much a symptomatic language as any of our obsessions. The symptom *is* the voice of the unconscious which speaks through the gaps in our conscious discourse. The critical awareness of the symptomatology in all our discourse should preclude the mastery of the overtly clinical eye, a psychoanalytic master discourse, while it should also belie the literary critic's interpretive mastery of the material of culture. What I have attempted to compile in this volume, then, is a product itself symptomatic of a desire to produce a text that can at once discharge the contradition and controversy within the discourse of applied psychoanalysis, while at the same time defend the inevitable "family" resemblances which the bonding of historical conflict guarantees.

Works Cited

Freud, Sigmund. *The Standard Edition of the Complete Psychological Works of Sigmund Freud*. Ed. and trans. James Strachey. 24 vols. London: Hogarth, 1953–74.
Forrester, John. *Language and the Origins of Psychoanalysis*. New York: Columbia UP, 1980.

"Me Jane, You Tarzan": On Meaning

Robert Silhol

What do we actually do when we speak, or write? We produce sounds—
phonemes, morphemes—which amount to words, and these words are
sometimes written down. We therefore replace objects, the world around
us (to begin at the simplest level), with sounds (recognizable by others)
or with written words. This replacing has long been studied and com-
mented upon by linguists, and we know what is implied by notions such
as "referent," "sign," "signified," and "signifier." Linguistics has also
taught us that what seemed at first a simple enough operation is, in fact,
so complex that we find ourselves faced with several awkward questions,
the nature of meaning being one of them. It is this concept that I wish to
discuss.

We have the thing, then, and we have the word. Meaning, here, is, or at
least seems to be, no other than the mental "content" of the word as a
phonetic or graphic unit; it is the reference. Thus, when I say /tābəl/ or
write *table*, the operation is accompanied by, or rather includes, the image (thing-presentation, *Vorstellung*) of a particular object. As we
know, to speak supposes this operation of abstraction by which the word
can replace the thing. Between word and thing, however (unless the
speaker is psychotic), there is no relationship of resemblance or of identity; the sign is arbitrary—which is one more good reason why we can say
that the thing is not the word and the word is not the thing. But, of
course, while there is no identity between the two, there is a correspondence, a relationship: our linguistic activity does indeed function *as if*
the word were precisely the thing. A replacement has occurred, a substi-

tution, and I want to emphasize straightaway that this illusion ("as if") is essential to the process of substitution. None of this is new. It has been known for quite some time,[1] and we call it "representation,"[2] but it does not precisely tell us what meaning is and where, at any rate, it can be found.

Now, although there is no pure state of language where one finds a close, absolute, one-to-one correspondence between word and thing, I shall accept, at this stage of our enquiry into meaning, the old and somewhat oversimplified model: linguistics speaks of referent and sign.

Because the world is out there, because objects are separated from us, "on the other side," and not *in us*, meaning, by definition, cannot be said to lie within the referent.[3] From this it should follow that meaning can only be found in the sign. If not in the latter, where else indeed?

We can at this point appreciate the ingenuity of Ferdinand de Saussure's model made of a mental image (the concept) and of sounds: what was at first transmitted to the infant in order that he become a speaking subject was not just sounds, but the indication that these sounds are related to specific objects. And in Saussure's model,[4] the one and the other are shown as inseparably related, united.

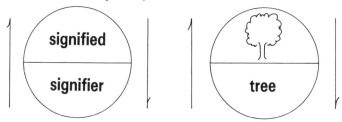

Thanks to the arrows on either side, the diagram clearly insists on how meaning does not lie within the image (apart from the word), as, of course, it does not either lie within the sounds (separated from the image), which is not to say where meaning is to be found, but simply that it cannot appear or be produced without this two-in-one element. These two little arrows constitute, in fact, an essential element of the model, and it is important that we do not forget the inseparability they stand for. This should be stressed, I think, because we quite naturally tend—at least this is the point I wish to make—to forget this inseparability, particularly when we equate meaning with the signified. But Saussure's theory enables us to introduce the notion of relationship. Between signified and signifier we can say there exists a relationship, and in this I see a process, an event which takes some time to develop and is not forever given.

Let us carefully note the two elements we have so far obtained from our model: an inseparability and a relationship. One of these two notions we observed when examining the referent and the sign: we saw how, between thing and word, there was a correspondence, a link. But the notion of relationship might imply distance, separation, and indeed word and thing are separated from one another, separated by a space that cannot be bridged, exactly as a subject is separated from objects, that is, from the world. (And, as I have already hinted, we might also add that they are separated inasmuch as their "correspondence" does not rest on identity or resemblance, the sign being arbitrary.) Perhaps this is the reason why, when pointing out the correspondence, we did not insist on the inseparability which is yet just as much a necessary part of the model.

Does the model seem too contradictory, then, or can I speak both of an abrupt, radical separation and of a link? This is, of course, the central point of the argument I am developing, but already a first brief answer can be given: it is precisely because, as subjects, we are separated, cut off, hopelessly isolated from the world, that we cannot survive without establishing a link with it. Thus can we realize the structural identity of the notion of unconscious and of language. Yes, it is as simple as that, and if Jacques Lacan's famous formula is so often misunderstood or even violently rejected, it is simply because it points out with precision what we all, as humans, unconsciously refuse to acknowledge: the hopeless separation I have just mentioned.

No wonder, then, that we should find such words and notions as "link" and "gap" in Freud's paper, "The Unconscious." Discussing the possible influence of Herbart on Freud and showing how "Freud the neurologist" was finally "overtaken and displaced by Freud the psychologist," the editors of the *Standard Edition* write in their introduction to "The Unconscious":

> He seems from the first, it is true, to have felt the force of the argument . . . that to restrict mental events to those that are conscious and to intersperse them with purely physical, neural events "disrupts psychical continuities" and introduces unintelligible *gaps* into the chain of observed phenomena. But there were two ways in which this difficulty could be met. We might disregard the physical events and adopt the hypothesis that the *gaps* are *filled* with unconscious mental ones. (14: 162; emphasis added)

And while we may agree with the neurologist's comment that the "psychical continuities" cannot be "disrupt[ed]," we can also sense with Lacan, after Freud, how fundamentally unacceptable this notion of gap, of disruption, is for us. Today, psychoanalysis can be interpreted as an attempt "to fill gaps"—whether through theory or practice—and it is an attempt which is both realistic and symbolic as it paradoxically describes the ultimate and ontological gap as unfillable. In Freud, too, we have Saussure's "little arrows": "A word . . . acquires its *meaning* by being linked to an object-presentation; at all events if we restrict ourselves to a consideration of substantives. . . . The pathology of disorders of speech leads us to assert that *the word-presentation is linked at its sensory end (by its sound-image) with the object-presentation*" (14: 213, 214).

This brings us back to linguistics and to our discussion of meaning. Here, too, we have gaps and links; the linguistic model provides us with a good example of our attitude toward separation. We saw what distinguished the original pair from Saussure's more elaborate formula.

We can now observe what feature they have in common. In the first case, sign and referent are separated, while the necessity of a correspondence maintains a link, a relationship, however abstract. In the second case, signified and signifier are conceived as an unbreakable unit (neither signified nor signifier can function on its own), while the notion of relationship (the arrows) is not only kept but guarantees the solidity of the unit. What has been left out between the two stages, or rather subdued, "repressed," is separation. Obviously, from the linguist's point of view, there is a reason for this; Saussure was introducing the notion of signified as a necessary condition of speech, and it had to be conceived not as an independent element but as part of a larger process. Also, and more generally, we can say that the accuracy of his description enables us today to distinguish features of which he was unaware. For what has been repressed always comes back, one way or another, and it does so in Saussure's diagram in the shape of the line which separates signified from signifier. Separation is therefore also present in the linguistic model, which explains why we can still work with it. (Lacan's "subversion" of the formula, by which signifier comes to be written on top and signified below, is his own way of acknowledging this, while pointing out the essential difference between psychoanalysis and the description made by the linguist: separation, *coupure* [cut], *béance* [abyss, void].) Both models thus insist on the existence of a link, but vary greatly in their representation of separation. True, Saussure does account for it in a way, but he does so within a close, "secure" structure, while the "cut" is more strongly stressed in the sign-referent model, to the point, in fact, of being part of the structure—word/separation/word—and this is sufficient to introduce a major difference between the two representations.

If we review the main features of Saussure's diagram, we have: (1) an insistence on relationship (and we know it is a necessary condition of language) $\uparrow \frac{sied}{sier} \downarrow$; (2) the conception of the sign as a unit, where I see the realization of a fantasy of fusion $\mathbf{O}$;(3) and finally the reminder, but carefully enclosed, tucked away in the "egg," that image and sound, as representatives of thing and word, are to be kept apart as indeed things and words are in reality. Everything is there, each element at work has been carefully itemized, but I find that the insistence on what unites, on what links, and the closed, enclosing design of the "egg" somewhat temper the force the separating line may have. *La coupure* is represented, but in no way does it seem so radical as it is in reality. As we remarked earlier, there is much less distance between signified and signifier than between sign and thing: this points out the unconscious desire behind the diagram, a desire that the gap should be closed. Such is the fantasy, I think, which inhabits Saussure's model—a model, as we saw, which operates quite correctly on the level of a linguistic description of speech; it is as if a sewing up of the split (*suture de la béance*) had occurred. In this unconscious desire to deny the reality of separation I see one of the functions of language: just as much as words can be said to reveal, they also conceal.

Perhaps it is not too difficult to understand why such an unconscious repression should have occurred in the second case: it is the function of language to "bridge the gap" between humans and the world, and between humans themselves (the person out there, to whom I speak, is part of the "world"). It is because separation is unbearable that such a bridging of the gap is so essential; whenever we study man's and woman's relationship to the world, which amounts to a study of the object-subject relationship, we come across this naturally human attitude. This seems equally true of the production of linguistic theory, of literary criticism—whatever the school—and even of psychoanalysis (but this time *paradoxically*, and the specification matters a great deal) as this discussion on the meaning of meaning should make clear.

To sum up this last point, I shall say with Lacan that as "subjects"—and the concept will have to be defined very carefully—we speak because we are separated, cut off from the world. By definition, the notion of subject implies an incompleteness, which can also be read as division within the individual; between subject and object, the difference cannot be reduced, and between the two the distance is insuperable, which is simply to say that from my particular place and point of view I shall never be an object, except for others.[5] Hence the need to imagine, invent, create a link with objects. But the link is an illusion, although an illusion we cannot recognize as such (except theoretically) since confronted by the *real* it is all we have; it has the value of a hallucination, and what characterizes a hallucination is that one believes in it. Language is effective because of this suspension of disbelief, and so is art. Even though theory keeps repeating to us that the word is not the thing, we stop being conscious of this when we speak (or read or write), and this forgetting constitutes one of the necessary conditions of the production of language.

Indeed, even before any specific meaning (whatever that is) can be envisaged, the very structure of language is made of this double necessity to *reveal*, stand in the place of, and to *conceal* that the replacement is only hallucinatory.[6] One is reminded of Kurosawa's *Kagemusha:* each of our words is like a double, hired to take the place of a famous person, and one of its two functions is to prevent the discovery of the substitution.

What consequence can this have on our reflection on the concept of meaning? Again, what is meaning? It seems we can now turn to the process described above as a relationship. We found it in Saussure's model, to my knowledge the best we have at our disposal, and we can ask ourselves in what manner this representation of the speech process may help us. Hence the question: "Where is meaning?" We noticed how meaning had to lie within the sign rather than within the referent, if only because the object to be represented, the world out there, cannot be confused with its representation. (This is the whole point of this discussion of a mental operation taking place in a thinking, speaking subject.) But where in the sign? In the signified? Can I call meaning this effect of what I see, hear, feel, smell, or taste, and, for instance, the image of that tree out there? The image of the tree on the surface of my retina has no meaning in itself, as meaning cannot be reduced to this. The "reproduction" of an absence—the object out there—however real itself as an image and presence in me, has no more meaning than the "thing" it reproduces. But Saussure's description implies a process more elaborate than the simple mechanical reproduction given above and cannot be dismissed so lightly. For the concept of signified in the diagram must be understood mainly as the result of an operation of abstraction and generalization whereby a visual, oral, and tactile (and so on) experience undergoes a transformation and becomes a mental entity; thus the mental "image" *tree* calls to mind all possible trees; a whole class of objects, as does *noise,* for instance, or *odor,* or *wound, burn, caress.*[7] The signified, therefore, appears as the joint result of an inscription and an interpretation, as the result of a stimulation *that is recognized.* I would like to restrict "meaning" to this part of the process, to this operation of an abstraction-generalization which implies the "treatment" of an impression coming from the exterior: a recognition that the specific sensorial signal I received does represent a specific object in the world out there—in short, the acknowledgment of an adequation (between thing and "image," and also between objects of the same class). It then seems we have a succession of homothetic representations of the original relationship between thing and word, itself a representation: referent and sign (thing/word), signified and signifier (mental image/sound), and finally a relationship between duplication and thing which sums up what I call recognition, acknowledgment of a correspondence.[8] When we pronounce /trē/, when we use a *signifier,* that is, we acknowledge the correspondence above. I place meaning *not* in the representation, in the duplication as such, the "image," but in the recognition of a relationship: as the indication of a correspondence between word and thing, meaning is a mediation, a process.

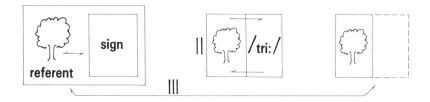

It can, of course, be argued that this operation is part of the concept "sign" and that many linguists precisely interpret "sign" in this way, and I would agree. It is true that "sign" may be said to express the relationship I have tried to point out, but in this case, it is simply the signifier of the mental operation I am describing; as such, it represents the process, the relationship, which is not in the sign but outside of it. Thus, we can still say that meaning is neither in the world nor in the sign but in a correspondence between the two. When we correctly explain that the

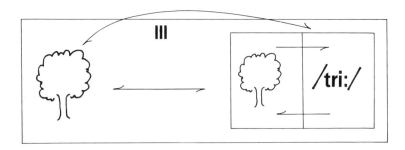

sign "sign" *is the expression of,* we are implying that the concept "sign" is nothing but the signifier of the existence of such a relationship, the link we have been discussing; and, of course, it is the illusion also, necessarily masked, that this link is not just a projection of desire but an actual bridge over the gap, a bridge through which fusion with the world and with others can be achieved. Meaning is the (necessary) illusion that the word is the thing which reminds us in passing that there is no metalanguage and enhances the importance of the signifier, for, indeed, "il n'y a que du signifiant." In Saussure's diagram (which is not really Saussure's but his disciples'), the arrows, which represent a necessary relationship, are in a way the signifier of the notion of meaning. But it is a masked signifier, a subverted one (by linguists), since it may be read as insisting only on relationship while forgetting distance and exteriority. All the same, the word—*tree,* for instance—is the indication of the fact that a particular relationship has been established between me as a subject and the object I recognize out there.

At this point, although the problem cannot be dealt with at length in this paper, I find it unavoidable to introduce Freud's and Lacan's "subject." For it is obvious that the process of recognition amounts to a subjective judgment. We all know that whatever sensorial signals we receive have to be analyzed, interpreted, before they are given a meaning. In *The Interpretation of Dreams,* Freud presents us with a new model of interpretation, one which takes "memories" and regression into consideration (5: 538).[9]

Thus, it can be seen that what is perceived is given a signification which largely depends on the nature of the perceiving subject. (And in order to stress the difference from phenomenology let me say that interpretation, here, results from an interaction, from the dialectical encounter taking place between the subject and the world. What makes this

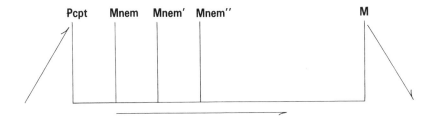

process so difficult for us to understand is that we tend to think in terms of "oneness," of "either/or," and remain unconsciously reluctant to accept such paradoxical notions as "two-in-one": subject and world.) Whatever signal comes from outside (and also from inside) has to go through the various "memories," screens or sieves which constitute the subject in each of us. Meaning is nothing but what this (unconscious) subject chooses to "perceive": in the process, the world out there may be taken into consideration, and generally is, but always it is the subject which "decides." Such a view is not new, of course, and in this respect we owe a lot to Norman Holland, who saw all this in his *Five Readers' Reading*. What remains to be settled now is what goes under the heading of "subject," and it is here that Lacan is so strikingly effective. In language, and in literature, meaning is this particular process where I reveal myself as a subject, which explains why we tend to obscure that part of the process. Whenever a critic speaks of meaning, he unconsciously does so in order to avoid speaking of himself and of the author as subjects. Such is the meaning of *meaning;* the discourse on meaning provides us with a convenient screen behind which the unconscious subject can remain hidden.

But what is a subject? Once again, it seems we can best approach the notion by looking at the way language functions. As we just saw, when I produce the signifier *tree*, I indicate that a relationship has been established between me as a subject and the object recognized out there. Such an operation, which, of course, can only be carried out thanks to a process of nomination, implies a triangular situation.[10] If we can use signs it is because they were once transmitted to us, and the establishing of a relation between sign and object is only possible for us because a signifier was first taught to us. To come into existence, the relationship I have just mentioned depends upon a correspondence which preceded it: that which constitutes any given linguistic code.

The replacement of the thing by the word repeats an initial establish-

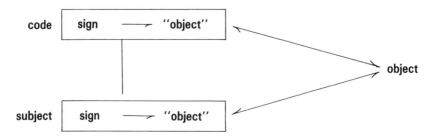

ment of relationship, and I find it striking that this transmission of a signifier marking the existence of an object-presentation should be of the same nature as what happens in the mirror-stage between infant and mother. This is where Jane and Tarzan come in.

Strictly speaking, there is no nomination yet in the mirror-stage, only the apprehension by the child of his unity and identity, but we are dealing with the same type of process.

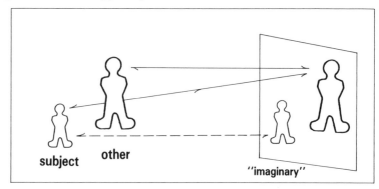

In the same way as an *other* provides the infant with an image with which it can identify, an other first taught me to designate things by their names. This is to say that even before the notion of unconscious desire comes to mind, the sign, in its very structure, already expresses what Freud discovered and theorized: the human's tragic, incomplete status as a subject—always estranged from others (fusion) and from the world out there (objects)—, and his unending attempts, his irrepressible desire, indeed, not only to compensate for his separation, through language and through art, but also to hallucinatorily refuse to acknowledge that he is separated.

When the ape man—in the Hollywood movie, *Tarzan, the Ape Man* (MGM, 1932), with Maureen O'Sullivan and Johnny Weismuller—

meets Jane, he is not yet a human. But with Jane—a woman, significantly—he is given an image, a model, somebody "like him": this is the mirror-stage. The baby (ape-man) thus acquires an identity through this encounter with an *other*, that is to say a sense of his unity and exterior identity, which does not make a subject of him (if it may be permitted to isolate in this way, and to separate, concomitant moments of a complex process), but at least ensures him of his existence. Then he is given a name—in the movie, more specifically, he is given the chance to pronounce his name—and this is the introduction to language, to the symbolic order, and it always comes from the *Other* (with a capital *O* this time, to distinguish it from the other in the mirror-stage where the Imaginary precedes, so to speak, the Symbolic). But before this highly symbolical giving of a name can occur, fusion has to be coped with. We must notice how the experience implies separation, a cutting off from the mother's body.

Tarzan's first human word is "me?" as a query after Jane herself has uttered "me." The exchange goes like this:

JANE: Thank you. Without you, this beast [an ape] would have attacked me.
TARZAN: Me?
JANE: I said: without you this beast would have attacked me.
TARZAN: Me?
JANE: Me is me. I am me only for me.
TARZAN: Me?
JANE: No, I am you, you for you.
TARZAN: You?
JANE: No, my name is Jane Parker, do you understand? Jane, Jane.
TARZAN: Jane, Jane, Jane.
JANE: Yes, Jane, and you? And you, you?
TARZAN: Jane.
JANE: And you, you?
TARZAN: Tarzan, Tarzan, Tarzan.

The infant has to go through separation before coming to the realization that there is such a thing as "me" and such a thing as "you," and Jane is here to help. She insists, "I am me only for me," and she adds a "no" in her next sentence, which also introduces "you" and the opposition you/me. Tarzan can then repeat "you," although with a question mark again, to which she replies: "No, my name is. . . ." By pronouncing her own name, she completes the "session," showing what a name is and how it is attributed to one person only: "Yes, Jane, and you?" And to do so, she has had to teach Tarzan what difference is: *No,* "you" cannot be a name for him; *yes,* her name is "Jane." We can say she points the way to Tarzan, encouraging him, in fact, to use his own name, which I interpret as a symbolic acceptance on his part of a name for himself. Note the progression of signifiers (me, you, Jane, Tarzan), and how the dialogue, almost musically, first rather insists on a repetition of "me" and then shifts to "you" in the same way. It is after this insistence on difference (yes/no), on separation, that names can appear: after the Imaginary (mirror-stage), the Symbolic. For only "Jane" and "Tarzan" point to subjects; their names transform the objects they were (me, you) into subjects.

But, of course, a subject is also the object of an Other's desire, for it is the Other who has chosen the name. In the film, the accuracy of the psychoanalytic metaphor stops when Tarzan proves such a good "pupil" and replies "Tarzan" when asked what his name is. Had Jane said (as many spectators afterwards believe, and as I myself erroneously believed when I started on this paper): "Me Jane, you Tarzan" it would have been perfect for my demonstration. The fundamental ambiguity of the notion of subject must be stressed: my name made me a subject, but it was given to me, and this makes me the object of an Other's desire.

Psychoanalytic theory is also a representation, of course; it is nothing but a discourse on separation, on the void, but because it has attracted our attention to *la coupure,* it is a discourse with a difference. Now at least we know that separation is at once unacceptable and unavoidable, and we have grown somewhat more[11] conscious of our need constantly to deny this. Psychoanalytic theory is a representation which *does not quite* have the same attitude toward illusion as other representations have. Finally, it implies the knowledge that it is a discourse which cannot be heard, or which, at any rate, is never heard clearly.

Notes

1. See André Chervel's remarkable paper, "Le débat sur l'arbitraire du signe au XIXe siècle" (1–33).

2. I keep Freud's term *Vorstellung* (presentation) for psychical processes and use *representation* when speaking of the relationship between subject and object, that is, when a subject produces a signifier.

3. The extreme case being, of course, that of words which do not have an "objective" referent.

4. I am aware that what I am calling "Saussure's model" may only be Bally's and Seche-
haye's representation of what these disciples learned from their master. On this particular
problem, see Robert Godel's *Les Sources manuscrites du cours de linguistique générale de
F. de Saussure* and Tullio De Mauro's edition of Saussure's *Course (Corso di Linguistica
Generale)*.

All the same, there is an "arrow," and even "arrows," in the model left us by Saussure. I
find it remarkable that Saussure should have started with an egg-shaped figure:

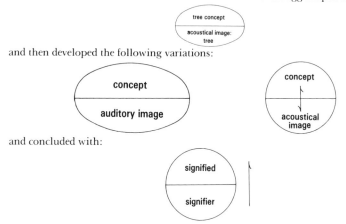

and then developed the following variations:

and concluded with:

Here is part of Saussure's commentary (quoted by Godel [238], and taken from G. Dugal-
lier's notebooks): "La flèche marque la signification comme contrepartie de l'image auditive" ("The arrow marks the signification as counterpart of the auditive image"); and
Godel's own commentary: "Dans le premier schéma du signe [Saussure 114] . . . la flèche
ne figurait pas—non plus, d'ailleurs, que les mots *signification* et *contrepartie* dans le
contexte. A la fin du chapitre sur la limitation de l'arbitraire une flèche à double pointe
marquait la réciprocité de la relation intérieure" (122). ("In the first schema of the sign,
there was no arrow—and the words *signification* and *counterpart* were not used either in
the context. At the end of the chapter on the limitation of the arbitrary a double-headed
arrow marked the reciprocity of the inner relationship.")

5. This poses the problem of the basis on which the investigation of such an elusive
"subjective" object can ever be carried out. Briefly, then, let me say that such an investigation can only be carried out properly if it incorporates an awareness of its relative inability;
psychoanalysis is not a positivistic science; as new scientific knowledge, it can only be
relative and paradoxical.

6. This is developed in the introduction and first chapter of my *Le Texte du désir*.

7. This is true even though each of us always gives these notions a personal
interpretation.

8. Again, this is not new. Cf. Chervel's observation: "Le signe des Idéologues [au début
du XIXe siècle, en France], c'est donc à la fois un son et une relation" (6). ("The sign of the
Idéologues [at the beginning of the XIXe century, in France] is therefore at once a sound
and a relationship.")

9. Strictly speaking, it is not a model of interpretation, and Freud here is mostly concerned with regression in dreams. But I think we can use his conception of the psychical

apparatus in our discussion of language and the unconscious. Lacan does so in his en-
lightening development on regression and the subject in *Le Seminaire II* (163–75).

    10. See, for instance, K. Buhler's Organon-Modell (1931) and B. Malmberg's comment
in his *Analyse du langage au XXe siècle* (284).

    11. I use "somewhat more" because progress is always relative.

Works Cited

Chervel, André. "Le débat sur l'arbitraire du signe au XIXe siècle." *Romantisme.* Paris, N 25–26, 1979.

Freud, Sigmund. *The Standard Edition of the Complete Psychological Works of
Sigmund Freud.* Ed. and trans. James Strachey. 24 vols. London: Hogarth,
1953–74.

Godel, Robert. *Les Sources manuscrites du cours de linguistique générale de F.
de Saussure.* Geneva: Droz; Paris: Minard, 1957.

Holland, Norman. *Five Readers' Reading.* New Haven: Yale UP, 1975.

Lacan, Jacques. *Le Séminaire II.* Paris: Seuil, 1978.

Malmberg, B. *Analyse du langage au XXe siècle.* Paris: P.U.F., 1983.

Saussure, Ferdinand de. *Corso di Linguistica Generale.* Ed. and trans. Tullio De
Mauro, Bari: Editori La Terza, 1967.

Silhol, Robert. *Le Texte du désir.* Paris: Cistre/Ecrits, 1984.

Tarzan, the Ape Man. Dir. W. S. Van Dyke. With Maureen O'Sullivan and
Johnny Weismuller. MGM, 1932.

Redefining the Revenant: Guilt and Sibling Loss in Guntrip and Freud

Peter L. Rudnytsky

Harry Guntrip's (1975) record of his analytic experiences with W. R. D. Fairbairn and D. W. Winnicott is at once a moving auto-biographical document and an important theoretical discussion of the nature of therapeutic action in psychoanalysis. Central to Guntrip's paper, and his motivation for seeking analysis in the first place, is "a total amnesia for a severe trauma at the age of three and a half years, over the death of a younger brother," Percy (447). Recognizing that it was this trauma which led him to become a psychotherapist, Guntrip convincingly argues that "it seems that our theory must be rooted in our psychopathology," and instances as proof of this interplay between personal suffering and scientific insight "Freud's courageous self-analysis at a time when all was obscure" (467). Although Guntrip's was not literally a self-analysis—he had over one thousand sessions with Fairbairn in the 1950s and over 150 with Winnicott in the 1960s—part of his purpose is to investigate the continuing effects of an analysis after termination in order to assess its therapeutic efficacy. Emulating Freud's courage, Guntrip distills the lessons of his encounters with two masters in a luminous piece of self-analysis.

In addition to the self-analytic component of his essay, Guntrip resembles Freud in the biographical accident of sibling loss. As is well known, Freud was profoundly affected by the death in infancy of his younger brother Julius, at a time when he himself was just under two years of age. Although mentioned in the memory-laden letter to Fliess of 3 October 1897, and later recalled in a 1912 letter to Ferenczi, the death of

Julius is nowhere alluded to in any of Freud's published writings. Max Schur has elucidated the importance of the *"non vixit"* dream in terms of Freud's recurring experience of the "guilt of the survivor" (153–71); and Ernest Jones has drawn upon Freud's own paper, "Some Character Types Met with in Psycho-Analytic Work" (1916), to depict Freud as one who was himself "wrecked by success" through the fulfillment of unconscious death wishes against Julius (146).

A comparison between the experiences of sibling loss in Guntrip and Freud provides the focal point for the present inquiry. My thesis can be stated relatively simply: whereas in Freud the death of a brother gives rise to the conflict between ambivalent feelings of love and hatred which leads to guilt, Guntrip's inability to recall and hence to mourn his brother's death is indicative of arrest at a more primitive stage of emotional development. This contrast between Freud's unresolved ambivalence and Guntrip's "absence of grief" (Deutsch) is all the more remarkable in that Guntrip was more than eighteen months older than Freud at the time of the loss of their respective siblings.

The example of Guntrip, moreover, who unblocked his amnesia in 1971 after learning of the death of Winnicott, allows us to reconceptualize Freud's persistent struggle with the ghosts or revenants of his unconsciously murdered rivals. Instead of being merely a curse or burden, guilt may be viewed rather as a positive achievement, heralding an arrival at the depressive position (Klein). The sense of guilt, as Winnicott remarks, "even when unconscious and even when apparently irrational, implies a certain degree of emotional growth, ego health, and hope" ("Psycho Analysis" 19).

Although Guntrip seeks to maintain an evenhanded attitude toward both of his eminent analysts, calling Fairbairn more innovative in theory and Winnicott more spontaneous in practice, and expressing gratitude for what he had received from each, his paper in fact offers a devastating critique of Fairbairn's limitations as a therapist and a corresponding tribute to the genius of Winnicott. Not only were Fairbairn's interpretations excessively intellectualized, but the rigidity of his manner—symbolized by his placing the patient's couch in front of a large desk, and seating himself on the other side—had the effect of stymieing Guntrip's analysis at the experiences that took place when he was between three and a half to seven years old, and rendering inaccessible the earlier double traumas of his brother's death and his mother's failures of empathy. In the highly applicable terms of Balint, Fairbairn conducted the analysis at the level of Oedipal conflict without reaching to the breakdown of the primary love relationship that defines the area of the basic fault.

I shall summarize the salient details of Guntrip's personal history. His mother, the eldest of eleven children, had already played the part of careworn "little mother" to her younger siblings and did not want any children of her own when she married Guntrip's father, an eloquent and protective Methodist preacher, in 1898. In his teenage years, Guntrip was told by his mother that she had breast-fed him because she believed it would prevent her from having another pregnancy; she then refused to breast-feed Percy and was reproached by her husband that Percy would have lived if she had done so. After Percy's death, Guntrip's mother withheld further sexual relations from her husband.

The Kleinian aspects of these issues of breast-feeding, in which the breast becomes consolidated as a "bad" object, and hence no "good" loved object can be installed within the ego, are transparent. Because no good object can be introjected, moreover, the ego remains arrested at the schizoid position and, in Deutsch's words, "is not sufficiently developed to bear the strain of the work of mourning" (13). Both regressive anxiety and a mobilization of defenses—above all, the blocking of affect—are responses to the threat posed by object loss to the immature ego. But a Kleinian analysis purely in terms of internal objects needs to be supplemented by an emphasis on the failure of environmental provision. For, as Winnicott has shown, the infant's attainment of the depressive position "is not so much dependent on the mother's simple ability to hold a baby, which was her characteristic at the earlier stages, as on her ability to hold the infant-care situation over a period of time during which the infant may go through complex experiences" ("Psycho-Analysis" 23). It is precisely the inability of Guntrip's mother to "hold the infant-care situation" which lies at the crux of his difficulties and for which the struggles over breast-feeding are but the most striking metaphor.

Upon seeing Percy naked and dead on his mother's lap, as he was informed later, the three-and-a-half-year-old Harry rushed up and called out, "Don't let him go. You'll never get him back!" He then fell victim to a mysterious illness, from which he would have died had he not been sent temporarily to the family of a maternal aunt. But all memory of his brother's death and his leaving home was totally repressed, though, Guntrip adds, "it remained alive in me, to be triggered off unrecognizably by widely spaced analogous events" (455). Both at the ages of twenty-six and thirty-seven, separation from a brother-figure gave rise to an inexplicable exhaustion illness. By the latter occasion, in 1938, Guntrip had studied classical analytic theory and realized intellectually that he lived, as it were, atop the buried memory of Percy's death. He reports a dream: "I went down into a tomb and saw a man buried alive. He tried to get out but I threatened him with illness, locked him in and got away quick" (456). This search for a hidden traumatic scene, "triggered off unrecognizably by widely spaced analogous events," is a paradigm for the psychoanalytic quest, which evokes Oedipus' assembling the clues to his past in *Oedipus the King.*

Upon returning to his parents' home, Guntrip tried to coerce his mother's love, first by various psychosomatic ailments, and then, after the age of five, by more active defiance. This misbehavior in turn provoked brutal rages and canings from his mother. It was to the dissection of this "world of internalized libidinally excited bad-object relations" (457) that his analysis with Fairbairn was dedicated, and Guntrip derived considerable benefit from it. But, as I have indicated, he came increasingly to realize that he was not making progress on the more important underlying problems of the period before Percy's death, and indeed his conflicted relations with his mother served as a defense against this deeper material. In addition, Fairbairn fell ill—shortly after the death in December 1957 of Guntrip's friend whose departure thirty years earlier had caused the first adult eruption of the illness modeled on his response to his brother's death—and the analysis was interrupted for six months. By 1959 Guntrip reached a crucial insight, though he did not impart it directly to Fairbairn: either remaining in analysis and awaiting Fairbairn's death or losing him by ending the analysis would cause a repetition of the trauma of Percy's death, with no one to help him through it. In view of Fairbairn's declining state of health, Guntrip phased out his analysis during that year.

Part of the courage needed to terminate his analysis with Fairbairn came from Guntrip's decision to seek analysis with Winnicott, with whom he had begun corresponding at Fairbairn's instigation in 1954. Guntrip writes: "By 1962 I had no doubt that he was the only man I could turn to for further help" (459). In this eminently well-placed confidence in Winicott's healing powers the sixty-one-year-old Guntrip echoes the distressed plea of the Piggle, two years and four months old, before her first consultation: "Mummy take me to Dr. Winnicott" (Winnicott, *Piggle* 7). Despite the limited number of sessions, Winnicott allowed Guntrip "to reach right back to *an ultimate good mother, and to find her recreated in him in the transference*" (460). In so doing, and in a way that would only become clear in the fullness of time, he gave Guntrip access to the inner strength needed to face his double traumas of sibling loss and maternal deprivation.

Winnicott's gifts as a clinician are legendary, and readers familiar with any of his case histories or vignettes need not be surprised to find corroboration coming from yet another quarter. Yet Guntrip's account is unusually poignant as it is written from the patient's point of view. As an analogue, I turn to the illustrative case included in "Creativity and Its Origins." In this paper, Winnicott tells of a man who feared to be called mad for thinking himself a girl, to whom Winnicott responded: "It was not that *you* told this to anyone; it is *I* who see the girl and hear the girl talking, when actually there is a man on my couch. The mad person is myself." As a result of enabling the patient "to see himself as a girl *from my position,*" Winnicott achieved a breakthrough: "He and I have been driven to the conclusion (though unable to prove it) that his mother (who is not alive now) saw a girl baby when she saw him as a baby before she came round to thinking of him as a boy" (74).

Guntrip's symptoms do not include the feature of split-off female elements, but his interaction with Winnicott is otherwise very similar. Essential in both instances is Winnicott's inclusion of his own uncertainty as part of the analytic discourse, while at the same time remaining extraordinarily attuned to the anxieties of the patient. He told Guntrip near the end of their first session: "I've nothing particular to say yet, but if I don't say something, you may begin to feel I'm not here" (460). It was not long before he divined the root of Guntrip's discomfort at silence and his need to talk hard: "You feel silence is abandonment. The gap is not you forgetting mother, but mother forgetting you, and now you've relived it with me. You're finding an earlier trauma which you might never recover without the help of the Percy trauma repeating it. You have to remember mother abandoning you by transference on to me" (461). Winnicott thus took the place of the "good breast mother" at the point where Guntrip's actual mother had failed him. Both in Guntrip's case and in that reported by Winnicott in "Creativity and Its Origins," it is only through the transferential encounter between patient and analyst that it is possible to relive and hence to reconstruct the primordial trauma of maternal madness or abandonment.

In addition to becoming the "good-enough mother" Guntrip never had, Winnicott permitted Guntrip to cultivate his own nurturing powers. Acknowledging his own vulnerability, he went so far as to say: "You too have a good breast. You've always been able to give more than you take. Doing your analysis is almost the most reassuring thing that happens to me. The chap before you makes me feel I'm no good at all. You don't have to be good for me. I don't need it and can cope without it, but in fact you are good for me" (462). By providing a holding environment and refusing to retaliate or be destroyed, Winnicott transformed the meaning of Percy's death and likewise helped Guntrip to resolve his dilemma concerning termination.

In true psychoanalytic fashion, the most enduring results of Winnicott's interventions only manifested themselves after the event, through deferred action. Guntrip last saw Winnicott in July 1969, and in February 1970 Guntrip was told by a physician that he was seriously overworked. But rather than accept retirement, he continued to write feverishly, until in October he contracted pneumonia and spent five weeks in the hospital. Guntrip did not fully realize that his hyperactivity was still a result of his struggle to assert himself as a living being in the face of his mother's apathy. Early in 1971 Guntrip learned that Winnicott had had a flu attack and so dropped him a line. Winnicott called soon afterwards to thank him for his note. Two weeks later Winnicott's secretary called with the news that he had died.

Winnicott's death precipitated in Guntrip an extraordinary series of dreams. In the first, *"I saw my mother,* black, immobilized, staring fixedly into space, *totally ignoring me* as I stood at one side staring at her and feeling myself frozen into immobility" (463). In previous dreams, his mother had always attacked him. Although he first assumed Winnicott's death to represent a repetition of the loss of his brother, Guntrip soon recognized that he had not dreamed of his mother in this way on the two previous occasions when he had been separated from someone who had reminded him of Percy. Now, moreover, he did not fall ill, as he had both in 1927 and 1938. The dreaming of his mother's indifference was thus a sign that Guntrip was beginning, for the first time, *to remember the events of the period before his brother's death.* In "Dreaming, Fantasying, and Living" (1971), Winnicott makes the unexpected point that "dreaming and living have been seen to be of the same order, daydreaming being of another order" (26). In being able to dream of what he had previously forgotten, Guntrip was making contact with his dissociated past and, as a result, learning to live.

The next two months led Guntrip through a "compelling dreamsequence which went on night after night, taking me back in chronological order through every house I had ever lived in" (463). The climax came in two dreams in which Guntrip clearly saw himself as he was during his brother's life and death. In the first, he was three, and holding a pram with his one-year-old brother; their mother was staring vacantly into the distance. The second dream is even more startling:

> I was standing with another man, the double of myself, both reaching out to get hold of a dead object. Suddenly the other man collapsed in a heap. Immediately the dream changed to a lighted room, where I saw Percy again. I knew it was him, sitting on the lap of a woman who had no face, arms, breasts. She was merely a lap to sit on, not a person. He looked deeply depressed, with the corners of his mouth turned down, and I was trying to make him smile. (464)

In this dream, Guntrip actually recaptures the memory of trying to reach out to his brother when he beheld him dead on his mother's lap, and in both dreams he also breaks through to the earlier period before Percy's death "to see the faceless depersonalized mother, and the black depressed mother, who totally failed to relate to both of us" (464).

Through his death, Winnicott enabled Guntrip to summon his emotionally absent mother and prematurely deceased brother back to life in his mind. As Guntrip writes, *"He has taken her place and made it possible and safe to remember her in an actual dream-reliving of her paralysing schizoid aloofness"* (464-65). Thus, the ghosts of the past become, rather than tormentors, a reassuring sign of the persistence of memory, a confirmation of one's power to grieve over lost objects. In Kleinian terms, Guntrip negotiates the transition from the paranoid-schizoid to the depressive position. Through his belated introjection of Winnicott as a good mother, Guntrip in old age achieved what Freud, likewise confronted by sibling loss but sustained from infancy by his mother's love, struggled with for a lifetime—the ambivalence accompanying the "guilt of the survivor."

In his second climactic dream Guntrip refers to standing with "a double of myself." This "double" is, most evidently, a recollected image of himself as a child. But it may also represent his dead brother Percy, no less than the repressed portion of his own past. The consequence of the very idea of the double is to break down distinctions between self and other, or between interpersonal and intrapsychic relations. When, in the *"non vixit"* dream, Freud makes the famous declaration, "My emotional life has always insisted that I should have an intimate friend and hated enemy" (5: 483), he defines his life in terms of a series of encounters with revenants of his nephew John, beneath whom lies the shadowy figure of the dead Julius. As I have argued in *Freud and Oedipus* (44-49), the constant ambivalence in Freud's dealings with male counterparts is paralleled by the oscillation between "delusions of inferiority" and "megalomania" in his own self-esteem.

In thinking about the implications of the common experience of sibling loss in Freud and Guntrip, I find it helpful to invoke Bion's notion of the "imaginary twin." In the case of a patient whose sister, his elder by eighteen months, died when he was one year of age,[1] Bion observes the tendency to invent an imaginary figure, a twin, who stood for "the bad part of himself from which he wished to be dissociated" (9). But this menancing doppelganger is also that which must be reintegrated if amnesia is to be overcome and the self is to be made whole.

From the "imaginary twin," it is a short step to a contemplation of the phenomenon of actual identical twins. I rely here on the fascinating autobiographical paper by George L. Engel. Engel's paper is germane in the present context both because it is a venture in self-analysis, displaying courage comparable to that of Guntrip and Freud, and also because it turns on the death of a brother.

Unlike the brothers of Guntrip and Freud, however, Frank Engel, George's elder by five minutes, died not in early childhood but at forty-nine years of age. But this difference is of only secondary importance. The Engels' father, like Frank, died unexpectedly of a heart attack at the age of fifty-eight. Though already forty years of age, Freud, as I have documented elsewhere, (18–23), was inordinately afflicted by the death of his father in 1896 because it reawakened the "germ of reproaches" implanted by the premature death of Julius. The death of Engel's father precedes that of his brother, as one would expect in the normal course of events, and likewise lacks the infantile factor. But the psychological dynamics of the interplay of survivor guilt toward his sibling and paternal rivals are otherwise closely akin to those found in Freud.

In his paper George Engel describes his mourning process, including anniversary reactions and parapraxes. He includes some astonishing photographs taken of himself in April 1972 and of his father in April 1928, when each man was fifty-eight years of age, as well as of Frank Engel, on the same day in April 1928, when he was fourteen years old. The poses of the three men reading are truly uncanny in their likeness. Engel ponders the question: "Had I unconsciously begun to fuse the images of my father and my twin? Indeed, had he in my unconscious become my twin?" (29).

One example of a parapraxis committed by Engel must stand for many. When presenting the material orally at the University of Rochester, Engel misspoke and said, "December 10th, 1971, was my ninety-

eighth birthday," instead of his fifty-eighth birthday. After being con-
vulsed with "uncontrollable laughter," in which his audience joined
wholeheartedly, he interpreted his slip as expressing "my wish to live to
a ripe old age, or better still, forever." The age of fifty-eight was, of
course, a highly charged milestone because that was the age at which his
father had died. But, as a perceptive medical student in the audience
pointed out, the slip of ninety-eight was overdetermined by the fact that
it represented twice forty-nine, the age at which his brother had died. As
Engel sardonically comments, "By doubling his life span I shall live his
life for him and enjoy the twinship for both of us. What a triumph! What
a marvellous joke! No wonder the uncontrollable laughter and tears"
(29).

Very few people have an identical twin, or even a sibling who dies in
infancy. But the exceptional individuals to whom such a lot befalls may
show us in bolder relief the patterns that likewise shape our own lives.
From identical twins, through "imaginary twins," we return to the in-
dubitably universal phenomenon of the double. Following Rank, Freud
has argued that the idea of the double—including belief in an eternal
soul—was "originally an insurance against the destruction of the ego,"
but then "reverses its aspect," and "from having been an assurance of
immortality, it becomes an uncanny harbinger of death" (17: 235). The
same ambiguity attaches in reverse form to the revenant. The ghost of a
loved or hated person who haunts us from beyond the grave, it carries the
promise that we, too, may be remembered after death.

When the Piggle asks about Winnicott's birthday, he does not hesitate
to interpret in terms of opposites: "What about my death day?" (Winnicott, *Piggle* 124). Whether in the analysis of a little girl or an elderly
man, the end of life joins up with the beginning. By addressing the hidden anxiety in the Piggle's question, Winnicott was in the most tactful
way preparing her for not only for the eventual termination of her
treatment but also for his own death, which indeed occurred within five
years. In the same way, he seems to have wrought a miracle in the analysis of Guntrip, bestowing in his death the gift of freedom.

Puzzled as to what gave him the strength to face the "basic trauma" of
his mother's failure, Guntrip concludes: "It must have been because
Winnicott was not, and could not be, dead for me, nor certainly for many
others" (464). According to Hans Loewald, "The extended leave-taking

of the end phase of analysis is a replica of the process of mourning"
(259). For Guntrip, this proved to be literally the case. But even those
whose contact with Winnicott can only take place through the medium
of books may know what it is like to have their lives changed by his. In
mourning his loss, we may console ourselves with the thought that, like
Freud, Winnicott has become part of our permanent analytic and cultural heritage.

Notes

1. In his retrospective commentary on the case, Bion states that this information is "fac-
tually inaccurate," but that it "approximates closely" (120) the true state of affairs. It
should be added that Bion does not develop the theme of sibling loss in his paper.

Works Cited

Balint, M. *The Basic Fault: Therapeutic Aspects of Regression.* 1968. New York:
    Brunner/Mazel, 1979.
Bion, W. R. "The Imaginary Twin." 1950. *Second Thoughts: Selected Papers on
    Psycho-Analysis.* London: Maresfield Reprints, 1967. 3-22.
Deutsch, H. "Absence of Grief." *Psychoanalytic Quarterly* 6 (1937): 12-22.
Engel, George L. "The Death of a Twin. Mourning and Anniversary Reactions.
    Fragments of Ten Years of Self-Analysis." *International Journal of Psycho-
    analysis* 56 (1975): 23-40.
Freud, Sigmund. *The Standard Edition of the Complete Psychological Works of
    Sigmund Freud.* Ed. and trans. James Strachey. 24 vols. London: Hogarth,
    1953-74.
Guntrip, Harry. "My Experience of Analysis with Fairbairn and Winnicott."
    1975. *Essential Papers on Object Relations.* Ed. P. Buckley. New York: New
    York UP, 1986. 447-68.
Jones, Ernest. *The Life and Work of Sigmund Freud.* Vol. 2. New York: Basic,
    1955. 3 vols.
Klein, Melanie. "A Contribution to Psychogenesis of Manic-Depressive States."
    1935. *Essential Papers on Object Relations.* Ed. P. Buckley. New York: New
    York UP, 1986. 40-70.
Loewald, H. W. "Internalization, Separation, Mourning and the Superego."
    Papers on Psychoanalysis. New Haven: Yale UP, 1980. 257-76.
Rudnytsky, Peter L. *Freud and Oedipus.* New York: Columbia UP, 1987.
Schur, Max. *Freud: Living and Dying.* New York: International UP, 1972.
Winnicott, D. W. "Creativity and Its Origins." *Playing and Reality.* 65-85.

———. "Dreaming, Fantasying, and Living." *Playing and Reality.* 27–37.

———. *The Piggle.* New York: International UP, 1977.

———. *Playing and Reality.* 1971. London: Tavistock, 1984.

———. "Psycho-Analysis and the Sense of Guilt." 1958. *The Maturational Processes and the Facilitating Environment.* New York: International UP, 1965. 15–28.

The Uses of Literature in the Psychoanalytic Process

Frederick Wyatt

Today when we address the subject of literature in psychoanalysis, we are reconsidering a relationship which, in fact, reaches back to the beginnings of psychoanalysis.[1] One could well date its origin with Freud's letter to Fliess of 15 October 1897 (Freud, *Letters*) and arrive at results which may still strike us as surprising. I shall give a summary of this letter, then cite several passages from it. Initially, Freud reports upon the continuation of his self-analysis and in the process begins to talk about his old nursemaid, who was discovered to be a thief and was therefore discharged. He then reflects upon a dream of his own which concerns taking money from the mother of a doctor. He conjectures that, as a small child, he must have heard that the nursemaid was a thief but then forgot this information. Her disappearance must have had some effect on him. What happened to the memory of her disappearance, he asks himself in that letter to Fliess. At this point he recalls a thought which from time to time takes possession of him: "I can't find my mother. I cry in despair. . . . Brother Philipp, twenty years my senior, who was evidently supposed to take care of me, opens (probably to satisfy my demands) a locked wardrobe, *Kasten* in Austrian parlance, and not finding mother here either, I cry even harder until she comes through the door, slim and beautiful."

Subsequently, Freud explains this sequence of memories as follows: "I must have been afraid that mother had disappeared just like the old nurse-maid. I must have also heard something to the effect that the latter was locked up because of her stealing—'eingekastelt' [Austrian dialect, pun on "Kasten," being locked up in jail] as my brother liked to say even many years later—and I must have feared, therefore, that something similar could have happened to mother." Freud says then: " . . . one single thought of general value [relevance] came to me. I found I, too, was in love with my mother and jealous of my father, and I now consider this to be a universal event in early childhood." He continues: "If that is so, one can understand the irresistible power of King Oedipus despite all objections of the intellect to a preordained fate . . . as this Greek myth seizes upon a force of universal scope that everyone recognizes, because he can sense its existence within himself. Each individual (in the theater) was once, inchoately and in his own fantasy, just such an Oedipus and from the fulfillment of the dream presented here everybody shrunk back to the extent of the repression which now separates one's present condition from one's erstwhile infantile one." And, he goes on, "it passed through my head that the same problem might also be at the base of Hamlet. I am not thinking of Shakespeare's conscious intent but prefer to believe that the real event roused the poet to create its presentation, with the unconscious in him understanding the unconscious of the hero."[2]

It may be concluded from this letter that literature was instrumental in defining the classical model of conflict in psychoanalysis. Having grasped this condition, Freud, guided by literary paradigms, addressed it from the beginning as the "Oedipus complex." The connection between literature and psychoanalysis thus starts out on an extensive and auspicious development. It took its origin from the introduction of the Oedipus complex by example, as a prototypical event important both on an individual as well as on a social and historical level. Literature thereby stands at the beginning of the discovery of the continuous effects and consequences of these early involvements, namely, the rivalry with the beloved, vitally important—from the place of the boy, the father—for the sole possession of an equally beloved and vitally important person— the mother. It stands at the beginning of recognizing function and necessity of repression as well as role and scope of the unconscious. Inasmuch as Freud considered overcoming the Oedipus complex as the foremost criterion for the presence of, or the freedom from, neurotic disturbances and had already touched upon this point in the letter to Fliess, one could rightly say that the connection between psychoanalysis and literature also occupied a significant place in the unfolding of psychoanalytic psychopathology. Finally, the letter of 1897 and the well-known section in the "Traumdeutung" (Freud, *Interpretation* vol. 3) both refer to Oedi-

pus and Hamlet and thereby represent the first statement in what was to
become the most significant aspect in the relationship between psychoanalysis and literature, namely that literature provided psychoanalysis with crucial prototypes.

By interpreting the mythopoeic patterns passed on in literature, psychoanalysis would, in return, affirm the cognitive value of literature
which in other respects must necessarily reach far beyond the scope of
psychoanalysis. The unique faculty of literature for enlarging consciousness had certainly been acknowledged before; but now, through
the basic psychology of psychoanalysis, this faculty was established and
explained systematically for the first time. Through this preconscious
relationship to psychoanalysis, literature is by no means reduced to a
museum of psychoanalytic ideas and hunches. The vast resources of literature supplement the empirical observation of the psychoanalytical
clinic and often serve as touchstones for new hypotheses. Expressed in
this way it may first sound like an exaggeration, but in the letter to Fliess
from which I quoted, we do indeed find the manifest starting point for
the psychoanalytic study of literature (Holland, *Freud* and "Postmodern
Psychoanalysis"). Naturally, when we read it now, we do so with the
knowledge of what happened in following decades. Yet the fact is clear:
the letter does point to a new approach, the psychoanalytic study of literature which is still in the process of being realized. The letter as well as
the remarks in the "Traumdeutung" also refer to the unconscious reaction of readers or of an audience to the repertory of conflicts and developmental crises presented to them (Erikson). Literature has a special
competence when dealing with unconscious and, therefore, with essentially unacceptable topics. It is possessed of insights—one would like to
say "born with them"—for which psychologists and psychoanalysts
must laboriously toil.

However, the scope of literature in psychoanalysis is even larger and
more varied than presented so far. Most of the examples mentioned before are discursive and didactic. We want to examine once more the
prospects and potentialities for the application of literature in psychoanalysis and, if it can be done, arrive at a unifying concept. In the dialectics of the psychoanalytic procedure literature is most frequently employed for comparison and exemplification. King Oedipus, as well as
Hamlet, belong to a configuration which Freud first identified as an
elementary developmental crisis of his own life, then generalized from it
to the notion of a universal stage and crisis of growth. At the same time
he noticed that figures of classical literature might lend themselves both

to clarify and to exemplify these generalizations more effectively than a single-minded description of events, memories, and dreams. Here Freud touched upon something which in the writings of the next two decades he worked to explain more fully.

Not every member of the audience watching the plays *King Oedipus* and *Hamlet* may have experienced what Freud in the throes of a monumental discovery had surmised. Nevertheless, his remarks confront us with the question: why, in the theater and in the literary arts, it should be possible to live out what in ordinary life is strictly forbidden for the individual? Literature obviously works as a catalyst to individual psychological dispositions, in order to make possible what otherwise would be impossible. Certainly, when we are in the theater we are also participating in a collective experience. In the process of sharing it with others, we identify with each other, uniting against the instinctual danger of what is arousing us, as well as against the threat of conscience which, for just that reason, could painfully encroach upon us. On the level of subjective experience, literature has the power to transform that primordial subjective element, the daydream, by giving it a new structure: while broadening and deepening it, literature also succeeds in taming its potential explosiveness. The special faculty of literary arts appears to lie in their capacity for condensation, the meaningful arrangement of elementary experiences on various interrelated levels, extending from concrete representation to metaphorical and to discursive abstraction.

When we speak of the esthetic quality of literature, however, we are also bound to speak of what one might call its functional or psychoanalytic quality. This also means that we include the anthropological peculiarity and singularity of the literary arts, their meaning for mankind, and their place in civilization. How should we define it? As an institution? But that would deviate too far from conventional sociological usage. We can't very well call literature a cultural artifact, borrowing that descriptive term from ethnology. Perhaps we should assign to literature the status of a basic and very nearly universal category of planful articulation by special means. We should, therefore, define literature first of all with regard to the peculiar manipulation of language employed to transform experiences, memories, and daydreams, reanimated in fiction and condensed in reflection. The communication of experience resulting from this transformation then becomes itself a source of new experiences.

Doesn't all this have something to do with the obvious use of literature when we analyze? We often look for an opportunity to utilize an example from literature in order to clarify the psychoanalytical nexus we want to convey. We need not be surprised, therefore, if analysts from the very beginning have tried to draw from literature for both the understanding and the communication of their enterprise, when they felt the need for the psychoanalytic *mot juste*. The reference to literature, the quotation, might accomplish the analyst's aim by making his point more concrete, while at the same time deepening its allusiveness, exactly as literature does with the original experience from which it springs.

The analyst, it appears, points to parallels in literature as they occur to him. "By the way, what you have just reported reminds me of particular themes in a classical play. It reminds me of instances that may have occurred to you, too. I am speaking of the anger of a young man over a figure of authority who suddenly appears to block his way, so that a violent confrontation is unavoidable. To be sure, in connection with what you have just recounted, it also looks as if this confrontation could well have been avoided. Obviously, it has had its origin in the tensions arising from your own needs and conflicts and not only from external events. It does sound like Oedipus at the crossroads! By way of another example: your bitter feeling because you find yourself incapable of showing up your blustering step-father when he throws his weight around, that you still can't put him in his place although you have been independent of him for several years—and in particular your vexation because of your mother's involvement with him—doesn't that remind us a bit of Hamlet?"

The aim of such a remark—of which one hopes that in a real therapeutic conversation it would sound less artificial and "dragged-in-at-the-heels" as it may sound here—lies in the expectation that invoking a familiar context, the repertory of world literature, will help clarify the peculiar coherence of a number of events just related. The comparison should assist in the understanding of a context and, additionally, deepen the analytical alliance. Here is a subliminal invitation for the analysand to identify himself with the analyst through the joint experience of a literary paradigm, and hidden in the pretext of clarification through concrete imagery is the prompting (Wyatt, "Narrative") to go on reflecting further than before on whatever else in the patient's life might have something to do with the authoritarian figure at the crossroads. The connection might similarly be made between *Hamlet* and the short-sighted decision of one's own mother to marry that uncle—a mother, incidentally, by whom one had felt vaguely disappointed much earlier, without ever knowing quite why. The comparison with Oedipus and

Hamlet clearly aims to help the patient become aware of the pattern of his own life, then expand and deepen that awareness.

Literature often comes into the analytical dialogue when the patient makes reference to it. (Introducing literature in this manner will complement what has been said before about the inherent capacities of literary expression.) Both patient and analyst are looking for opportunities to close in on the patient's early experiences. Both see to it that they may accomplish this by means of a variety of images, a quasi-experimental series of pictures and allusions which should help to recover or reconstruct what had been repressed a long time ago. The patient doesn't merely want to distract and evade the analyst-pursuer, as analysts not too long ago would have concluded. The analysand's reference to a literary text wants to communicate something which goes far beyond intellectualizing. When the patient refers to literature, several things may have happened. He may wish thereby to come closer to the analyst. The patient is also looking for ways to make something clear to himself. Without comprehending it explicitly, he intimates that he would want, first, to share something with the therapist in order to be able, then, to communicate it. So far he has not been able to penetrate the fog-bank of his self-alienation. Groping his way verbally, he indicates that he is looking for signs which might aid him in orienting himself. Good examples for this are to be found throughout Hilda Doolittle's book, *Tribute to Freud.* She says there: "I must find new words as the professor found or coined new words, to explain certain states of mind or of being as yet unrecorded."

I grew up with the experience that through quotation I could declare a kind of belongingness which, in turn, would give me support. Only the grave historical interruption of this, one must add, somewhat playful and rather magical game, showed me that there must be more to quoting from literature than self-confirmation. In the United States where I lived from 1938 to 1974 I soon had to give up the habit of quoting, not because the people on whom I had tried it out rejected it as a symptom of educated, middle-class snobbery, but because too often it met with polite bewilderment and sheer ignorance of the quotation and its frame of reference. Sense and purpose of quoting became, as it were, defused. In the process of learning anew, which living in another culture will exact, I also became acquainted with a characteristically American concept. The phrase "conspicuous consumption" is so common that it is even cited in regular dictionaries and transliterated as follows: "ostentatious standard of living for prestige reasons" (Langenscheidt). The phrase comes from

Thorsten Veblen, a social scientist whose impact was strongest in the first quarter of this century. In the book which made him famous, *The Theory of the Leisure Class* (1899), Veblen describes behavior patterns whose aim and goal is to gain prestige. The consumption of goods, above all, in this group-specific behavior pattern is supposed to help gain social status. A few decades later an ethnologist, Ruth Benedict, took up the same theme in a different context. She described the giving and destroying of goods for reasons of prestige among the Quakiutl, an Indian tribe on the northwestern coast—a "conspicuous consumption" of sorts in Veblen's sense, who considers the use of quotations as being among the "rules of the game" for an "ostentatious standard of living."

Was the rejection, more exactly the nonreception, of my attempt at calling upon the great names of the European past an indirect demonstration of Veblen's rule? As if somebody had said to me: "Don't give yourself airs like that! You just want to obtain status by appearing supereducated." No, I don't think so. *Bildung,* that special ideal of a universalist European education, means too little to Americans. Veblen, I would say now, judged wrongly because of his own sociopersonal bias. Most important among its components was a deep-rooted anti-intellectualism which, though it came from Puritanism originally, in Veblen's own time tried to hide behind a technocratically colored populism. Veblen, perhaps without being aware of it, helped find a new rationale for the opposition of country people, supposedly safely cradled by their tradition, against the corruptions of the big cities. Because Veblen was caught up in his own unconscious prejudices, he missed entirely what quotation is all about—the search for the *mot juste,* the right word. In quoting we seek to utilize images, metaphors, and formulations which will clarify connections or establish new ones. Quotations are memorable not because they are in verse but because they represent a typical experience: "Yes, that's it! That is the sense and true meaning of this thing!" The rhyme doesn't just complacently ring; it shows, as Karl Kraus put it, that two thoughts are in accord with each other. When one calls upon such a successful formulation, one refers at the same time to the elementary task of form-giving articulation: How can I hold on to and fix experience before it becomes evanescent again? Or, as we might put it in the language of psychoanalysis, before it falls prey again to being undone by repression? Certainly, that which we finally preserve by having expressed it is never exactly what we have really experienced. Quoting means, therefore, attempting to catch up with experience mostly by means of metaphorical language. It also means participating in a universal endeavor obsessed with formulation, with all the psychological consequences of affirmation of the self.

Montaigne is instructive here. In quoting the ancients, it was certainly important to him to present the reader tokens of a lost Golden Age. As he was not free of vanity, it may have mattered to him to show his readers that he was familiar with the best that the human spirit had discovered and articulated. But in the end, he was always concerned with the power of quotation to approach what could neither be grasped head-on nor understood by will alone. With each classical quotation he expresses a feeling of wistful admiration: these ancients could always find the right expression for it, better than we have been able to ever since. It is as if Montaigne had said: "Don't let yourselves be deceived by what may seem transitory and historical to you, by an elevated, alien language, by pagan images and mythological themes, in short, by a world which may appear strange. When you allow the words of my quotations to touch you, you will realize that they are still as valid for our cares and uncertainties as they once were for theirs." Montaigne was right. Not only has at least the essence of what one strains to understand been felt before but, most importantly, it has been *expressed.*

More than four hundred years after Montaigne the problem presents itself anew to psychoanalysis. How can we transfer inchoate experience (*Erleben*) into orderly awareness (*Bewβtsein*)? The purpose of analytic procedure is to find some expression forever so many things in experience which could otherwise be neither stated nor mastered. This includes, above all, an effective grasp of the context, of motives manifest in experience; to find flexible interpretations of impulses and inhibitions, which is what we are mainly concerned with when we do therapy. To this end we also would need modes of expression capable of approaching the original experiences, that is, when they need help to be articulated at all. That is exactly the appeal of literature and the peculiar function of its language in the conduct of psychoanalysis. In other words, psychoanalysis needs the competencies of literature in order to accomplish its own purpose.

In what follows, I should like to present two examples of the use of literature in the process of analysis and in the thinking of the analyst. I should like to relate experiences which demonstrated to me impressively the goal of literature in psychoanalysis. A younger colleague who, some time ago, had been in a training analysis with me, reminded me of an image that I had used several years ago during his analysis. He found himself at that time in a period of great loneliness and spent the hours not claimed by his therapeutic work mostly in a state of despondent isolation. His need was that of a sullen but also mournful state of dejection. While complaining about his isolation, he was inclined to despise other people. At the same time he longed for close relationships. At that time the picture of Lucifer in the fourth book of Milton's *Paradise Lost* suddenly had occurred to me in an analytic hour—for more than one reason, as I discovered upon reflection. The following text illustrates my point:

> And like a devilish engine back recoils
> Upon himself. Horror and doubt distract
> His troubled thoughts, and from the bottom stir
> The Hell within him, for within him Hell
> He brings, and round about him, nor from Hell
> One step no more than from himself, can fly
> By change of place. Now conscience wakes despair
> That slumber'd; wakes the bitter memory
> Of what he was, what is, and what must be
> Worse; of worse deeds worse sufferings must ensue.
>   (17–26)

> O sun, to tell thee how I hate thy beams,
> That bring to my remembrance from what state
> I fell, how glorious once above thy sphere;
> Till pride and worse ambition threw me down;
> Warring in Heaven against Heaven's matchless king!
>   (37–41)

> What could be less than to afford him praise,
> The easiest recompense, and pay him thanks,
> How due! Yet all his good prov'd ill in me,
> And wrought but malice. Lifted up so high
> I'sdain'd subjection, and thought one step higher
> Would set me highest, and in a moment quit
> The debt immense of endless gratitude,
> So burthensome, still paying, still to owe;
> Forgetful what from him I still receiv'd,
> And understood not that a grateful mind
> By owing owes not, but still pays, at once
> Indebted and discharg'd— . . .
>   (46–57)

> O, then, at last relent! Is there no place
> Left for repentance, none for pardon left?

> None left but by submission; and that word
> Disdain forbids me, and my dread of shame
> Among the spirits beneath, whom I seduc'd
> With other promises and other vaunts
> Than to submit, boasting I could subdue
> Th'omnipotent. . . .
>
>   (79–86)

This is obviously "great Milton" (Hildebrandt). This passage confronts the reader with the fantastic contradiction between compulsive, desolate Puritanism and an extraordinary capacity for imagery and for a language of unparalleled concentration and power. Milton's unique mastery of the language holds these adverse partners together and succeeds in reconciling them again and again.

When my former analysand reminded me of the literary passage I had used in his analysis, I was greatly impressed. What had touched me now, years after the event, was the confirmation of its effect. Two people, analysand and analyst, must have experienced the power of these images in the same way. Why should just this scene have helped to deepen the analysand's understanding of self by an incisive step which finally contributed to the overcoming of his chronic isolation and inadequacy? It did have the effect I had expected from a many-layered literary reference—more of it, I am convinced, than could have been achieved through a discursive statement in conventional language about a psychological nexus. Yet Milton's message as he intended it for his day was as remote for the analytic tandem as can be. How, then, did it achieve the purpose I had assigned to it in a flash of association? My colleague emphasized that he was grateful for the image, the gift not only of a special and uncommon power of the imagination, but of literature as such, for he knew us to be in agreement about the importance of it for our kind of work. He also reminded me that the imagery and metaphoric quality the reference to Milton had lent to my interpretation had certainly helped him to perceive his own condition more clearly and more intensely, more than a merely discursive explanation would have done. He had suddenly experienced awareness—something even a very sensible interpretation does not always accomplish.

What holds for the contemplation of self in therapy also holds for the contemplation of literature: that which you can discover for yourself will carry more conviction and have a more lasting effect than even the superior insight as it was worked out by others and transmitted to you on paper. I had discovered for myself that a profound if clandestine admiration informed Milton's image of God's rebel. Quite naturally, this admiration is secured and made safe by ever new invocations of orthodox zeal—loyalty oaths, so to speak, before the very pinnacle of authority. It began to dawn upon me how much subtle knowledge of the loneliness that dwells in such a sorrowful defiance is contained in Lucifer's image, how much candid psychological perception of rage, despair, and tentative submission is to be found in the concrete, sensory presentation of the scene. Milton must have been fascinated with God's enemy, and the roots of this fascination ought to reach deeply into his own life and development. The young Milton, already a poet of some repute, his imagination quite possibly alive with images of the future poem, wrote of visions of horror and guilt in the diary he kept during a trip to Italy. Even if they are judged by the standards of a century especially haunted by psychological dread (think of Pascal), Milton's states of abysmal anxiety and overwhelming guilt were uncommonly great and appropriately anguishing.

Milton would have shuddered if he had had an idea that in the images of Lucifer he could have staged some of his own clandestine wishes and fantasies. Had he seen fit to respond to such a challenge, which surely was as foreign to his mind as to his age, he might have said, as did his later exegetes, that only a magnificent Lucifer could be the proper counterpart of a still more magnificent Creator-God. What Lucifer must have meant to him unconsciously emerges from the text. One could formulate it, albeit in a thoroughly post-Miltonian manner, as follows: behind spite and excessive pride lies more than jealousy of the greater and rivalry with the more powerful overlord. What is at stake is the preservation of self before that awesome, if kind and forgiving God-Father. Pride in depravity may be all that is left then, especially in real life and in the enormous susceptibilities of childhood, unadorned by the comforting image of an all-forbearing God. Indeed, wherever this image is cultivated, it seems to be as much the result of guilt as of hope. Rebellious pride surely has other meanings beside serving as a last redoubt of one's own integrity. But it will, in any case, represent an insurmountable obstacle against accepting the support from others, which, if mutuality had worked, in time should be returned to others. There is enough reason in all this for a basic mood of melancholy. Only when the inner logic of such a character is understood may he suddenly be able to transform himself from a ferocious mask into a suffering being, accessible to empathy. Suddenly we recognize in him something that is deeply hidden in all of us, therefore comprehensible, therefore approachable. Lucifer asks, in effect: Why must I be like this? Why did it have to come to this? And Milton, who displaced his own affects onto a mythological figure whose defeat is certain, can for one long, poetical moment allow a part of himself otherwise silenced and shut away to gain voice and expression.

There is so much in these moving and at the same time so adamantly faithful, orthodox passages. For example, that one will never cease to love that focal person, whom one so demonstratively hates—it makes no difference whether one is aware of it or not. Or that one will always have to display one's own valor and push one's own worth when one has been hurt too early in life by the fickle tenderness and the ambivalent support of a parent. One will be prone, then, to shift one's own insecurity onto others, ready to be hostile to any and all who might threaten one's own self-esteem—even before anybody might do so. If there is no visible detractor, one must create one in order to relieve one's own unrest. However, once one has begun to withdraw from others, one will soon be isolated from oneself, too, and through this alienation will quickly set off a new round of the old dismay.

In Milton's amazing poem which is now more than three hundred years old, one can find that yearning for affection may still be confessed, even when it is loudly protested: "I have felt enough disappointments; from now on I shall protect myself against them!" One will find poetic insights far beyond the seventeenth-century vision of man, but will have to read *à rebours*, against the current of the narrative and against its manifest aim. All this endows Milton's Lucifer with attraction—a marvelous poetic achievement and a highly personal one as well. For how could the rebellious angel be more plausible than by attracting the reader nearly as much as he once did with a defecting host of fellow angels? Milton also bestows upon him the dignity of a universal fate in which we all have a share.

Seen in this perspective, Milton was astute enough to anticipate Melanie Klein (see also Segal) by about three hundred years. He knew to the last and bitter analytical end about the heavy burden of gratitude: that it has to cope first with the envy of another person who already has so much that he can give to others. Milton, even though officially dedicated to ethics of self-abnegation, was able, nevertheless, to understand intuitively that it is not the greater power but the greater goodness of God which is so hard to bear. He knew what kind of contortions and distortions human beings, powered by narcissism and shaped by the Oedipus complex, will undertake in order to convince themselves that it is their natural right to hate those who are better, kinder, and more generous than they can ever hope to be. It seems that the adversities of early life restrain people and make it impossible for them to settle between envy and gratitude. The elementary human pursuit of seeking love against the weight of such conflict is transformed into something like: "Apparently I am supposed to submit and prostrate myself—never!" Lucifer, like a good analysand, has already some inkling that what he pictures to be submission is, in reality, something else. Milton also knows something about the heavy weight of shame upon discovering that one desires exactly that which so far one has insisted on despising.

All this and more seem to have resonated when I referred to Milton's Lucifer in that analysis. Today I am inclined to think that what mattered most was that it could be taken not only as an image of a singular defiance, but as a general predicament with which one can empathize. For only in this way can a truant from affection—the analysand for whom the image in the quotation was intended—look at himself differently and begin to wonder about his customary attitude and stance in life. Obviously, Milton's picture of the first and ultimate rebel contains positive features, too. Behind defiance there is the torturing certainty of his fall, of his own corruption. Has he not been unworthy of his loving protector? Isolation loosens when it is recounted again and again with its causes and varying connections to the analytic listener and interlocutor who, by and by, seems to become a part of the process. It is no longer necessary, then, to maintain isolation and to sit like Lucifer in desperate defiance at the barren, outer edge of human fellowship. This is why my patient could translate the quotation from *Paradise Lost* into an effective insight. What made the reference to Lucifer's rejection of any loving concern—the "debt" of which he spoke—so important, was the opportunity it afforded my analysand to reflect on his unspoken anxiety that quantities of devotion and gratitude might be exacted as a price. If he didn't have Lucifer's spectacular position, he had nevertheless at his disposal a much greater latitude of reflection and choice than the Prince of Darkness in his eschatological obsession. Finding out why he had to react as he had been accustomed to do, and to what construction of his imagination, my analysand also gained more freedom to modify his response. What mattered in the end was the belief in the possibility of a personal, psychological liberation in which the analysand and the analyst could share.

The following vignette reports an incident of the unspoken use of a literary image in the reflections of the analyst. Shortly after Ulrich M.

had entered into psychotherapy with me, I found myself calling him "Tonio Kröger" in my thoughts when reviewing his situation and personality. He really did come from an upper middle-class family in the north of Germany. By now, several generations of his family had prospered. The pattern of living developed under these circumstances shaped Ulrich just as it had shaped his parents and siblings—without obliterating the neurotic problems which distinguished each of them.

Ulrich M. actually looked just about as one would imagine Tonio Kröger to look. To be sure, he was taller and more robustly built than his Hanseatic model and, according to the custom of his day, was more sportive and more savvy about life. Ulrich, like Tonio, had excellent manners. Up until the beginning of his professional studies he had played the viola da gamba with considerable success. He stopped playing when he began to be paralyzed by comparing what he could actually do on his instrument with what he demanded of himself. He did not pursue literature, as did Tonio Kröger, but his ironical reports about his own problems and his amusing anecdotes about family and acquaintances gave evidence of some narrative talent. It took some time until it became clear that these amusing stories might yet have other functions than to entertain me in a pleasant and uncommitted manner.

Up to this point I had tentatively accepted Ulrich's similarity with Tonio. The idea stimulated me to search for further correspondences. Where so many external features seemed to be in accord with the celebrated model, they ought to reveal something in the end of a configuration of character, too—or so I thought, confident in the wisdom of literature. Naturally, I was influenced by the fact, too, that I had for many years engaged in the studies of Thomas Mann's work (Wyatt, "Creative Career," "Themenwahl").

It is the nature of the analytic process, however, that the outline of the individual personality will assert itself in the end as he or she is, by reason of life history, character structure, and, last but not least, through the uniqueness in the composition of features. The individual will come out as he or she really is if the observer will allow it, that is, if he will not distort him by the power of his own preconceptions. I had to find out soon that Ulrich, although possessed of several characteristics approximating those of the fictitious Tonio, was beset by entirely different problems. For the therapist they would necessarily lead to different propositional questions. As I pondered my initial notions and playful fantasies, it occurred to me that the Tonio Kröger of the novella also is in contradiction with his well-argued official dilemma. The reader will not no-

tice it at once, and I am not sure whether Thomas Mann was aware of it
himself. That Tonio became a writer and drifted about looking conspicuously melancholy and alone can certainly not be attributed only to
his life history or to the role and function of the artist. Tonio's girlfriend,
Lisaweta, comes closer to the point when she calls him a misguided
member of the bourgeoisie. What strikes us as genuine in his characterization to this day is still not sufficiently explained by Lisaweta's curt
judgment.

Thomas Mann attaches motives to Tonio Kröger which, as we know,
he has taken up in ever new variations in all his writing. It would appear
that he tried to give expression to prototypical patterns of his own experience, unconscious images and constellations of fantasy—to express
them in order to integrate them and gain mastery over them through the
act of articulation. When he pressed Tonio into the service of his concern
about artist and society, preformed as they were by the discourse of the
fin de siècle, he also passed on to Tonio his own dilemma. Tonio was
supposed to represent something that in reality he was not made to be
and could not be—just as his creator displaced onto a distant topic what
subjectively preoccupied him and, one would surmise, frequently op-
pressed him. Mann attempted to foist it all onto the dilemma of the artist
and succeeded thereby in rationalizing his own unconscious motives. Of
course, he didn't want to write about himself and his afflictions. Years
later we learned about them through his diaries. He wanted to disasso-
ciate himself from what burdened and upset him, and so forced himself
anew to find expression for it by transforming it into orderly fiction.

The two bits of insight, that Ulrich was quite different from Tonio
Kröger and the fictitious Tonio would therefore be no help in understanding the real Ulrich, and that the Tonio of the novella cannot be
sufficiently understood on the basis of his own rationalizations, both
helped me quickly to relocate therapy where it belonged. I had sensed the
hidden contradictions in Ulrich's personality without clearly being
aware of them, and so had attempted for a moment to solve my ambiguity by borrowing from a skillful literary paradigm. Only the disclosure of Tonio Kröger's own contradictions as well as those of his author
led me finally to apprehend the real conflicts of my real patient.

By way of conclusion: I began these reflections on a rather subjective
level and want to end them that way, too. To be sure, in the analytical
dialogue this irrefutable, primal subjectivity is also subject to a continuous examination—a cautious assertion, as it were, that things begin in

the id but, by and by, they ought to become ego. Quite naturally, the analytic comprehension will have to correct itself again and again: it transcends itself in the light of every new observation. The analytic process should, therefore, be capable of bringing about changes not only in the analysand's state of consciousness but also in the conduct of his life. The task of the analytical process consists in finding out about needs and motives in the on-going stream of experience so that they will be registered by the ego and eventually take their place in its conscious inventory. Immediate experience will thereby become part of a secondary, yet highly important and effective context, that of reasoning, judgment, and meaning. Literature and psychoanalysis have similar aims in this respect, different though their endeavors may be in many others. What they have in common is that by means of language they work to hold onto and put down fleeting experience, ultimately, to make sense of it and give it meaning. As psychoanalysts, we should be able to concede cheerfully that literature brings more experience and competence to this task than most of us can claim.

I cannot imagine, therefore, psychoanalysis without literature, just as it cannot do without history, sociology, anthropology, and certainly not without biology. Literature may have a more particular relationship to psychoanalysis, but surely not one less complex. Both want to create awareness. Beyond their primary specific intents which, of course, are different, each of them works on giving shape and form to experience. Both want to secure "was in schwankender Erscheinung schwebt . . . in dauernden Gedanken" ("what floats through ever-changing appearance, secure in enduring thought," from Goethe, "Faust I"). Patient and analyst on the one side and writer on the other struggle to transform experience into enduring form and thereby attach it to orderly consciousness—in the last analysis, in order to manage the business of living, in order to survive. In one instance, as we have seen, an analyst may draw from literature for his enterprise; in another, an analysand may prove to be especially accessible to literary expression, perhaps because representation through language played a special role in his personal development. But we hardly need these examples to declare that literature remains inseparable from psychoanalysis. Literature, is, so to speak, implicit in analysis as much as analysis is incontrovertibly implicit in literature. As analysts, we only have the choice either to close our eyes to this fact and play blind, or to take for granted the common roots of literature and psychoanalysis and in our work act accordingly.

Notes

1. The occurrence of literature in the psychoanalytical process has concerned me for some time, especially the quoting from literature in the process of interpretation. I am obliged to Professor Carl Pietzcker for prompting me hermeneutically to transform these observations into the present report.

2. At this point it could also be considered to what extent the familiar relationship in *King Oedipus* and in *Hamlet* may have contributed to the formulation of the Oedipus complex as we now understand it. Freud's letter to Fliess appears to say: first came the observation, then came the comparison with the literary model (or paradigm) and provided the name for the principle derived from both. But wouldn't it be just as plausible to suggest that the literary text was so well known, and especially to Freud, that it supplied the theme of a constellation into which self-observation and clinical experience could easily be fitted? Literary paradigms like Oedipus and Hamlet have in any case the advantage of explicitness and clarity. They become configurations of life history, comprehensible patterns of relationship. We were already accustomed to saying "as in *Hamlet*" or "a situation like that of King Oedipus' " long before the name became a byword for a central proposition in psychoanalysis. In the letter to Fliess, these paradigms appear—as if still uncertain of themselves—a little like a figure just emerging against the ground or backdrop of confusing clinical observations. They clearly offered themselves to the observer to help him organize what he had surmised. Because the paradigms were already established in the memories of many people, it seems only natural that a new idea would seek support of patterns of relationships already established in literature.

Works Cited

Benedict, Ruth. *Patterns of Culture*. Boston: Houghton, 1934.

Erikson, E. H. *Childhood and Society*. New York: Norton, 1950.

————. *Identity and the Life Cycle*. New York: International UP, 1959.

Freud, Sigmund. *The Interpretation of Dreams*. 1900. Vols. 3 and 4 of *The Standard Edition of the Complete Psychological Works of Sigmund Freud*. Ed. and trans. James Strachey. 24 vols. London: Hogarth, 1953–74.

————. *The Origins of Psycho-Analysis: Letters to Wilhelm Fliess, Drafts and Notes: 1887–1902*. New York: Basic, 1971.

HD [Hilda Doolittle]. *Tribute to Freud*. Boston: Godine, 1974.

Hildebrandt, Karl. *Zeiten, Volker und Menschen*. Vol. 4. Berlin: Profile, 1878.

Holland, Norman N. *Freud, Physics and Literature. Journal of the American Academy of Psychoanalysis* 12(1984): 301–20.

————. *Poems into Persons*. New York: Norton, 1975.

————. "Postmodern Psychoanalysis." *Innovation/Renovation: New Perspectives on the Humanities*. Ed. Ihab Hassan and Sally Hassan. Madison: U of Wisconsin P, 1983. 291–309.

Klein, Melanie. *Contributions to Psychoanalysis*. London: Hogarth, 1948.

————. *Envy and Gratitude*. New York: Basic, 1957.

Kohut, Heinz. "Thoughts on Narcissism and Narcissistic Rage." *The Psychoanalytic Study of the Child* 27(1972): 360–402.

Milton, John. *Paradise Lost.* Chicago: Henry Regnery for The Great Books Foundation, 1949.

Segal, Hannah. *Introduction to the Work of Melanie Klein.* London: Heinemann, 1964.

Wyatt, F. "Anwendung der Psychoanalyse auf die Literatur: Phantasie, Deutung, klinische Erfahrung." *Seminar: Theorien der kunsterischen Produktivität.* Ed. M. Curtius. Frankfurt: Suhrkamp, 1976. 335–57.

——. "The Narrative in Psychoanalysis: Psychoanalytic Notes on Storytelling, Listening and Interpreting." *The Narrative.* Ed. T. Sarbin. New York: Praeger, 1986.

——. "Zur Themenwahl in der Literatur. Gefahren und Gewinne." Vol. 4 of *Freiburger Literaturpsychologische Gespräche.* Frankfurt: Peter Lang, 1984.

——. "The Theme of the Artist's Creative Career." Paper presented at the Austen-Riggs Center, Stockbridge, Mass., 1967.

Delusions and Dreams:
Freud's Pompeian Love Letter

Jan Ackerman

Freud wrote his "little book" Delusions and Dreams in Jensen's Gradiva in 1906 at a critical moment in his life and in the life of his "new science."[1] Looking back from our vantage point, it is difficult to realize that this was a time when the institution of psychoanalysis as we know it might not have come into existence. Freud was still in desperate need of official recognition and also in need of followers or disciples. Publication of his infamous Dora case study and his "shockingly wicked" *Three Essays on the Theory of Sexuality* had recently made his name "almost universally unpopular" in the scientific community (Jones 12). But Freud was also in need on a more personal level. His long friendship with Wilheim Fliess had come to an end, and Freud needed another close ally with whom he could continue his "self" analysis. Most important of all, at age fifty he needed a "friend and heir" to inherit and perpetuate the institution of psychoanalysis.[2]

At this moment Carl Jung was a promising young (thirty-one years old) assistant staff physician at the University of Zurich's respected Burghölzli Hospital. He had recently sent Freud a volume which contained work that Jung knew would meet with Freud's approval.[3] And indeed Freud did respond quickly and enthusiastically. Not surprisingly he singled out for special praise Jung's essay "Psychoanalysis and Association Experiments," which "pleased [Freud] most"—for good reason. In it Jung explicitly identifies himself as a follower of Freud and presents a case study parallel to Freud's Dora in its technique, "psychoanalysis strictly on Freud's lines," and in its result, "sexual history" (Jung 2:

304, 306). Understandably, Freud discovered here his hope for the much-needed disciple and friend. Commenting on this essay, he observed to Jung: "You argue on the strength of your experience that everything I have said about the hitherto unexplored fields of our discipline is true. I am confident that you will often be in a position to back me up, but I shall also gladly accept correction" (*Freud/Jung Letters* 3).

Thus by the time of Freud's writing of *Delusions and Dreams,* Jung was already in the process of becoming a disciple and perhaps even the "friend and heir." At the 1906 Congress of Neurologists and Psychiatrists he championed Freud against the attacks of the influential Gustav Aschaffenberg and later published this same defense. No wonder Freud wrote *Delusions and Dreams* in the spirit of an address to Jung.[4] Viewed in the context of this spirit and against the background of Freud's professional and personal needs, this essay takes its place as a crucial chapter in the drama of the institutionalization of psychoanalysis. It served as a catalyst both for the relationship between Freud and Jung and for the emergence of Freud's new science. A measure of what it meant to Freud personally can be glimpsed in the following euphoric response to Jung's favorable reception of the essay:

> Many thanks for your praise of *Gradiva.* . . . This time I knew that my work deserved praise; this little book was written on sunny days [summer] and I myself derived great pleasure from it. . . . I believe it enables us to enjoy our riches. Of course I do not expect it to open the eyes of our hide-bound opponents. . . . To tell the truth, a statement such as yours means more to me than the approval of a whole medical college; for one thing it makes the approval of future congresses a certainty. (*Freud/Jung Letters* 51-52)[5]

Inherent in Freud's embrace of Jung as a collaborator and, especially, as a disciple can be seen a certain expectation about the possibilities of friendship, intellectual relationship, and the founding of a tradition. Freud's response to Jung was turned toward the future: Jung would back Freud up and make future approval certain. It is not by accident, then, that the principal focus of *Delusions and Dreams* is on the idea of transference, that is, the question of love in both the personal and therapeutic senses and, by extension, the broad question also of the transference of authority, the relationship between master and disciple. Freud's essay, however, not only addresses the *idea* of transference; it is also, as we have seen, a personal appeal *for* transference. It functions in two registers.

This doubleness of style and purpose in *Delusions and Dreams* is not a mere coincidental conjunction that could just as well have been otherwise. Freud's divided aim here points up a crucially enabling but problematic doubleness in the idea and practice of the transference cure itself.[6] On one hand Freud scientifically investigates *Gradiva* as if he were doing a case study. On the other hand he addresses a "love letter" to Jung that promises collaborative friendship and a successful marriage of minds.[7] Freud speaks in the registers of both distanced objectivity and intimate identification. But this doubleness was also precisely the hallmark of Freud's new science and its method of knowing and curing.

Even by this early date it was becoming evident that Freud was in the process of claiming a territory for his infant science of psychoanalysis that lay somewhere in between empirical science and the traditional domain of art or literature. One of the main reasons behind Freud's favorable response to Jung was that the younger man was following Freud and emphasizing—already in the essay Freud liked best—that the analyst should develop a "way of thinking that is innate in a poet but is carefully avoided in scientific thought" (Jung 2: 289). In *Delusions and Dreams* Freud himself continues this line of argument, noting that "description of the human mind is indeed the domain which is most [the creative writer's] own; he has from time immemorial been the precursor of science, and so too of scientific psychology." The psychiatrist, on the other hand, restricts his interest to "severe" illnesses, failing to attend to "deviations from health which are slighter and capable of correction"— and, most important, through the medium of which alone can be understood "either normal states or the phenomena of severe illness." The "strict psychiatrist" tends to "coarsen everything" and to develop "systems of nomenclature and classification [that] . . . have something precarious and barren about them." In contrast, the author of *Gradiva,* for instance, does not put his disturbed hero "at a distance from us"; instead, Jensen brings him "closer to us so as to make 'empathy' easier" (43–45).

Freud's psychoanalytic method, then, requires that the patient be brought closer to the analyst in the way that the creative artist enlists our sense of identification with his characters. In fact Freud maintains that the patient must first "love" the analyst before his arguments can "carry conviction" (*Introductory Lectures* 445). Once this therapeutic relationship of mutual proximity has been established, however, what is the basis upon which the analyst's knowledge rests—beyond the patient's emotional accreditation? Once Freud has brought the objectifications of science and the identifications of art into such close alignment, how does he propose to keep them separate? Where does he plan to draw the line between knowledge and love, science and art? Freud is ready to grant that "creative writers are valuable allies . . . [who] are apt to know a whole host of things between heaven and earth of which our philosophy has not yet let us dream . . . sources which we have not yet opened up for science." But he also wishes that "this support given by writers . . . were less ambiguous" (*Delusions* 8).

Freud turned to *Gradiva* in order both to corroborate his own work and to differentiate his new science from the creations of art. His interest in the novel was first aroused by an anonymous "one" (probably Jung)[8] who noticed that the dreams described there "looked at him with familiar faces and invited him to attempt to apply to them the method of *The Interpretation of Dreams*" (*Delusions* 9–10). The story gripped Freud's attention for many reasons, but perhaps most crucial is the fact that *Gradiva* recounts the adventures of a trip to Pompeii made by a phantasy-ridden archeologist in quest of an idealized love. The novel is subtitled *A Pompeian Phantasy.* Freud's own interest in Pompeii is well known.[9] For here it is sufficient to recall more generally his understanding of the psychoanalytic uncovering of the unconscious as analogous to the excavations of archeology.

The novel (and Freud's interpretation) opens with the German archeologist Norbert Hanold's growing erotic obsession with a Roman bas-relief on the wall of his study, the same replica Freud soon placed in his own consulting room (see fig. 1). This statue of a young woman in flowing robes perhaps catches Hanold's eye because, as Freud suggests, she has an "unusual and peculiarly charming gait" (10). In other words, she looks alive. And Hanold further intensifies this illusion by phantasizing a name for her, Gradiva, and also a personal history detailing her noble Grecian birth and her eventual demise in the catastrophe of Pompeii.

Hanold then is gradually drawn to the ruins of Pompeii by the lure of this imaginary Gradiva. But while there he in fact encounters a real woman who appears to him to resemble his idealized vision in every respect. Uncannily this woman turns out to be Hanold's childhood girl-friend Zoe Bertgang, who over the years has continued to love him. Seeming to understand the nature of his delusion, Zoe plays the role of Gradiva in order to bring Hanold back to health and reality—and to open the possibility for him of an erotic relationship with a real woman. In their final encounter Hanold is able to accept Zoe's analysis of his neurosis because his love for her in the role of his Gradiva imago has

Fig. 1. The *Gradiva* relief. Vatican Museum.

made him a willing collaborator in his own cure. Thus Jensen's novel tells a tale of repression and transference that serves to corroborate Freud's own method of analysis and cure.

In fact the story of *Gradiva* so closely seems to follow from Freud's own work that the "one" who first noticed these similarities took it upon himself to question Jensen concerning the author's possible prior knowledge of such "scientific theories" (*Delusions* 91). Jensen, however, denied any such awareness—and so paved the way for Freud's own explanation that the similarity between the work of the "writer and the doctor" resulted from the common "source" of their investigations and so independently proved the accuracy of each other's efforts. Freud is happy to admit that his own "views on repression, on the genesis of delusions and allied disorders, on the formation and solution of dreams, on the part played by erotic life, and on the method by which such disorders are cured . . . [are not] the common property of science"—but rather also can be found in the possession of art (91–92).

On the other hand, Freud cannot allow art to usurp the authority of science. Art can corroborate psychoanalysis and help to make it "new," but art must remain clearly separable from science and also clearly subordinated to it. Just as art can serve as the "precursor" of science but not its equal, so also Jensen and Freud can be in possession of a "common property"—but not in possession in the same way. Not only need Jensen "not state these laws [that Freud has revealed in *Gradiva*], nor even be clearly aware of them," Jensen as artist *cannot* be in possession of this knowledge. It is the prerogative of doctors or scientists alone to be able to "discover these laws by analysing [the novelist's] writings just as [they] find them from cases of real illness" (92).

The line between science and art that Freud draws here, however, blocks not only the artist from true possession of his knowledge; it also blocks the analyst from identifying with that "way of thinking that is innate in a poet." In protecting his science from the encroachment of art, Freud appears to be condemning the analyst once again to those barren systems of thought that deny the possibility of empathy. Moreover, Freud seems also to be forgetting the main lesson of Jensen's text. The real curer of *Gradiva* is not the scientist. It is the scientist Hanold who is sick, who has lost the capacity to know phantasy from reality (or perhaps art from science). Nor is it simply the "real" Zoe who cures him. The true doctor in this story is Zoe-Gradiva, the "real" woman in the guise of the phantasy.

Where Freud discovers a *law*, Jensen finds an instability. Where

Jensen softens or blurs the line that separates phantasy and reality, Freud seeks to establish a clear line of demarcation, not only between phantasy and reality but also between art and science, doctor and patient, master and disciple. Freud is ready to open his new science to the potentially destabilizing effects of art only as long as science remains firmly in control. But with the risks so minimized, are the equally potential curative powers of art still accessible to the doctor or scientist? Can Hanold be cured without first losing control? Can the Freudian analyst cure without relinquishing his position of mastery? Can the master himself perpetuate "his" institution through a disciple without losing control of the disciple and the institution? If Jensen and Freud together possess a "common property" or source in the unconscious, they nonetheless envision the relationship between phantasy and reality in different ways, just as they also propose different methods of cure.

In the process of subordinating the *other*—both artist and disciple—to his scientific mastery, Freud punctuates *Delusions and Dreams* with a series of attempted codifications of his laws of resistance and transference, the all-important "facts" that validate his new science ("From the History of an Infantile Neurosis" 16). In the opening section of his study, for instance, he defines these laws with reference to an etching by the Belgian painter Félicien Rops, *The Temptation of St. Anthony* (see fig. 2). In this etching, in Freud's words,

> [St. Anthony] has fled . . . from the temptations of the world to the image of the crucified Saviour. And now the cross sinks down like a shadow, and in its place, radiant, there rises instead the image of a voluptuous, naked woman in the same crucified attitude. . . . Rops has placed Sin in the place of the Saviour on the cross. He seems to have known that when what has been repressed returns, it emerges from the repressing force itself. (35)

The Rops artwork and the Jensen love story are both called on to support Freud's claim that "the source of the driving forces of neurosis lies in sexual life" ("From the History of an Infantile Neurosis" 12). Transference works, Freud argues, because analysis uncovers the real sexual drive beneath its phantasy substitute (in the way that the real latent dream-thoughts are found beneath their manifest content). In this view of St. Anthony's temptation, the penitent tries to repress what he indeed sees—that his love of Christ is a substitute for physical love. But this trauma—although painful for the neurotic and difficult to resolve for the analyst—both confirms Freud's law of repression and suggests

Fig. 2. Félicien Rops. *The Temptation of St. Anthony.* Royal Albert Library, Brussels.

the possibility of cure. For once the real sexual trauma is restaged in transference, the analyst-mediator can then transfer his understanding of the neurosis onto the patient and send him, cured, into the real world to find a real love-object. The enabling premise of this dialectical under-standing of transference is thus the real sexual repression, the negative force that through analysis can be transformed into a positive erotic drive.

While Freud was insisting on this "fact" of sexual repression as the ground of his science, his "hide-bound opponents" were arguing that

Freud's patients were just inventing "stories" to support his equally phantasy-ridden laws.[10] But instead of his new science having become too compromised by art, certain difficulties in *Delusions and Dreams* suggest that Freud was not compromising enough. Rops's etching, for example, illustrates more than Freud's law of repression. This St. Anthony might never give up his substitute for reality for the simple reason that he experiences reality not in the flesh but in the spirit.[11] In other words, the real and the phantasmal are intertwined in uncanny ways.

As a follow-up to his interpretation of this Rops etching, Freud tells the story of one of his own patients, a young student who had repressed his sexual desires through a series of substitute satisfactions—first an "intensified . . . zeal for learning," then an "exaggerated . . . dependence on his mother," and finally an absorption in mathematics. These substitutes failed, according to Freud, because each of them revealed as well as concealed the erotic drive the student was trying to repress. So at last "when he felt that he had been betrayed by mathematics as well, he took flight from it too" (*Delusions* 36). Freud abruptly concludes his discussion at this point. But the reader might continue to speculate with the Rops etching still in mind. Where will this series of substitutions end? Where did it begin? Will the student be truly cured when he is able to love a "real" woman? Would this be a final resolution of his problem or just another substitution?[12] Freud's theory of repression opens up rather than resolves the general question of the relationship between phantasy and reality.[13]

Freud reads *Gradiva* as a "commonplace love-story" (*Delusions* 22) and also as the "model of a cure by love" (90). But there is nothing commonplace about this cure. Zoe-Gradiva remains an uncannily double figure throughout the transference cure—and even after the cure is supposedly over (as we will see).[14] Upon first having actually seen the real Zoe, Hanold stares in wonderment: "Had what had just stood before him been a product of his imagination or a reality? He did not know that, nor whether he was awake or dreaming, and tried in vain to collect his thoughts" (Jensen 49). Even after he begins to return to "sound reason" and to the realization that "Gradiva was only a dead bas-relief," he continues to believe also that "it was equally beyond doubt that she was still alive. . . . [T]his dual nature remained enigmatic. . . . Yet to this incompatible duality there was joined a similar one in him" (Jensen 102–03).

It is this strange precise resemblance between the statue and the real woman that disturbs Freud most about the story. Like St. Anthony coming face to face with his primary repression, Freud too faces his own deepest "scientific" repression, the exclusion of phantasy from the realm of reality. It would of course be more consistent with Freud's interpretation of *Gradiva* were there to be a marked *dis*similarity between the two figures. This fact would clearly establish Hanold's problem as wholly delusional while also clearly identifying Zoe as a real woman entirely separate from the delusion. In rendering these figures—the phantasy and the reality—as all but indistinguishable, Jensen introduces an uncanny dimension into the novel which Freud's interpretation evades.

Freud's confrontation with this issue is worth following in detail. Even though Jensen "expressly renounced the portrayal of reality by calling his story a 'phantasy,' " Freud finds that it is "so faithfully copied from reality that [he] would not object if *Gradiva* were described not as a phantasy but as a psychiatric study." Only two of Jensen's premises "do not seem to have their roots in the laws of reality." The second (the coincidence of the meeting in Pompeii) Freud is able to explain away. But he is perplexed in the extreme by the first premise, the nearly exact resemblance between the dead statue and the live woman. This premise "seems to lean more towards phantasy and to spring entirely from the author's arbitrary decision." And yet Freud acknowledges that it is this premise "on which all that follows depends." He wishes, though, that Jensen had made a "more sober choice" by limiting the resemblance perhaps to the "single feature of the posture of the foot." But in the absence of such a choice on the author's part, Freud himself feels called upon to offer his own scientific explanation for this strange coincidence—an explanation so extreme that instead of solving the riddle it provides rather a measure of the extent of Freud's own perplexity. In brief, Freud hypothesizes that the German Bertgang family was "descended from a Roman family one member of which was the woman who had led the artist to perpetuate the peculiarity of her gait in the sculpture." But of course this explanation explains nothing of the cause behind the exactness of the overall resemblance between the two figures. And so Freud decides to give up such "speculations" and suggests that it would be "wiser . . . to enquire from the author himself" in order to prove that "what was ostensibly an arbitrary decision rested in fact upon law." Except for this single "improbable premise," Freud concludes, "the author has presented us with a perfectly correct psychiatric study . . . a case history and the history of a cure" (*Delusions* 41–43).

This cure, however, also poses a difficulty for Freud—and for the same reason. Elsewhere he first observes the "striking preference for ambiguous speeches in *Gradiva*" and then goes on to provide the rational explanation that in the case of Hanold the ambiguity is a symptom arising from the "double origin" of his illness and its unstable "compromises between the conscious and the unconscious." But the ambiguous speeches of Zoe, on the other hand, exhibit an *"intentional* ambiguity" that enables her to rise "above the delusion." Such intentionality, of course, depends upon the presupposition of Zoe's singular identity. A dual Zoe-Gradiva would speak ambiguously without intention. Freud goes on to parallel Zoe's conscious use of double meaning with the analyst's own intentional employment of ambiguity, which, Freud adds, "is apt to raise the greatest objection in the uninitiated and to give rise to the greatest misunderstandings" (*Delusions* 84–86). Freud thus continues to make use of the methods of art while attempting also to set (rational) limits to its unsettling doubleness. But in so doing, he continues also to strengthen the barrier between analyst and patient, normal and abnormal—the same barrier that the artist Jensen, in contrast, tends to dismantle.

This univocal flattening out of the ambiguous complexities of *Gradiva* and especially of the analyst figure Zoe-Gradiva is evident in Freud's evasion of the delicate suggestiveness of the novel's concluding scene. After pledging their troth to each other and planning, perhaps, a honeymoon in Pompeii, the hero (now supposedly cured) and heroine walk together through the streets of Pompeii until Hanold stops and "with a peculiar tone" asks Zoe to walk ahead of him. Zoe complies with a "merry, comprehending, laughing expression" while "raising her dress slightly with her left hand" (as in the Gradiva bas-relief) as she crosses the street with her "buoyant walk" under the view of Hanold's "dreamily observing eyes"—truly a "Gradiva *rediviva,*" as the author describes her here for the last time (Jensen 117–18).

Freud explains this enigmatic climax by observing simply that "with the triumph of love, what was beautiful and precious in the delusion found recognition as well" (*Delusions* 40). But what is suggested by this episode is not the mere ornamental addition of the beauty of the phantasy to the reality of the love but rather an infusion of the phantasy into the sphere of the love itself. Phantasy and reality interpenetrate in this climactic passage, just as they do throughout the whole of this love story. This is precisely what Jacques Lacan means when he points out that the "subject can never reach its sexual partner, which is the Other, except by way of mediation, as the cause of its desire. . . . [T]his can only be a fantasy" ("Love Letter" 151).[15] No wonder that in terms of her intimacy with Hanold, then, Zoe will also remain Gradiva as well. Who can doubt that they will always honeymoon in Pompeii, the site of the Other where past and present, phantasy and reality intertwine?

Despite his overtures toward Jung and toward the poetic "way of thinking" that leads to "empathy" Freud wrote *Delusions and Dreams* largely for the purpose of setting ground rules to safeguard the analyst's scientific authority and also in order to sustain his own personal mastery in his relationship with his new disciple. Although Freud does in fact recognize a difference between Jensen's fictional analyst and the practicing Freudian analyst, it is not the same difference that we have just observed. Rather it is simply the practical difference that, following the successful cure, "Gradiva was able to return the love [of her patient] . . . but the doctor cannot. . . . The doctor has been a stranger, and must endeavor to become a stranger once more after the cure" (90). Neither *Gradiva* nor *Delusions and Dreams*, however, is concerned with what happens after the cure. Both focus on the role of love during the cure. Freud is not interested in the practicality of whether or not the analyst can or should love the patient after the analysis is over. He is suggesting limits to the doctor's empathic loss of control during the analysis, but he is not telling us what those limits are. The analyst "must endeavor to become a stranger once more." But how has he not been a stranger during the cure?

This question of empathy and mastery—as well as the allied issues of literature and science, phantasy and reality—is a far-reaching dilemma that of course continued to baffle Freud throughout his career and continues today to confound psychoanalytic thought.[16] My purpose here has been to raise this question in relation to *Delusions and Dreams*. But our story does not stop there. For Freud and Jung continued their discussion of *Gradiva* and its author in the course of a number of letters written after the publication of Freud's study. Their mutual excitement over the issues raised by *Gradiva* both intensified their friendship and perhaps contributed to their eventual estrangement. As in *Delusions and Dreams*, there is more at stake in these letters than their "intentional" cognitive content. In a sense, Freud and Jung "perform" their friendship through the mediation of *Gradiva*. But this is not the place for a detailed consideration of this correspondence.[17] I would, however, like to conclude by pointing out briefly how *Gradiva*'s unanswered question of love and mastery returns to haunt the Freud-Jung friendship.

Jung's enthusiastic acclaim of *Delusions and Dreams* (which we noted at the outset) was part of a larger pattern of adulation for the person of Freud and for Freud's new science. Jung's letter of 30 May 1907 provides a typical instance of the manner in which the scholarly subject of *Gradiva* coalesced with the rhetoric of a disciple: "Thanks above all for the news about Jensen. . . . In my entourage *Gradiva* [*Delusions and Dreams*] is being read with delight. The women understand you by far the best. . . . I would gladly write something for your *Papers* [*Papers on Applied Psychology*]. . . . Anyone who knows your science has veritably eaten of the tree of paradise and become clairvoyant" (*Freud/Jung Letters* 55–56).

Jung's final hyperbole points up the extent to which this developing friendship was early cast in the mold of a master-disciple relationship with a religious aura. In another letter to Freud, Jung observes: "It seems to me that one can never quite understand your science unless one knows you in the flesh. Where so much still remains dark to us outsiders only faith can help; but the best and most effective faith is knowledge of your personality" (30). Other letters indicate that this mold included also codes from priest-confessor and doctor-patient forms of relationship. Freud's stated expectation to Jung that all his "followers" should be "able to overcome their own inner resistance to the truth" (6) was a veiled appeal for confessions from his patient-disciple, an appeal Jung answered on 28 October 1907: "I confess this to you with a struggle—I have boundless admiration for you both as a man and a researcher. . . . [M]y veneration for you has something of the character of a 'religious' crush. . . . I still feel it is disgusting and ridiculous because of its undeniable erotic undertone." Jung's next letter begins: "I am suffering all the agonies of a patient in analysis, riddling myself with every conceivable fear about the possible consequences of my confession" (*Freud/Jung Letters* 95).

If this patient-disciple, however, loves in order to believe (an analytic requirement noted earlier), then with the failure of love (or lack of return of his emotional investment) the belief too falters. Thus it was over this same question of love and mastery that the Freud-Jung friendship eventually foundered. Jung explains on 18 December 1912: "Your technique of treating your pupils [disciples] like patients is a *blunder*. . . . You go around sniffing out all symptomatic actions in your vicinity thus reducing everyone to the level of sons and daughters who blushingly admit the existence of their faults. Meanwhile you remain on top as the father, sitting pretty." Jung goes on to question whether Freud has really achieved the self-containment he pretends to, whether indeed he has been able to overcome his neurosis through self-analysis alone:

"You know, of course, how far a patient gets with self-analysis: *not* out of his neurosis—just like you. . . . Do you *love neurotics* enough to be always at one with yourself? But perhaps you *hate* neurotics" (*Freud/ Jung Letters* 534-35). Jung recalls elsewhere an experience with Freud that was due to become "the most important factor in [Jung's] relation with him"—namely, Freud's refusal to continue his analysis with Jung: "Our analysis, you may remember, came to a stop with your remark that you 'could not submit to analysis *without losing your authority.*' These words are engraved on my memory as a symbol of everything to come" (526 and n.).

"But," Freud might have remarked in response, "the doctor must remain a stranger." Unlike Zoe-Gradiva, Freud's doctor cannot love. The analyst's "scientific" authority derives from his capacity to explain phantasies, not to indulge in them. But this is not to suggest that Jung himself was innocent of the ambition to explain phantasies. In a sense his own truly psychoanalytic thought began during this period with a questioning of Freud's views of regression and transference—and with a "teleological" revalorization of phantasy as the "first beginnings of spiritualization" (Jung 4: 179-80). Recalling our discussion of Freud's analysis of the painting of St. Anthony, it should come as no surprise that Jung's final flare-up with Freud was triggered by the master's unsympathetic response to a paper by Jung on the subject of mysticism (*Freud/Jung Letters* 524-27). Both Freud and Jung aspired to explain phantasy.

Perhaps in some Pompeian space beyond Freud's appropriation of phantasy for science and Jung's appropriation of phantasy for religion, Zoe-Gradiva continues to beckon us with the promise of a poetic way of knowing and curing that is neither true nor false, but no less effective.

Notes

I would like to thank Robert Ackerman for assistance in revising this essay.

1. Freud considered his science "new" in its investigation of and application to the "normal" as well as the pathological. See, for example, *Autobiographical Study* 47 and "A Short Account of Psycho-Analysis" 205.

2. On the basis of his "periodic law," Fliess calculated that Freud would die at fifty-one, a prediction Freud did not take lightly (*Complete Letters* 245; see also *Interpretation* 513 and *Freud/Jung Letters* 6). For "friend and heir," see *Freud/Jung Letters* 172.

3. Jung claims that this volume of the *Diagnostic Association Studies* was published with the aim of opening up "new avenues to Freud's body of knowledge," which was "far too advanced for the understanding of his time" (*Collected Works* 2: 291). Freud credits this volume directly in *Delusions and Dreams* 53n.

4. Jung himself was aware of this personal aspect of the essay and claimed that Freud wrote it "to give [Jung] pleasure" (Jones 341). See also note 8.

5. In his reference to "hide-bound" opponents, Freud quotes Jung in a letter written to Freud two days earlier: "Your *Gradiva* is magnificent. I gulped it at one go. The clear exposition is beguiling, and I think one would have to be struck by the gods with sevenfold blindness not to see things now as they really are. But the hide-bound psychiatrists and psychologists are capable of anything!" (*Freud/Jung Letters* 49).

6. For further discussion of this doubleness in *Delusions and Dreams* (which often, I think, takes Freud too much at face value), see Kofman. For an interesting brief discussion of the same issue, see Jacobus 119-27, 136-37. On the general question of transference, see Chase and Copjec (who also briefly treats *Delusions and Dreams* on 85-90).

7. On a general level Freud longed for an "alliance between the Vienna and Zurich schools" ("From the History of an Infantile Neurosis" 27), while on a personal level Freud came to think of Jung affectionately as the "spirit of [his] spirit" (*Freud/Jung Letters* 115). For more on the subject of the "love letter," see Lacan, "Love Letter" and Derrida, *Post Card* 63, 197.

8. Ernest Jones identifies Jung as the "one" who had interested Freud in Jensen's *Gradiva* (341). James Strachey speculates that the two references to the "one" in *Delusions and Dreams* are to Jung—both the "one" who called *Gradiva* to Freud's attention and the "one" who questioned Jensen on his prior knowledge of Freud's *Interpretation of Dreams* (see *Delusions* 4, 9, 91). Further support for this view comes from the positive identification of Jung as the "friend" and collaborator (in analysis of the Jensen question) mentioned by Freud in his postscript to the second edition of *Delusions and Dreams* (94).

9. See, for example, Freud's references to Pompeii in *Complete Letters* 214, 236, 440, *Delusions* 4-5, 40, "Notes upon a Case of Obsessional Neurosis" 176-77, and "Constructions in Analysis" 260.

On the spelling of *phantasy*, I have preserved the *ph* largely for the reasons listed by Laplanche and Pontalis in *The Language of Psycho-Analysis*. The spelling avoids the connotations of triviality or eccentricity while emphasizing the word's association with the imagination and with literature, as well as its etymological identification with the Latin *phantasma*. This spelling also accords with the *Standard Edition*.

10. Freud often felt it necessary to defend his practice against such charges. See, for instance, "From the History of an Infantile Neurosis" 49-50, 103 and *Introductory Lectures* 368, 452.

11. In his discussion of the *Jouissance* of the mystic, for instance, Jacques Lacan stresses the desire not for sexual but for spiritual union. For the mystic the Real is within. "As long as soul souls for soul [l'âme âme l'âme]," Lacan concludes enigmatically, "there is no sex in the affair" ("Love Letter" 155).

12. Freud is more suggestive concerning the far-reaching implications of such substitution in certain very late essays. See "Fetishism" 152-54 and "Splitting" 275-77.

13. "One may say," Jacques Derrida observes, "that Freud's text has scientific value or claims a scientific status, that it is not a literary fiction. But what is the ultimate criterion for such a division? . . . If the truth inhabits fiction, does this make fiction true or the truth fictional? Is that a real alternative, the true vs. the fictional?" ("Purveyor" 38, 41).

14. For a later discussion by Freud of such ambiguous doubling of selves in literature, see " 'Uncanny' " 232, 235-36.

15. Laplanche and Pontalis conclude similarly: "Sexuality is detached from any natu-

ral object, and is handed over to fantasy, and, by this very fact, starts existing as sexuality" (17).

16. Lacan once observed, for instance, that Freud "to his great astonishment . . . could not avoid participating in what the hysteric was telling him, and that he felt affected by it. Naturally, everything in the resulting rules in which he established the practice of psychoanalysis is designed to counteract this consequence, to conduct things in such a way as to avoid being affected" (quoted in Felman 23).

17. This paper is part of a book-in-progress (about Freud's struggle with the question of art and literature) wherein I investigate the Freud-Jung correspondence in more detail.

Works Cited

Chase, Cynthia. " 'Transference' as Trope and Persuasion." *Discourse in Psychoanalysis and Literature.* Ed. Shlomith Rimmon-Kenan. London: Methuen, 1987. 211–32.

Copjec, Joan. "Transference: Letters and The Unknown Woman." *October* 28 (1984): 60–90.

Derrida, Jacques. *The Post Card: From Socrates to Freud and Beyond.* Trans. Alan Bass. Chicago: U of Chicago P, 1987.

_____. "The Purveyor of Truth." Trans. Willis Domingo et al. *Yale French Studies* 52 (1975): 31–113.

Felman, Shoshana. *Jacques Lacan and the Adventure of Insight: Psychoanalysis in Contemporary Culture.* Cambridge, Mass.: Harvard UP, 1987.

Freud, Sigmund. *An Autobiographical Study.* 1925. *Standard Edition* 20: 7–74.

_____. *The Complete Letters of Sigmund Freud to Wilheim Fliess 1887–1904.* Trans. and ed. Jeffrey Moussaieff Masson. Cambridge, Mass.: Harvard UP, 1985.

_____. "Constructions in Analysis." 1937. *Standard Edition* 23: 255–70.

_____. *Delusions and Dreams in Jensen's* Gradiva. 1907. *Standard Edition* 9: 7–95.

_____. "Fetishism." 1927. *Standard Edition* 21: 152–57.

_____. "From the History of an Infantile Neurosis." 1918. *Standard Edition* 17: 7–122.

_____. *The Interpretation of Dreams.* 1900. *Standard Edition,* vol. 5.

_____. *Introductory Lectures on Psycho-Analysis.* 1916–17. *Standard Edition,* vol. 16.

_____. "Notes upon a Case of Obsessional Neurosis." 1909. *Standard Edition* 10: 155–249.

_____. "Observations on Transference-Love." 1915. *Standard Edition* 12: 159–76.

_____. "On the History of the Psycho-Analytic Movement." 1914. *Standard Edition* 14: 7–66.

———. "A Short Account of Psycho-Analysis." 1924. *Standard Edition* 19: 191–209.

———. "Splitting of the Ego in the Process of Defence." 1940. *Standard Edition* 23: 275–78

———. *The Standard Edition of the Complete Psychological Works of Sigmund Freud.* Ed. and trans. James Strachey. 24 vols. London: Hogarth, 1953–74.

———. "The 'Uncanny.' " 1919. *Standard Edition* 17: 219–52.

Freud, Sigmund, and Carl Jung. *The Freud/Jung Letters: The Correspondence between Sigmund Freud and C. G. Jung.* Trans. Ralph Manheim and R. F. C. Hull. Ed. William McGuire. Bollingen Series 94. Princeton: Princeton UP, 1974.

Jacobus, Mary. "Is There a Woman in This Text?" *New Literary History* 14 (1982): 117–41.

Jensen, Wilhelm. *Gradiva: A Pompeiian Fancy.* Trans. Helen M. Downey. New York: Moffat, 1918.

Jones, Ernest. *The Life and Work of Sigmund Freud.* Vol. 2. New York: Basic, 1955. 3 vols.

Jung, C. G. *The Collected Works of C. G. Jung.* Ed. Sir Herbert Read et al. 19 vols. Bollingen Series 20. Princeton: Princeton UP, 1967–76.

Kofman, Sarah. "Delusion and Fiction: Concerning Freud's *Delusions and Dreams in Jensen's* Gradiva." *The Childhood of Art: An Interpretation of Freud's Aesthetics.* Trans. Winifred Woodhull. New York: Columbia UP, 1988. 175–99.

———. "Résumer, Interpréter." *Critique* 305 (1972): 892–916. Rpt. in *Quatre romans analytiques.* Paris: Galilee, 1974.

Lacan, Jacques. *Feminine Sexuality: Jacques Lacan and the école freudienne.* Trans. Jacqueline Rose. Ed. Juliet Mitchell and Jacqueline Rose. London: Macmillan, 1982.

———. "God and the *Jouissance* of The Woman." *Feminine Sexuality* 61–73.

———. "A Love Letter." *Feminine Sexuality* 137–61.

Laplanche, Jean, and J.-B. Pontalis. "Fantasy and the Origins of Sexuality." *The International Journal of Psycho-Analysis* 49 (1968): 1–18.

Lacan's Seminars on James Joyce: Writing as Symptom and "Singular Solution"

Ellie Ragland-Sullivan

My purpose is to try to convey in some detail the fruit of Jacques Lacan's seminars given on James Joyce, principally in 1975 and 1976, but also as early as 1971. When Lacan first spoke at Yale University in 1975 he began: "Ce n'est pas facile" ("It is not easy for me") ("Kanzer Seminar"). Indeed Lacan's words on Joyce depict a Joyce that will be perfectly strange for many, including Joyce scholars. You will hear ideas such as these. There are Real knots in Joyce's prose that are not metaphorical, but have to do with metonymical signifying chains surrounding the Name of the Father. These knots denote the "thing" (*das Ding* or *point de capiton*) stuck at a point of impasse or encounter. But what is a knot? For Lacan the knot has the structure of a symptom, defined in at least three ways. But for the moment we will describe it as that in a person's life history which conscious knowledge does not account for, but which leaves its imprint anyway. That is, the symptomatic knot is Real, extrinsic in the first place to the cord it ties. It has to be put in. As such it is a Real referent. Thus one can say that psychoanalytic resistance has the shape of a knot, the structure of a symptom, the structure of something that is an obstacle or blockage in various aspects of a person's life.

In 1987 Jacques-Alain Miller described the symptom in *Joyce avec Lacan* as an enigma written in secret characters which in and of themselves say nothing to anyone ("Préface" 11). Secondly, the symptom is also the pure *jouissance*—which Freud discovered as the limit of the power of interpretation—of an *écriture* that Lacan called the Real ("La psychanalyse" 445). Among other things, Lacan says fantasy is separable from *écriture* and gives rise to desire [($\cancel{S}$ ◇ *a*)]. Miller adds later that both interfere in language ("Préface" 11). In Joyce's case, the effects are knots that denote an unconscious memory bank of signifying associations particular to James Joyce alone, actively suspended within his prose, but resisting his knowledge of them as unconscious truth. Jacques Aubert has suggested that Joyce, like Lacan, developed an "art of suspension" ("Galeries" 83). In such a context "truth" is the *savoir* of a particular subject's unconscious and serves a paradoxical function: to provide a knowledge base and to stop up a hole in the Other from which a subject's *jouissance* arises, not as a signifier, but as an effect of the Real. The unconscious signifying chains or *savoir* contain some elements that make sense and others that are nonsensical, the nonsensical "significations" producing a *jouissance* effect rather than a clear grammatical or informational communication.

I shall speak of Joyce's prose, then, as arising from the discourse that constituted the author in the first place as a subject poised between oblivion and the signifier. Jacques-Alain Miller once called "discourse" a process of language that truth constrains ("Avertissement" 5). In his 1975 Kanzer lecture at Yale, Lacan spoke of the truth in Joyce's discourse by referring to an article that had just appeared in a French literary journal whose thesis was that the English language did not exist any longer after Joyce's prose. Lacan's opinion was that, on the contrary, up until *Finnegans Wake*, Joyce had respected what Noam Chomsky has called grammatical structure ("Kanzer Seminar"). His own interest in Joyce was not in the linguistic intricacies of his prose, Lacan said, but rather in the connection of the "truth" that is Joyce's unconscious *savoir* to Joyce's language. One of Lacan's many characterizations of truth is of some *thing* that affects the place from which we are speaking ("The Freudian Thing" 121). Freud understood that the unconscious produces symptoms, but did not grasp that those same symptoms cannot be easily revealed as meaningful truths because they do not arise from anticipated models or meanings such as the various ones Freud proposed in trying to relate mind to body and truth to an unconscious.

Freud's assumptions of what constituted identity and mentality were typical of the positivistic thinking of his day, assumptions that led him to overlook the meaning (*jouis-sens*) in nonsense that he cast aside as irrelevant by 1923. He chose instead an id-ego-superego model to replace his earlier search for the cause of symptoms in dreams, jokes, wordplay, slips of tongue and pen (*The Psychopathology of Everyday Life*), in myth (*Totem and Taboo*), or even in the "pathological" sublimation of art. While Freud saw the artist as necessarily neurotic, Lacan meant something quite different from Freud when he attributed symptoms to artists. While Freud elevated the artist to a sacrificial position, one whose repressed neurosis provides others with cathartic release, Lacan argued the opposite. The purpose of art is not to permit repression, but to pose a question that the artist him or herself has not answered or resolved. Artistic productions are not then in and of themselves pathological or neurotic.

Lacan taught that symptoms return retroactively as the *objet a* in a person's life, an effect of the Real as distinct from fiction. But what are the *objet a*, first derived from Imaginary identificatory material and Symbolic order language and codes? They are the Ur-objects of desire and "drive": the breast, the feces, the urinary flow, the (imaginary) phallus, the voice, the phoneme, the gaze, and the void ("Subversion of the subject" 315). By "object" Lacan never meant the phenomenologically totalizable object, but something to do with desire and *jouissance* as they inhabit language and the body, joining them. The *objet a* dwell in *jouissance* at the limit of the powers of conscious interpretation. As a surplus or *jouissance*, the *objet a* link the Real to the Symbolic and Imaginary by the Symptom, a fourth order that permits the unknotting of the material that holds symptoms together in the first place. Slavoj Zizek has defined the symptom as a particular element which gives the lie to the Universal of which it is a part ("The Marxist Symptom" ms. 12). Some such particulars show up as fictions, desires, or prohibitions whose final referent is the signifier of the "Father's Name," the first countable signifier as a referent for identity. Yet these very symptoms make it seem there is no lack in the universe of self, image, language, or consciousness. The human tendency is to try to explain what *is* by things from the outside or by impersonal innate tendencies, rather than by deficiencies and dissymetries in being and knowing.

Unlike many critics who comment on Joyce, Lacan was not interested in the images in Joyce's work. He argued in his Kanzer Seminar that like any other apparent unity, images always block truth. In Lacan's teaching, grammatical language and images merely produce the illusion of a consistent universe. But the unconscious disrupts these illusions, by disassociating meaning that only seems full from our pretenses that it functions smoothly. The unconscious produces, instead, a glimpse of the void underlying our sense productions. On the other hand, truth does show up in spoken language, just as in dream or literary language, when it is linked to the *objet a* as they lean against chains of signifiers. Lacan taught that signifiers lean against the primordial objects of desire or *objet a* and enable us to think against a backdrop of desire. If language is, indeed, infiltrated by *objet a* as Real punctuation points around which articulable matrices of desire cluster, it becomes clearer what Lacan meant when he described truth as that which makes knowledge stumble. Fiction may have the structure of truth, but it is not truth per se.

In 1975 Lacan gave a seminar titled "Joyce le symptôme" at the Fifth International James Joyce Symposium.[1] In this lecture Lacan considered the difficulty of *Finnegans Wake* through describing a split in Joyce himself, but not the famous split of the subject divided between conscious and unconscious awareness. Rather, Lacan pointed to a split between a Real *jouissance* with which one is familiar, and truth which is repressed as an unconscious *savoir* ("Agency of the letter" 169). Moreover, the Real is stronger than the true (Kanzer Seminar, *Scilicet 6/7* 42). Joyce, he suggested, was more attached to the Real suffering caused by the *jouissance* that lies beyond repression than to any wish to ascertain the true reasons for his own psychic pain. It will perhaps be helpful to recall a definition of *jouissance* given by Jacques-Alain Miller: "Truth resisting knowledge of *jouissance*" ("A and a" 25).

In his 1987 introduction to the screening of Lacan's *Television*, Jacques-Alain Miller points out that *jouissance* is not Other-related, but is egotistical ("Introduction to *Television*" 14). Joyce's deteriorating eye condition (glaucoma), his daughter's psychosis, and his increasingly arcane prose were all symptoms of a man whose desire was encumbered by an excessive oppression of *jouissance*. And *jouissance* always concerns the relation of desire to the position of the Father's Name (or the phallus). The issue of fathers was paramount in Joyce's life and work. His own father had been an alcoholic, indebted, and an embezzler. Catholic church fathers were also constantly disappointing Joyce. In Lacanian terms, his masculine identity was continually beseiged by questions regarding the worthiness of his (father's) name, the worthiness of his national identity, and so on. Disappointed by Imaginary order models and by the Symbolic order itself, Joyce sought to make a *name* for himself chiefly as an artist, thereby depending on his own creativity rather than what others had created for him. Lacan argued that the character Stephen Dedalus was Joyce's alter ego through whom he fictively and unconsciously sought to decipher his own life enigmas. This argument is developed at length by Hugo Rotmistrovsky in "Joyce, el nombre." When an enunciation contains the enigma of the *énoncé* (or unconscious knowledge), Lacan denoted this phenomenon in his mathemes as E^e. A particular enunciation is not just talk or information, but itself announces that an enigma is in play. Rotmistrovsky refers to one such enunciation from *Portrait of the Artist as a Young Man:* "The cock crew, the sky was blue, the bells in heaven, were striking eleven, It's time for this poor soul, to go to heaven?" (35).

By the time he wrote *Finnegans Wake,* shattering his ego into dispersed voices, Joyce had dispensed with Imaginary and Symbolic fathers. Leaving sense behind, the Lacanian Real father (otherwise thought of as *jouissance*) takes over Joyce's language. Lacan described *jouissances* as unassimilated pieces of knowledge that act as symptoms and cause people to invent myths concerning their origins, bodies, desires, being, and so on. The Real symptom or *objet a* is a universal "negative" positivized as *das Ding* that is terrifying in its full presence—a lack of lack—and thus obscured by the *savoir* that generally masks it for the purpose of protecting a subject from knowing what constitutes his being and desire in reference to a cause. The symptom is the more-than-us in us which destroys us. But we cling to our symptoms because they are familiar and give us a sense of being unified and consistent. In the case of Joyce, Lacan described one of his symptoms as his doubt. He was a Saint Thomas who progressively demonstrated what Lacan taught: that our sins, like our uncertainties, place all of us on the same side as analyst and analysand. We all live behind the wall of language, inhabited by a fault or flaw or lack, or in the language of the Church, a sin. Every subject is an effect caused by this wall of language (Lacan's structure of alienation) behind which he or she lives more or less confidently, not knowing that they retrieve the words by which they live at the expense of a lack in being that constitutes them as speaking beings. Lacan gave Joyce a new name, "Joyce the symptom." By rewriting the spelling of symptom (a late-learned Greek borrowing) with the letters of its archaic Old French spelling—*sinthome*—Lacan said he was giving Joyce a new (old) name. The *sinthome* is that which is singular in each person, as ordered by every subject's experiences of taking on a gender identity.

As early as 1953 in his "Discourse of Rome" Lacan described a symptom thus:

> The symptom is here the signifier of a signified repressed from the consciousness of the subject. A symbol written in the sand of the flesh and on the veil of Maia, it participates in language by the semantic ambiguity that I have already emphasized in its constitution. But it is speech functioning to the full,

for it includes the discourse of the other in the secret of its cipher. It was by deciphering this speech that Freud rediscovered the primary language of symbols, still living on in the suffering of civilized man (*Das Unbehagen in der Kultur*). ("The function and field of speech" 69)

By the 1970s Lacan spoke of the symptom as a happening of the body where language joins symbol in such a way that the Imaginary and Real bodies combine appearance and enigma. It is important to note, however, that he does not make a simple symbol of the symptom. The symbol gives rise to the symptom, and the symptom refers to the symbol that gave rise to it. These are pulled along by the Real with which the Imaginary combines by passing above the symbol (representation of the sun, an elephant, etc.), and below the symptom (the fantasy that interprets the symbol). The link between an unsymbolized Real and a representational Imaginary is thus expressed by an opposition: *they must be taken together.*

In Lacan's redefinition of terms symbol does not mean a second sense or a hidden meaning, but as I have put it elsewhere: "a discrete unit, both autonomous and irreducible, which speech sounds endow with meaning in reference to other units" (*Jacques Lacan* 170). One sees that Lacan has rejected neopositivistic symbologies and argues for symbols as the lowest common multiple of meaning that imposes itself through projection/introjection in the building up of unconscious networks of signifying ensembles. In Lacanian terms, when one encounters an enigmatic use of language such as Joyce's *Finnegans Wake,* the author's language speaks an opaque symptomatology: a *jouissance* of the Real where language conceals (and reveals) the presence of a blockage within itself.

Joyce has called such a phenomenon "consubstantiality," referring to the theological theory that the three persons in the trinity or Godhead— Father, Son, and Holy Ghost—are of the same substance. Their flesh made word is celebrated in communion (*Ulysses* 32). Lacan frequently spoke of the word made flesh. Yet one cannot read the unconscious of a text, but rather the symptom which has the structure of metaphor. We remember that in metaphor one thing substitutes for another, in Lacan's view. Joyce substitutes the materiality of the voice for a cohesion between language and a lacking identificatory signifier for a worthy Father's Name. One can read this through the materiality of the voice as *objet a,* linked to the signifier for the Father's Name. Put another way, the unconscious bites into language. Lacan named this stylistic phenomenon common to Rabelais, Joyce, and himself an *écrit:* a place between speaking and writing where the timbre and resonance of the voice as a libidinal organ resides. As symptoms wax and wane they are linked to the voice. As *objet a* the voice is a cause of desire that refracts the tension between desire and *jouissance*. It produces an echo in the body of the fact that something resonates in language, demonstrating that the word has impact both as cause and effect. *Finnegans Wake* is, for Lacan, a dream, an enigma of signifiers and the silence of a *jouissance* bequeathed us by Joyce. This monumental work is not an awakening, but a dream full of sorrow and death: a wake. After Joyce's other works the *Bildung* or substitute ego that Lacan designated as Dedalus was finally ready to collapse in the sense that Joyce's own ego was fading, unraveling, abandoning Joyce to the unconscious signifying networks that spoke him as if from afar.

Lacan loved Joyce for his attempts to shred academic myths and conventions, to make litter of the letter, to put bits of verbal garbage in the can of *poubellication*. But he loved him most for his ability to live with his symptoms through a sheer will of words. Joyce's discourse was one of contingency, said Lacan, going so far as to suggest that Joyce published *Finnegans Wake* in order to become Joyce the *sinthome:* that is, Joyce the *enigma*. In this effort Joyce gained a mastery over the signifying deficiency in subjecthood that Lacan attributed to a foreclosure of the signifier for the Father's Name. Joyce's art became a supplement that would give birth to Modernism as that which provokes, but does not answer, and thus pushes "supposed" masters to interpret, according to Slavoj Zizek ("Limits" 38).

The inert presence of a *jouissance*, both unsymbolized and empty yet totally dense and full, that Lacan attributes to the Real, constitutes the painful, silent symptom behind Joyce's language. Lacan sees this symptom as the flip side of the signifier, one side giving life, the other showing death or an "extimacy" that he described as an intimate alienation emanating from within us (Miller, "A and a" 25). The life-giving side of a word suggests that infinite meanings are possible. Yet when a word ceases to mean, we confront the side of a text or an author that is not open to all meanings. On the contrary, one finds here the point at which all meanings can be abolished. The limits of a language are the limits of the subject. For Lacan this means that the signifier can occasionally, as in dreams or psychotic discourse, take over and begin to function either agrammatically or without reference to a listener, as if functioning on automatic pilot. In these contexts the signifier speaks the subject in such a way as to reveal the Other speaking, as if for no one.

In Joyce's texts that Lacan read and reread over a period of decades, he found both sides of what Jacques-Alain Miller has clarified as the Lacanian symptom. On one side, the symptom is a mark or tic that replaces or substitutes for a trauma (a knotting in the Real). The symptom may be a word, sound, event, detail, or image that acts in a way peculiar to a given subject's history. It will always involve some part of the body, if only as an *objet a*. On this slope, the enigmatic symptom belongs to the sign or the unconscious signifying chain of language because it is susceptible of being deciphered or decoded. But on the other slope, the symptom becomes more problematic because it concerns a *jouissance*— *hors-sens* or beyond language—that is both extrautilitarian and inaccessible and does not wish the "good" of the subject it inhabits. Insofar as James Joyce was concerned, Lacan ventured the theory that his first symptoms concerned an unconscious position taken toward the signifier for the Father's Name which he could still enunciate in *Portrait of the Artist as a Young Man* and *Ulysses*. Stylistically speaking, characters served Joyce in these two novels as metaphors—or the double structures that constitute ego or meaning—by negotiating the author's unconscious desire and taking up varying positions regarding his *jouissance*. But in *Finnegans Wake* Joyce had cancelled his subscription to the Other. His recognizable ego—with its double or metaphorical structure—disappears.

In *Ulysses* Joyce's father figures still ground him in a representational lineage, thereby giving him a way to subsist in language as a coherent (that is, desiring) subject. Up until *Finnegans Wake* the Father's Name signifier was represented by a country, a race, a religion, and a name for Joyce himself: *the artist*. On the first side of the symptom—the side signified by a signifier—Joyce's search for an identity adequate to his desire is only too visible in his texts. On the other side of the symptom *jouissens* comes into play as an excess left behind in the wake of the constitution of an ego, pointing here to the referent of the father. Although Lacan finds this key referent foreclosed, one could not determine that this was the "psychic" structure at issue before *Finnegans Wake*. Moreover, Lacan argues that Joyce is a curiosity like no other. Even the foreclosure of this central signifier is not necessarily sufficient to give rise to a psychotic rupture (Ragland-Sullivan, "La forclusion lacanienne" 199– 227). Joyce's great desire to be *the artist* makes a supplement (a kind of *objet a*) of the *sinthome*. In *Portrait* and *Ulysses* an Imaginary denigration of Joyce's own father becomes a Symbolic order deficiency which the son will try, albeit unconsciously, to rectify by creating Stephen

Dedalus. Taken as a cipher for Joyce's unconscious quest "to know," Stephen's ventures lead him along the path of trying to find out how to act, how to be "as a man." It is crucial to Lacan's importance for literary studies that one note his rethinking of creativity (sublimation). Unlike Freud, he did not view invention as neurotic displacement for Oedipal lack. Rather, a creation can function as a supplement or a bridge built between the "partial drives,"—the *objet a*—desire, and language. Art is a way to *dwell in* language as a subject of unconscious desire, as well as a way to adorn the void. Unlike psychosis or neurosis, art does not equate artist to symptom. Art offers an edifice built over suffering, a something extra that has a life of its own. Lacan theorized that the mental representations—the *Vorstellungsrepräsentanzen* or *savoir* (S_2)—which ground or frame every subject's identity question, his or her "who am I?", show up ultimately as a gender problematic that can be deciphered by a scanning of how language uses that subject.

It seems fantastic to suggest that the syntactical discontinuities in *Finnegans Wake* come from disturbances in Joyce's body and being, and that these are traceable to insufficient representational grounding for a masculine identity. Lacan's idea that the *objet a* are woven into language, indeed, materialize language, from infancy on—language which structures being by the signifier in the first place—seems outrageous. Yet, Lacan argued from clinical data, from philosophical treatises, from literary texts, from artistic artifacts of all sorts, from theology, and from everything else, that unquantifiable effects and enigmas—*not substantive essences*—create human *being* as an alienated set of fictions and myths that only seem essentialized because our language and bodies are connected by the *objet a*. We are structured as the creatures of an Other desire from which the *objet a* fall. In *Joyce avec Lacan* Lacan reminds us of this when he speaks of the "drive" as an echo in the body to the fact that there is a *dire* which resonates through the agencies we call being or meaning ("Le Sinthome" 42). Lacan said the same thing in other words in "Joyce le symptôme I": "Subjects are spoken in a way that creates their destiny, surely not by chance" (23; my translation). A subject is predetermined—not entirely, of course—by the discourse of his origins.

But does this not return us to a retrograde version of Freud's Oedipus complex? No, we have, instead, encountered Lacan's rewriting of the Oedipal symptom as the paternal metaphor or the fourth term that links networks of associative and combinatory meanings, tying Imaginary identifications to Symbolic language. These are pulled along by the Real of symbol and symptom which Lacan defined as a universal lack or negative kernel at the heart of all being, meaning, language, and desire. The appearance of a symptom points to an imbalance in the interrelatedness of R.S.I. (Real. Symbolic. Imaginary.) and denotes what Lacan termed the particular negative. One sees that a Lacanian reading of texts will pay heed not only to jokes, puns, slips of the tongue, and so on, but also to the appearance of the gaze, the voice, the void, or to any equivocation which points to the issue of identifying signifiers. It is in this sense that Lacan proposed in his 1975–76 seminar *Le Sinthome* that the increasing difficulties of Joyce's prose represent the degree to which Joyce becomes progressively detached from the Symbolic or grammatical order ("Kanzer Seminar"). Yet, as Danielle Bergeron points out, Joyce's production of a work of art, viewed as an object presented to the gaze of the Other, served the author as an effort to inscribe himself in the Symbolic order (172).

An *écrit* as defined by Lacan is something which gives language weight and the semblance of autonomy. Such language is to be located somewhere between speech and writing. For Joyce an *écrit* might be said to reside between language and the voice. We know that he even called his wife "Nor Voice" (O'Brien, 33). If we look at Joyce's difficult prose within a Lacanian context, rather than from the recently familiar deconstructive one, we will end up with a different view of it. Whereas poststructuralist theories have privileged metonymy within language itself, often describing language as the search for metaphor, Lacan placed substitutive desire on the side of metaphor and recast metonymy as a fading into enigma. Language does not so much slip, according to Lacan, as it swims in the water of desire that functions like Freudian condensation, according to the primary law of metaphor. Metaphor spawns metonymies which do not simply open up to yet another signifier on to infinity. Rather, metonymies dwell on the side of the Real and the *objet a*, some of which can be pinned down. While desire is on the side of the unconscious, the Real is on the side of the ego. That is, its effects are palpably strong, albeit mysterious, such as in anxiety. Not only is the Other misrecognized as the unconscious subject of desire, but it is not realized that the Real causes of desire are themselves effects or products of loss marked in the Other as a hole. Lacan spoke of *Finnegans Wake* as language rushing in to fill up a hole in Joyce's being, a hole that revealed a void behind the appearance of unities.

Paradoxically the underweave of discourse in *Finnegans Wake* gave birth to an artist like no other. Here Joyce is *writing*. The metaphorical and metonymic slopes of language fade rapidly in and out of each other like kaleidoscopic plays of being and nothingness. Joyce is dispersed into bits and pieces of the *objet a* as phoneme, voice, gaze, and (imaginary) phallus. "The point of unintelligibility there is, however, the ladder by which one shows oneself as master," Lacan said in "Joyce le symptôme II," continuing,

> I am enough of a master of the roots of language [*lalangue*], the one called French, to have myself arrived at what is fascinating in bearing witness to the *jouissance* particular to the symptom. Opaque *jouissance* of excluding meaning [*sens*]. One suspected it for a long time. To be a post-Joycian, is to know it. There is no wakening except through this particular *jouissance*. . . . The extraordinary thing is that Joyce arrived there, not without Freud (although it would not suffice that he had read him), but without recourse to the experience of analysis (which would have trapped him into some flat ending). (36)

The two faces of the symptom as designated by Lacan appear clearly in *Finnegans Wake*. On the communicative side, one finds the radical *non-sens* of Other signifying chains. On the *jouis-sens* side, the Name of the Father shows up as destructive of law ("Joyce le symptôme I" 27). The Real, in other words, is an obstacle that fragments and shatters appearances of unity into chaotic bits, its final term being that of the contradiction of the signifier for authority, "Father." When annulled, this signifier shows its structural underpinnings. "Father" signifies desire only in reference to prohibition. Such is Lacan's interpretation of Freud's myth in *Totem and Taboo* in which the primal hoard wishes to destroy the father, yet feels guilty for this desire. This myth, like many others, served Lacan as a setting out of the conditions of meaning and being, seen as things that will not run smoothly. In this purview, every person's unconscious reserve is ordered by experiences that make of them a symptom, insofar as the symptom is a fourth order or final term by which a subject exists with any sense of being subject to or of some limit. In "Joyce le symptôme I" Lacan says, "All psychic reality, that is to say the symptom, depends on the last term, of a structure where the Name of the Father is an unconditioned element" (27).

Art is an artifice, Lacan suggested, that serves artists in singular ways. In *Portrait* Joyce used Stephen to ask for love, to hollow out a position for himself in the public sphere. But in *Finnegans Wake* language has itself become a kind of ego. Joyce's unconscious is no longer structured like a language that doubles as a "self" fiction. Rather, language contiguities link pieces of voice to letter and phonation, enabling Joyce to become master of the debris coughed up into his discourse from the Real. In his seminar *Le Sinthome* Lacan wrote: "One thinks against a signifier. This is the meaning I have given the word *appensé*. One leans against a signifier to think" (Lacan, *Ornicar?* 11: 9). So while Joyce's art may be the quintessence of modernism for literary critics, for Lacan his art elaborated an ego already positioned at the breaking point, but an elaboration that enabled him to live with some imaginary identificatory consistency in the world of others. Joyce's art did not cure his symptoms nor stop his suffering. For his readers Joyce's language is, however, an interpretative delirium that stretches to infinity, in the words of Slavoj Zizek, "from the time when each stable moment reveals itself to be only an effect of the congealing of a plural signifying process" ("Limits" 38–39).

Zizek has called Joyce the writer of the fantasy in Lacan's sense, where "fantasy" closes off the space of a painful inert presence he called "nondialectisable *jouissance*." The prose of *Finnegans Wake* becomes the fantasy of language knotting together images, words, and traumas to (re)constitute a knot into which signifying associative chains from the Real, Symbolic, and Imaginary can hook themselves. In this context Lacan described *Finnegans Wake* as a book about the "polyphony of the *parole*" that manifested Joyce's *sinthome* in all its pristine purity. *Finnegans Wake* is anything but a book about play and humor, as some Joyce critics have argued. It is a book about the *sinthome,* itself a kind of writing that is irreducible. Symptom and symbol coalesce in the Real at a place where a signifier's meaning is not intended to be communicated to another as interpretable ("Le Sinthome" 47).

Lacan's innovative conception of the *sinthome* refers to a kind of writing that is completely empty of meaning, noninterpretable, but still does not lose its aptitude for correlating the subject with something of the unconscious: the sexual nonrelation (Lajonquière, 23). Another innovation in Lacan's reading of Joyce's prose is the idea that *Finnegans Wake* is not intended to mystify readers, but is Joyce's desperate effort to try to keep a link to the Symbolic order intact. This writing on the slope of metonymy gave its author a way to live without falling into the abyss of psychotic *jouissance.* As long as he could chain letters together and substitute sounds for images and voices in prose that resembled metaphorical language (just as one can forestall psychosis in the transferential or Imaginary realm by imitating Imaginary order models), Joyce could reconstitute himself as a double structure for others, even if those others could not grasp what he meant. The polyphony of voices in *Finnegans*

Wake creates a kind of border or limit, a simulated superego, whose continuing murmurings allow Joyce to make a pact between the *objet a* as cause of desire and the foreclosure of the Father's Name in the Real (there where no clear limits are set).

In *Portrait* Lacan saw Joyce as still engaged in substituting others in sexual relations for the underlying nonrelation of each subject to his Other. Dedalus represented Joyce's effort to face the gaze of Woman who evoked in him the horror of the Other's desire. Although certain women—particularly those whose standing in the Church was worthy—portrayed the "essence of truth" for Joyce, sexual women threatened him with the "gates of hell." In this sense, Woman was for him, as for other men, a symptom of masculine fantasy relations to the *objet a* Lacan called the void. In a complicated set of arguments Lacan has argued that there is no the in Woman for she reaches into the ineffable realm of the Real and is, in consequence, vilified, deified, or in other ways symptomatic for men (see *Encore;* André; Aubert, "Avant Propos" 18). In a Lacanian interpretation of literary texts, one can never dismiss figurations of women. It is not that Woman (or women as figures) is synonymous with "truth" or is essentialized in any other way. But she is close to the realm of a "truth" that lives us mysteriously, as an inwardness we recognize but whose source or meaning we cannot quite grasp. In *Portrait* Joyce uses Stephen's voice to block out the female gaze with all its intimations of seduction and judgment. Yet not only do the names of Molly and Nora open onto feminine sexuality, Joyce goes beyond names or characters in his grasp of the feminine when he confronts Woman in his epiphanies. Catherine Millot has called the epiphanies "trivial vulgar moments" when they concern masculine desire or Woman and sexuality. They indicate Joyce's use of *jouissance* to show the emptiness of phallic meaning in a return that marks the place of *das Ding* as invisible space (Millot 94). By the time he writes *Finnegans Wake,* Woman is no longer Joyce's major threat. The Real or the hole in the Other is. Instead of making Woman the solution and battleground for his life epic, Joyce took the turn toward the Father, the turn that required him to try to contain the overspill of the unbarred gaze of the Real.

In 1976 Lacan's clinical and theoretical orientation toward the Real does not bear any longer on the Name of the Father, but on the foreclosure of meaning in relation to his axiom that there is no sexual relation at the heart of sexual relating. Rather there are "partial drives" that appeal to others after having gone through the circuit of the Other.

These drives constitute the unconscious desire that conditions each subject (Lajonquière 22–24). Joyce himself names the foreclosure of the signifier for a Father's Name "the legal fiction of paternity." Not only external invaders—the British Empire, the Church, and so on—but also Joyce's own deteriorating eyesight and his daughter Lucia's psychosis, give a certain meaning to his prose. To read Lacan with an artist is to read art with life. To read *Finnegans Wake* with Lacan's theory of the symptom is to rethink the question of identity in relation to the concept of a signifier for law or limits.

Although Lacan first theorized the potential infinitization of the signifier in 1953, his interest in Joyce in the 1970s bears on the death drive rather than on the play of the signifier. What Freud called the "silence of the drives" in *Beyond the Pleasure Principle*, Lacan named the Real points of an irreducible movement in a subject's primary symbolizations, concerning the residue surrounding the signifier of the Father's Name. A Real knot blocks Symbolic differentials and Imaginary collusions. But Lacan knew that neither analyst nor literary critic—nor author for that matter—can get to the Real (which never ceases writing itself) by simply deconstructing texts or merely by decoding enigma or making innumerable puns. Put another way, language produces a Real which does not have any *corresponding* reality. Thus, it is difficult even to know when one is in the presence of the Real. Yet, paradoxically, even though the Real is the expulsion of, even the aversion to, meaning, Millot points out that the only way it can be treated is by being symbolized (91). In this context perhaps one can better understand that Lacan would take Freud's allegory in *Totem and Taboo* of a mythic father to be a Real father who signifies the paradoxical circumscription of law by desire ("Le sinthome, Séminaire du 20 janvier" 66).

One enters the Symbolic order in the first place at the price of submission to an Imaginary father whose superego images are initially (for any child) incomprehensible, if not ferocious and obscene. No child is born understanding that someone must "lay down the law." Although one of the Names of the Father is "mother," Lacan's larger point is that father signifies law because he is the diacritical opposite of mother, making male/female seem a natural opposition or at least a differential. But the effects of this seemingly equal opposition are structured asymmetrically in terms of gender identity, not as a clear equality. Because law actually dwells in some third position apart from mother and father alike, never equal to itself, yet seemingly attached first to a family structure and then to a social one, the signifier for law always appears to be attached to familial requisites. Freud called it the internalized superego and saw it as necessary to social functioning. Lacan emphasized that without an internalized representation of a border or an identity limit, a subject is open to the chaos of the Real which wreaks havoc on subjects who have little or no sense of a self that has a name and some characteristic properties. Without our "legal fictions," Lacan argued, psychosis waits in the wings, attesting to the human incapacity to think oneself human unless one already has a firm conceptualization of a position in a given Symbolic order. When psychosis appears the individual and particular character of the Real destroys Symbolic systems and Imaginary pacts that seemed adequate to subject functioning when no severe challenge to identity—who are you and what are you worth?—occurred.

The Symbolic father is a pure signifier, for Lacan, to which there is no correlative representation. Insofar as the mother is a natural signifier, the father is the first signifier for culture, a human interpretation imposed on nature to structure and shape it. This signifier, sometimes called the phallic signifier, denotes its own lack, as well as the possibility of its denotation. "In this respect the Name of the Father is one of the minimal elements of any signifying network whatsoever. Lacan, like Freud, situates the Name of the Father in 'prehistory,' though he instead calls it 'transcendent,' a term that needs to be treated with caution. In calling this signifier transcendent he is claiming that while it has no correlate in any representation it is nevertheless a condition for the possibility of any representation" (Grigg 120).

In many of his own *Ecrits*, Lacan, like Joyce, pushed at normative linguistic borders where conventions and grammar rules point to some authoritative referent. By pushing style to its limit, both men created a language where the mark of a lack in the Other can evade the Imaginary and attach itself to the Symbolic by the Real. In turn, language can be used to hook into the Real in an effort to avoid and evacuate Imaginary relations. Such writing dwells outside the "human," as if suspended from nowhere. It reveals that language can play around the void of lost objects that return as *objet a. Finnegans Wake* dramatizes a "beyond" Joyce's aesthetic, into Lacan's Real. Joyce's efforts to construct an aesthetic remain mimetic and imitative—Imaginary images and Symbolic codes—while the Lacanian Real is a savoir faire linked to the practice of the signifier joined to the *objet a:* "An action planned by man which places him in the situation of treating the Real by the Symbolic" (D. Miller 34).

Insofar as an aesthetic implies distance and perspective, Lacan's the-

ory that metaphor and the subject of desire function by the same substitutive movement or law confronts us with a "materialization of language" where the word becomes the flesh of being, precisely because
meaning must take up the burden of supporting *jouissance* as well as the
unconscious signifying chains that speak us. When a signifier refers to
the Father's name, the Real suddenly becomes stronger than ordinarily
so. The *objet a* shows its face as a *point de capiton* (anchoring button),
making of the subject the same object that causes his desire. But since
desire and *jouissance* are at odds, human subjects are asymmetrical (that
is, dialectical or contradictory) within their very being. This is because
subjects are the causes of Real effects that inhabit them intimately, but as
if from afar. If a subject is his own *sinthome*, one can see that actions—
including artistic acts—that one performs without necessarily understanding why, may have a *cause* in an Elsewhere with its own meaning
and logic. It becomes possible to imagine that James Joyce could have
written *Finnegans Wake* to resist the void at the center of his being, as a
survival action. In this act his tools or weapons would be words and
sounds. In Lacanian terms, the return of the Real always perforates the
Symbolic and Imaginary as nonlinear interferences. But for those who
are potentially psychotic, the *objet a* can have the paradoxical function
of replacing a hole in representation and being, possibly forstalling a
psychotic episode or suicide. But would a "supposed" use of the Real in
language not merely be a stylistic trick played by Joyce? Worse yet, one
which might make of him a neoplatonist trying to unify his being and
thinking by seeking an aesthetic in essences thought to dwell in language, or in the Irish people, or in some ideal form? Lacan's answer
would be no. Joyce's goal is not to totalize, nor idealize, but simply to
escape the rawness of anxiety produced by the effects of the Real that live
him.

Lacan saw language as creative of being in the first place, leaving
certain minimal signifiers in its wake. When language, identifications,
and experience are not sufficiently tied together, the Real (or *objet a*),
which is usually obscured by apparent unities and by being tied to the
other orders, becomes visible. It returns as a gaze or voice or act. Thus,
even psychotic language is full of meaning, although its meaning might
seem chaotic or peculiar. Yet, the Real as we ordinarily experience it in
anxiety, dreams, *jouissance,* and so on, has no explicable meaning at all.
In this context, Lacan read Joyce as exemplary of his theory that the
Oedipal complex is a symptom that subsists only in relation to language: only because the Name of the Father is the father of the name, an

"at least one" element by which we knot together a fiction of being. Through his art Joyce gave life to the archaic fathers in his memory network. Dead persons and failed beliefs are joined to the vitality of the voice, making a signifying knot for the Father's name foreclosed in Joyce's unconscious. Lacan argued in his seminar on *Le Sinthome* that Joyce's writing actually established a secondary knot between the Imaginary, Symbolic, and Real that tied lack to voice, being, and letter. One might call this a prosthetic knot.

Although Lacan discounts most of Joyce's explanations of how he established his aesthetic, one aspect of his aesthetic did help him to turn *jouissance* or suffering into art: his creation of the epiphany. These joyful moments of mastery become less joyful in *Finnegans Wake* where puns are not so imitative of speech as they are exemplary of linguistic "free association" taken to its breaking point. Lacan's interpretation of Joyce's epiphanies looks at the flip side of what Millot termed trivial vulgarities. When brilliant irradiance is attached to these textual moments they unveil a manic joy of elation and liberation. Lacan called this, quoting Thomas Aquinas, *claritas*. Such "clarity" is a return of the Real, said Lacan, that shows the Wizard-of-Oz shibboleth of phallic law. As such the epiphanies are a "singular" writing, an *écriture* placed at the limits of the Real that touch on the mystical. In Millot's view, Joyce's epiphanies are like "holophrases," which Lacan redefined as the summing up of everything in a few words that seek to grasp an absolute: God, Woman, the All (Aubert, "Avant Propos" 15). Aubert writes that Joyce's epiphanies try to organize what Joyce does not consciously understand, although he seeks to construct what he cannot see or say by trying to control what actually controls him ("Galeries" 83).

Lacan says Joyce in *Finnegans Wake* gave up his belief in a substitute or pseudofather and took the third person position of one listening to oneself write, rather than the usual second person position of writer to text. The voice becomes palpable, if not visible, as a libidinal object that carries signifiers along. Indeed, for Lacan, Joyce identified with the underwoven vocal tones in his own discourse and in this way escaped the actual death of his ego. Moreover, his writing enabled him to maintain and reconstitute a seemingly unified Imaginary body. In Lacan's thought, the body is an Imaginary signifier that demarcates one kind of limit to thought and desire. By linking language, unconscious signifiers, and body, Joyce created a world where a relationship between ear and eye could exist, even though he had difficulties in seeing. He invented a prose reduced to the torsion of the voice joined to phonation.

Sayings such as "you are—very—baa-aa-dd" open up a split between words used for meaning and the voice as a desiring part of the body. In this final text Joyce fully assumes Lacan's name for him: Joyce the *sinthome.*

By viewing Joyce as one who poses his identity question in art, Jacques-Alain Miller sees him as one who succeeded in passing from contingency to a kind of consistency [$\mathcal{S}$---> (a)]. But the consistency at issue is not perverse or hypocritical because it entails building a language on the side of the *écrit:* something not written to be read in an ordinary way. As Zizek puts it, such language has the status of the *objet a* or cause of desire out of which signifying textures arise in the first place ("Why Lacan is Not a 'Post-Structuralist' " 31–39). One cannot, however, comfortably describe such language as a Lacanian signifier—that which represents a subject for another signifier—because it does not represent a subject coherently. More apt for Lacan is Philippe Solers's description of *Finnegans Wake* as an exploding and regrouping of language. The art object is no longer an aesthetic artifact, but an *objet a,* itself made of separable parts: voice, name, symptom, palpable *jouissance.* That Joyce could come so close to writing down the unwritable becomes an unwitting revelation of the *équivoque* that ordinarily characterizes language. That is, langauge can lie, pun, overdetermine meanings, make homophones, turn the phoneme into an empty letter. Seen this way, the letter no longer resides on the side of *l'être* (being), but on the side of trash or litter (Schreiber 10). This Real of the letter can be taken as an evisceration of meaning, a model of Joyce's epiphanies taken to their extreme point.

One might argue that when Joyce's unconscious desire and his *jouissance* come together in his writing he cannot offer a unified theory of aesthetics for the simple reason that he cannot close the space between the word and the "letter," insofar as the *lettre* is that of the *objet petit a* that goes beyond transparent meaning. When Lacan spoke at a colloquium on Joyce in France in 1975 he spoke of Joyce's symptom as a dream-wish to mark an end or final term with *Finnegans Wake,* linking the Symbolic, Imaginary, and Real by the Symptom in the form of a knot. One can speak of a knot, Lacan said, because it too has a limit ("Joyce le symptôme I" 29). Insofar as he accomplished the goal of showing himself to be *master of the English language,* one might ask what interpretation psychoanalysis might give such an achievement? If Lacan is correct in his theory that language is received by humans as an alienating wall from which they, nonetheless, take the meanings they live by, but can only ever speak as half-truths or as truths half hidden, James Joyce's art revealed that writers create or invent in order to live, not the reverse. Such an understanding of Joyce's art adds something to our comprehension of what the literary is or what the aesthetic might be. Moreover, Joyce reveals that *writing* at its own limits meets—and reveals—the *objet a*. His daughter Lucia's name stands for an *objet a:* the gaze. Lucia means the goddess of seeing or light. The choice of her name as well as the fact of her psychosis are evidence for Lacan that she herself is a clue to the enigma that is her father (Kuberski 49–66).

Lacan was also interested in Joyce's insistence that his daughter was not psychotic, but was telepathic. While Joyce meant that Lucia was endowed with superior intelligence, that she could inform him miraculously of future events through secrets only she knew, Lacan understood something different by "telepathic." Although Lacan found no magic in the idea of telepathy, he did not dismiss the phenomenon, and suggested in his 1953 "Discourse of Rome":

> That the unconscious of the subject is the discourse of the Other appears even more clearly than anywhere else in the studies that Freud devoted to what he called telepathy as manifested in the context of an analytic experience. This is the coincidence of the subject's remarks with facts about which he cannot have information, but which are still at work in the connexions of another experience in which the same psychoanalyst is the interlocutor—a coincidence moreover constituted most often by an entirely verbal, even homonymic, convergence, or which, if it involves an act, is concerned with an "acting out" by one of the analyst's other patients or by a child of the person being analyzed who is also in analysis. It is a case of resonance in the communicating networks of discourse, an exhaustive study of which would throw light on similar facts presented by everyday life. ("Function and field" 55–56)

In Lacan's estimation, Joyce unconsciously looked to his child, even as he chose her name, for help with what he could not see/understand. As his ego gradually unraveled, dissolving borders between whether or not he was controlling language or being controlled by it, it must have seemed to Joyce that he received words in a somewhat hallucinatory—if not telepathic—manner. Moreover, his glaucoma ebbed and flowed, depending on whether or not he was writing, giving it a strangely psychosomatic aspect (Guir 17). Insofar as *jouissance* is unpleasure, yet the secret satisfaction at the heart of a symptom that attaches a subject to his pain, even serving as the pivot around which he turns, in Joyce's case, not seeing would equal not wanting to know what was written indelibly

in his unconscious. Dominique Miller has written that "it is in the measure that the symptom makes an enigma for the subject that a knowledge, in the name of the unconscious, is suspended" (34).

Lacan speculated that Lucia's psychosis was an extension of Joyce's
own forestalled psychosis. She lived the suffering he was able to keep at
bay by his art. Of course many questions remain unanswered in such
speculations. Is Lucia schizophrenic as diagnosed, or severely hysterical? Lacanian analysts find many women hospitalized in the Anglo-
phone world and misdiagnosed as psychotic or borderline patients
because the diagnostic category of hysteria is not used clinically or theoretically by the analysts in question. Moreover, in a Lacanian purview, a
psychosis is passed on to a child through the mother's desire to close out
the father, not directly from the father's inadequacies. The recent book
by Brenda Maddox on Joyce's wife Nora, *The Real Life of Molly Bloom*,
suggests that the mother may well have been a cause of Lucia's psychosis, although Maddox's viewpoint is that given the difficulties of living
with James Joyce, Nora is not to be blamed for any problems she may
have caused her daughter (O'Brien 33). In any event, Lucia's letters to
her father reveal an extreme care to avoid a kind of "psychic incest," a
care that perhaps cost her a normal life. If Lucia's very life was constituted so as to protect her father's fragile ego, she dwells on the same side
as the fictional character Stephen Dedalus. Both would bear witness to
Joyce's final failure to project enough Imaginary material onto others in
order to survive in any mimesis of normalcy. Yet, by double I do not refer
to the split in the subject where conscious and unconscious *savoir* fades
in and out.

In *James Joyce and the Revolution of the Word* Colin MacCabe has
written: "To speak is to have accepted a symbolic castration; to have
accepted difference and absence. To enter into language is thus to have
denied to the father his self-sufficiency and it is this denial which constitutes the guilt associated with language" (145). Lacan teaches the opposite of what MacCabe has written. To speak or write with coherency or
consistency demonstrates adequate confidence in an unconscious paternal representation to be able to ignore its effects on language. Lacan saw
the relationship between symptoms and language as a kind of half-
speaking between primordially repressed representations and a master
discourse which is normative and based on further repression of the
paternal signifier for any lack or division at all.

In his third theory of the symptom, Lacan thought there was more to
jouissance than he had previously suggested. Even in analysis, he said,

excess *jouissance* remains excessive. It resists cure. Unlike unconscious *savoir*, it is another kind of truth that wants no knowledge of itself. No one, himself included, wants to be cured of their symptoms because the death drive—which Lacan translates as *jouissance*—lies beyond the pleasure principle and beyond the principle of repetition. Freud called this phenomenon negative transference or unconscious masochism. Lacan called it the Real, or the existence of displeasure, discontent, enjoyment in the breach of the pleasure principle that places a stubborn obstacle in every life and a discontent or malaise in civilization. Lacan called the satisfaction of this death drive, as distinct from instinct, *jouissance* (Miller, "A and a" 23). While unconscious desire is connected to speech, *jouissance* dwells on the side of the silence of the drives. Indeed, *jouissance* is the very principle of symptom formation that appears as the "drive not to know."

In Lacan's many lectures on Joyce, he mentions the extraordinary accomplishment of devising a magisterial *dire* that enabled him to avoid his own imminent dissolution. In thinking of this picture of Joyce, I envision a man carrying on his back a mountain of monumental proportions, actually carrying his own mountain with him, rather than merely rolling some mythic stone up and down a mountain like Sisyphus. Lacan has said that sometimes the only adequate way to speak about the adequacy of language to itself is to speak about the manner of its movement. In this concept, language is an affected action, a trajectory, a path-forger, a constituting and reconstituting medium. At first glance a Lacanian might take the movement of Joyce's language to resemble that of an obsessional discourse, a usually masculine structure where the feminine seems all-consuming and is to be avoided at any cost, even though obsessional men are paradoxically overly dependent on the women they hold at arm's length. The obsessional's goal is to use language as a weapon to close out desire. Information systems, encyclopedic knowledge, ritualization of words and things, the use of sex to avoid speaking of love, are all welcome in this use of language that tries to exclude the unbearable threat of desire. Language itself becomes a fortress with potentially double-barred doors from which the all-too-present Other discourse is denied entrance.

On the other hand, one might view Joyce's language movement as typically hysterical, although hysteria is generally the feminine version of obsession (although they act differently). While masculine normativity is based on an accepted identification between father and sons, where desire and law are united in an ego ideal, in hysteria the Imaginary father engenders frustration at the level of ideals and leaves usually the female hysteric with a ferocious superego. Her duty is nothing less than to unconsciously support the desire of a denigrated father who gains his power of death over her life by his very shame which she takes on as her special burden to bear. In the end result, as Jacques-Alain Miller has put it, hysteria is itself dissatisfaction with knowledge as it stands ("A and a" 20).

Although there may be hysterial and obsessional traits in some of Joyce's texts, in the overall movement of his language something else occurs. A kind of tape-recorded double of sounds and voices appears behind and within regular language. The shadow language points to a prepsychotic structure where language is broken down into pieces in order to serve grammar as a missing superego or border that will prop up the ego, lest it collapse into the sterility of psychotic speech where there is no distance from the Other, no metaphorical law of the double. In the 1970s Lacan argued that foreclosure of the signifier for the Father's Name was not enough to cause a psychotic breakdown. Although the Real returns in the symptom to satisfy the superego which demands the right to *jouir* in the field of the Symbolic, and the *objet* returns in the Real by way of the Imaginary in fantasy, in psychosis the Real becomes detached from the Imaginary and Symbolic. Thus when there is a failure of—in Joyce's case masculine—identity, when any semblance of phallic authority disappears, it is still possible for a person to identify with the symptom as the terminal point of a failure of their desire ("Journal . . ." 171–73). This theory led Lacan to rewrite his formula regarding the sexual unrelation, to say that there is no sexual relation which is not supported by the *sinthome* that supports the Other sex of a particular subject. That is, because every subject is the subject of a symptom, thanks to the particularity of a *sinthome*, he or she can have a relation to the Other, from which an identity is forthcoming. The *sinthome* can stand in for the "number" of the Father which Lacan called the fourth term (Grisolia 31). Only in the outbreak of a psychotic episode does the symptom become synonymous with itself because a relation to the Other disappears. When the ego breaks down and psychosis ensues, the psychotic person becomes the Other. Joyce died at age fifty-eight and never had a psychotic break. In the broadest conception of the symptom that one can find in Lacan's teaching, the *sinthome* played the displacement role for Joyce of building simulated relations to others, as in ordinary (sexual) relations, thus maintaining some distance from the Other. There may have been foreclosure of the signifier for the Father's Name in

James Joyce's unconscious, but Joyce never became psychotic as did Judge Schreber, for example, because Joyce's *sinthome* is itself the knot that ties together the Borromean topology requisite to subject functioning, creating the illusion of a relation to the Other.

We are no longer speaking of Oedipus, but of the difference between a *sinthomal* and a *nonsinthomal* structure where the foreclosure of the paternal reference is compensated for by art (Lajonquière 23-24). Perhaps we are speaking of the case of "one," if not the only one, at least one of few writers who have shown that literary art is not the unconscious, but can respond to unconscious drives to create against the odds. As such, artistic creation shows itself to be the highest merit of mankind. In speaking of James Joyce in Lacanian terms, we speak of the *sinthome* of invention, then, not the symptom of pathology. In this sense, does James Joyce not become a *saint homme?*

Notes

1. This lecture was first published in *Joyce & Paris: Actes Cinquième Symposium International James Joyce*, Paris, June 16-20, 1975, edited by J. Aubert & Maria Jolas (Paris: C.N.R.S., 1979). It is referred to in my essay from the most recent collection of some of Lacan's seminars given on James Joyce which have been edited by Jacques Aubert in *Joyce avec Lacan*. In Aubert's collection it is referred to as "Joyce le symptôme I." The article called "Joyce le symptôme II" in Aubert's collection was previously published in *L'Âne: Le Magazine Freudien* 6 (1982): 3-5. Many other selections on Joyce from Lacan's year-long seminar on *Le Sinthome* have been published in *Scilicet* and *Ornicar?* The early ones that I don't have and can't get, I refer to simply as "Le Sinthome" with the date of the weekly seminar.

All translations from French herein are my own.

Works Cited

André, Serge. *Que veut une femme?* Paris: Navarin, 1986.

Aramburu, J., et al. "Journal: 'Le Seminario Lacanio' de Buenos Aires." *Ornicar?* 33 (1985): 170-73.

Aubert, Jacques. "Avant Propos." *Joyce avec Lacan.* 13-18.

———. "Galeries pour un portrait." *Joyce avec Lacan.* 69-84.

———. "Le sinthome, Séminaire du 20 janvier 1976." *Joyce avec Lacan.* 49-67.

———, ed. *Joyce avec Lacan.* Paris: Navarin, 1987.

Bergeron, Danielle. "Jouer sa vie sur un semblant." *Folie, Mystique et Poésie.* Ed. Raymond Lemieux. Québec: Collection Noeud de GIFRIC, 1988. 161-82.

Freud, Sigmund. *Beyond the Pleasure Principle.* 1920. Vol. 18 of *The Standard*

Edition of the Complete Psychological Works of Sigmund Freud. Ed. James Strachey. 24 vols. London: Hogarth, 1953-74.

———. *The Psychopathology of Everyday Life.* 1913. Vol. 6 of *Standard Edition.*

———. *Totem and Taboo.* 1913. *Standard Edition* 13:1-162.

Grigg, Russell. "The Function of the Father in Psychoanalysis." *Australian Journal of Psychotherapy* 18 (1986): 116-26.

Grisolia, Adriana. "James Joyce y el nombre del padre." *Revista del cercle psico-analitic de Catalunya* 5 (1988): 29-31.

Guir, Jean. *Psychosomatique et cancer.* Paris: Points Hors Ligne, 1983.

Joyce, James. *Finnegans Wake.* New York: Viking, 1939.

———. *A Portrait of the Artist as a Young Man.* New York: Viking, 1964.

———. *Ulysses: The Corrected Text.* Ed. Hans Walter Gabler et al. New York: Random House, 1986.

Kuberski, Philip. "The Joycean Gaze: Lucia and the I of the Father." *Sub-stance* 46(1985): 49-66.

Lacan, Jacques. "The agency of the letter in the unconscious or reason since Freud." *Ecrits: A Selection.* 146-78.

———. *Ecrits: A Selection.* Ed. and trans. Alan Sheridan. New York: Norton, 1977.

———. "The Freudian thing or the meaning of the return to Freud in psycho-analysis." *Ecrits: A Selection.* 114-45.

———. "The function and field of speech and language in psychoanalysis." *Ecrits: A Selection.* 30-113.

———. "Joyce le symptôme I." Aubert, *Joyce avec Lacan.* 21-29.

———. "Joyce le symptôme II." Aubert, *Joyce avec Lacan* 31-36.

———. "Kanzer Seminar, Yale University." 24 Nov. 1975. Unedited lecture. Written down by some of Lacan's students from stenographed notes and from tapes. Published as *Jacques Lacan: Conférences et entretiens dans des univer-sités nord-américaines.* Later published in *Scilicet* 6/7.

———. "La psychanalyse et son enseignement." *Ecrits.* Paris: Seuil, 1966. 437-58.

———. *Le Séminaire: livre XX: Encore.* 1972-73. Ed. Jacques-Alain Miller. Par-is: Seuil, 1975.

———. *Le Séminaire: livre XXIII: Le Sinthome.* 1975-76. Text to be edited by Jacques-Alain Miller.

———. "Le Sinthome, Séminaire du 18 novembre 1975." *Joyce avec Lacan.* 37-48.

———. "Subversion of the subject and dialectic of desire in the Freudian un-conscious." *Ecrits: A Selection.* 292-325.

———. "Le Symptôme, Columbia University." 1 Dec. 1975. Unedited lecture. Written down by some of Lacan's students from stenographed notes and from tapes. Published as *Jacques Lacan: Conférences et entretiens dans des univer-sités nord-américaines.* Later published in *Scilicet* 6/7.

Lajonquière, Carlos, et al. "Quelques questions sur la prépsychose." *Clinique différentielle des psychoses: Fondation du champ freudien*. Ed. Lilia Mahjoub-Trobas et al. Paris: Navarin, 1988. 11–24.

MacCabe, Colin. *James Joyce and the Revolution of the Word*. London: Macmillan, 1979.

Miller, Dominique. "Sur le signifiant du transfert: des entrées en analyse—'Les trois transferts.' " *Ornicar?* 33 (1985): 31–36.

Miller, Jacques-Alain. "A and a in Clinical Structures." *Acts of the Paris–New York Psychoanalytic Workshop*. Ed. Stuart Schneiderman. 1986. New York: A Schneiderman Publication, 1987. 14–29.

———. "Avertissement." *Cahiers pour l'Analyse* 1 (1966): 4–5.

———. "Introduction to *Television*." *Newsletter of the Freudian Field* 3 (1988): 6–16.

———. "Préface." Aubert, *Joyce avec Lacan* 9–12.

Millot, Catherine. "Epiphanies." Aubert, *Joyce avec Lacan* 87–95.

O'Brien, Edna. "She was the Other Ireland." Rev. of *The Real Life of Molly Bloom*, by Brenda Maddox. *New York Times Book Review* 19 June 1988: 33.

Ragland-Sullivan, Ellie. "La forclusion lacanienne: les origines de la psychose." *Folie, Mystique et Poésie*. Ed. Raymond Lemieux. Québec: Collection Noeud de GIFRIC, 1988. 199–227.

———. *Jacques Lacan and the Philosophy of Psychoanalysis*. Urbana: U of Illinois P, 1987.

Rotmistrovsky, Hugo. "Joyce, el nombre." *Revista del cercle psicoanalitíc de Catalunya* 5 (1988): 33–39.

Schreiber, Françoise. "Sept remarques de Jacques-Alain Miller sur la création." Notes taken from Miller's Seminar on "Les psychoses et le sinthome." *La lettre mensuelle* 68 (1988): 9–13.

Zizek, Slavoj. "The Limits of a Semiotic Approach to Psychoanalysis." *Psychoanalysis And . . . .* Ed. Richard Feldstein & Henry Sussman. New York: Routledge, forthcoming.

———. "The Marxist Symptom." *Lacanian Theory: A Reader*. Ed. Mark Bracher et al. Urbana: U of Illinois P, forthcoming.

———. "Why Lacan is Not a 'Post-Structuralist.' " *Newsletter of the Freudian Field* 2 (1987): 31–39.

Anaïs Nin's Mothering Metaphor: Toward a Lacanian Theory of Feminine Creativity

Diane Richard-Allerdyce

Anaïs Nin, still known to many chiefly as a writer of erotica or as "Henry Miller's friend," has offered the readers of her diary an unprecedented portrait of what one might call a "feminine" perspective. Otto Rank, Nin's analyst during her twenties, acclaims her diary as, in Nin's words, "invaluable as a study of a woman's point of view . . . a document by a woman who thinks like a woman, not like a man" (*Diary* 2:24). It is the difference between feminine and masculine thought and experience with which much of the nearly lifelong diary deals, and although Nin is not primarily a theorist, I see a theory of feminine creativity emerging throughout her work which may be illuminated by a Lacanian view of gender difference.

Despite his admiration for Nin's perspective, Rank initially encourages her to give up the diary, believing that it keeps her subjugated to an ideal ego. By keeping a writer's sketchbook instead, he suggests, she might create artistic works for herself, apart from a need to fulfill her father's expectations (*Diary* 2:277–81). The conflict comes in his dismissing or not considering the possibility that the diary might be seen as a work of art in itself (2:25). After struggling with this issue for many months, Nin eventually rejects his advice and continues the work whose literary form might be considered to have boundaries as fluid as the feminine identity she describes.

By the time Rank changes his mind about the diary and admits that his theories were based on masculine models (2:24), Nin has already begun to formulate a concept of feminine identity. She combines her

ideas about women's intuition and mobility with her desire for a creative, active, and independent position, moving away from traditional
models of femininity based on motherhood and asserting a choice about
when and how to mother. In a way, she strives toward that which Adrienne Rich has written should be the goal of the feminist movement,
"to visualize and make a way for a world in which . . . female creativity might or might not choose to express itself in motherhood" (16).
Although the theory of feminine creativity which emerges throughout
Nin's works may posit motherhood as the feminine creator's position, I
believe her concepts point to a formulation of gender difference which
moves her out of a selfhood based on the reflection of male desire even as
it allows her to retain aspects of traditional femininity which she finds
valuable. While certain feminists may object to her depiction of woman
as relational, intuitive, emotional, and sensitive on the grounds that
such a view perpetuates stereotypical classifications, Nin is adamant in
stressing both that there is a difference between men's and women's
perspectives and that a woman need not become like a man in order to be
strong. She did adhere to certain traditional views of women, but she
also participated in a phenomenon described by Sandra M. Gilbert and
Susan Gubar, who argue that since the nineteenth century, women writers have used their writing to shatter the mirror in which they have existed throughout history as reflections of male desire (4–44).

Adhering, on one level, to what Gilbert and Gubar illuminate as the
patriarchal Western tradition of considering an author "a father, a progenitor, a procreator, and aesethetic patriarch" (6), Nin writes in volume
1 of her diary that "Dr. Rank had become himself a [metaphorical]
father, . . . written his own books, evolved his own theories" (1:280).
Then, as she strives to distance herself from him, Nin is able to begin
formulating an answer to a question later asked by Gilbert and Gubar:
"If the pen is a metaphorical penis, with what organ can females generate texts?" (7). For Nin, the "organ" which allows her to "parent" her
texts emerges not as a counterpart to the male penis, but, as in Lacan's
theory, a type of relation toward the Other.

As she attempts to forge an authorship for and of herself, Nin uses the
metaphors of mothering and childbearing to refer to the artistic process.
Yet she seems to go beyond the traditional comparison of works of art to
offspring suggested in the analogy of male authors as fathers of texts. For
her, "mothering" a text is metaphorical, but she recognizes, like Lacan,
that metaphor is inextricably related to corporal experience. Nin's formulation of femininity is similar to Lacan's in that for both this inmix-

ing of language to body remains stronger for a feminine subject than for
the masculine. As Ellie Ragland-Sullivan puts it, there *is* a difference
between the genders, and, in Lacan's theory, the difference makes a
difference.[1]

Essential to my argument is the recognition that for Lacan gender is
not reducible to biology; that is, "the relation of the subject to the phallus . . . is established without regard to the anatomical difference of
the sexes" (*Ecrits* 282). Both male and female subjects develop their
gender identity around the symbolic phallus, which positions the individual within a socially prescribed order. Identity originates in the subject's prehistory, since the human infant enters a prefigured reality as
structured through the parents' discourse. Thus it is the individual's
"unconscious castration complex" (281) functioning as a "knot" to position the subject in relation to the Name of the Father—and not biological difference per se—that determines one's position as feminine or
masculine within the social order. I shall argue that, for both Lacan and
Nin, the feminine position emerges in this order as more closely linked
to unconscious "truth" than does the masculine. I must emphasize,
though, that both male and female subjects may occupy either position,
and that for Lacan feminine and masculine are just that—subject
positions—rather than biologically determined categories. This does
not mean that the body is not significant in influencing gender positioning, but that rather than being a first-cause determiner, the body becomes a signifier of gender identity at a secondary level.

Although she does not have the theoretical basis provided by Lacan,
Nin seems to intuit the relations among language, representation, and
identity which are illuminated by Lacan's teachings. As she works out
her position in relation to men, Nin uses language in the form of literary
creations—including her diary which blurs the line between art and
life—to create and maintain an identity that goes beyond and through
what Lacan calls *moi* fixation and is established on the side of the feminine for its position in relation to desire.

During her pregnancy and especially through the stillbirth experience which she describes in the first volume of her diary, Nin develops
a way to mother metaphorically. Overwhelmed by the needs of others
and by her slavery to meeting them, Nin writes that there is no room in
her life for the child she is carrying. "I have, already, too many children"
(1:338), she says, referring to friends, family members, and lovers for
whom she feels responsible. In addition, Nin fears motherhood without
a responsible partner, a fear based, perhaps, on her own father's aban-

doning her when she was eleven years old. She writes: "I love man as creator, lover, husband, friend, but man the father I do not trust" (1:346).

It is significant that during her pregnancy she speaks to her unborn child, saying that it would be better off dead, for "there are no real fathers, not in heaven or on earth" (1:338). Better, she tells it, would it be to live in "the paradise of non-being" (1:338) than to suffer abandonment by a father, and she is sure that her baby's father (whose name has been edited out of the published diary) will leave as her own father did. After the child has died within her she thinks that perhaps the dead little girl she has evicted with much effort from her womb is a symbol of her role as "Lawrence's symbolic mother" instead of as a biological mother (1:346). Never able to have another child, Nin rejects a traditional mothering role even as it is denied her by nature, choosing, in a sense, not to recreate the Oedipal structure which led to her neurosis. That is, instead of recreating a pattern of slavery to a father's desire, Nin creates a self for herself through literature. This process, in turn, enables her to move away from the self-effacement which characterizes her early relations to others and to approach a relative freedom from father-identification.

Gradually, Nin begins to gain confidence in her writing style, which Lawrence Durrell tells her will come to be recognized as representing a feminine style not to be judged by male standards. With war breaking out all around her, Nin strives to create a world for herself in her diary, and at this point the nature of gender difference becomes based, for her, on the disparity between creation and destruction. In July 1936 she writes that the "world of man [is] in flames and blood" (2:98), but the "world of woman [is] alive as it is in this book, as it shall be forever, woman giving life, and man destroying life" (2:98). Later she will recognize the limitations of dichotomous opposition, but at this point, at least, this formulation enables her to assert the voice which has often been repressed.

In my interpretation, Nin uses this emerging feminine voice to articulate a self apart from others' desire by striving for both a sexual relation and a form of mothering which is both physical and metaphysical. While still pregnant, she writes in the first volume of the diary: "I have known a motherhood beyond biological motherhood—the bearing of artists and life, hope, and creation" (1:213). This statement may be linked to Lacan's concept of a *jouissance* that *goes beyond*. That is, Nin's going beyond biological motherhood may be formulated as her going beyond a *jouissance* of the body, which means, for Lacan, that she takes a position on the side of the Real, the hole in the Other. In going beyond the biological, feminine *jouissance* goes beyond a *"jouissance* of the body" to a *"jouissance* of being" (Lacan, *Feminine Sexuality* 142), and for Lacan the path is that of language: "If the unconscious is indeed what I say it is, as being structured like a language, then it is on the level of language that we must interrogate this One" (*Feminine Sexuality* 139). In March 1937 Nin writes that she is "becoming more and more aware" that she is "writing as a woman" (2:184), that is, that her style is valid apart from male standards. Most significantly, she writes that this kind of writing "happens in the real womb, not in the womb fabricated by man as a substitute" (2:184). As I understand her, she means that while male writers may produce literary offspring because they cannot bear children, it is those subjects who identify on the side of woman for whom language is truly creative. In my view, Lacan's theory makes much the same point.

I am not arguing, however, for an idealization of motherhood, an idealization which would perpetuate the conception of the ego's ability to be whole. As Ragland-Sullivan points out, "the conception of woman as a *toute* through motherhood is a contradiction in terms, since her value stems from the relationship to an-other and not from her own being" (290). For Nin, the crux of the feminine perspective is the awareness that one is not a unity and can only create by linking with the Other, for which Nin, like Lacan, uses God as metaphor. By contrast, the masculine position is identified with the symbolic phallus, an identification which "conveys the feeling that one is *tout*," or whole (Ragland-Sullivan 293). Nin's femininity is that which recognizes one's dependence on the Other, and it is through Nin's sexual metaphor that this recognition is attained. The idealization of mother may be seen to lie on the side of the masculine, then, for its belief in a fictional ego unity. The actual mother, in playing the role assigned to her in the Symbolic order, adopts a masculine version of femininity; one of the Names of the Father is the mother as law-giver. Lacan says: "What she busies herself with are other *objet a,* being children, in relation to whom the father does none the less intervene . . . in order to keep under repression . . . his own version of his perversion" (*Feminine Sexuality* 167). I understand Lacan to be saying here that through subjugation to law, a woman will adopt the masculine version of motherhood which becomes idealized for its conception of the possibility of a normative wholeness.

Nin does strive for unity, but I believe that it is a unity based on awareness of lack. By considering her metaphor of the womb, one can account for femininity from a feminine perspective. For Nin, as I interpret her, the womb becomes a metonymy representative of the unconscious which for Lacan is structured like a language; the womb imagery which appears throughout much of her work may also represent her attempt to signify void material. Lacan's theories, which show how language is reproductive, may thus illuminate Nin's figuration. He taught that words and attitudes produce the concrete set of circumstances into which a human subject is born. This prefigured set of circumstances structures the individual's identity and shapes his or her positioning in the social order. Since language is formative in creating its own meaning through the culture of which it is both creator and created, metaphor, by substituting one signifier for another, shows the creative and reproductive effect of signification. Once a metaphor enters the signifying chain as a substitute signifier, it becomes metonymous in the unfolding of language. Similarly, the physical offspring of speaking (human) beings function on one level as reproductions of their parents, but on another level, they enter the Symbolic order as signifiers themselves and thus become not only metaphors of their parents but metaphor-producing metonymies.

I see Nin's mothering metaphor and womb imagery as the creative application of what is itself creative or structuring—the Symbolic through which culture is perpetuated and structured—as humans use language to recreate their existence even as they are structured by it. In this correlation between language and one's experience we may see not only the structuring effect of language on identity but also its reproductive effect on sexuality, which, according to the circular and revolving nature of Lacan's three orders—the Real, the Symbolic, and the Imaginary—is in turn reproductive. Thus, literary creativity may be seen not only to be *like* mothering as physical reproduction, nurturing, and creation, but in some ways, to *be* a virtual form of mothering.

Lacan implied the creative function of the Symbolic when he said that "to make love, as the term indicates, is poetry" (*Feminine Sexuality* 143). While any speaking being might be considered, then, a "parent" of living language, Lacan defines gender difference—and thus the difference between a literary "mother" and a literary "father"—as the difference in one's relation to desire and to law. Nin's view is similar, I think, in her formulating literary motherhood as a type of relation to a fecundator, or God. For both Lacan and Nin, the feminine position emerges as more closely linked than does the masculine to unconscious desire, to "truth," to what Lacan calls the Other. It is a way of knowing, or more accurately experiencing, which is different from the masculine, an experiencing which Lacan links to the mystic who is, for him, on the feminine side: "There are men who are just as good as women. . . . Despite, I won't say the phallus, despite what encumbers them on that score, they get the idea, they sense that there must be a *jouissance* which goes beyond. That is what we call a mystic" (*Feminine Sexuality* 147). For Lacan, women's *jouissance* is of the body but it goes beyond that of the phallus as image of presence (*Feminine Sexuality* 145). That is, the body, rather than being a first-cause determiner of gender positioning, becomes, at the level of secondary effect, a signifier for the gendered being. Just as the mirror image becomes a signifier for the baby who invests in that image a notion of autonomy which becomes linked up to selfhood, the penis with its ability to rise and fall becomes for many males a signifier of power and law whose signification is reinforced by identification with the father. The phallus also comes to represent the subject's helpless impotence, for just as a human cannot control his or her existence and is in fact (according to Lacan) the object of unconscious desire, neither can the penis always be made to perform at will. Because it is potentially separable from the body, as boys especially realize if they see a girl whose "lack" they imagine to be the result of castration, the penis functions simultaneously as the image of presence and as the mark of lack. Such lack is the basis of existence itself, and the masculinely positioned subject will defend against it through *méconnaissance*, denying human fragility by investing in the image of presence provided by the phallus. Perhaps it is this investment which motivates the kind of male authorship traced by Gilbert and Gubar, who argue that male writers traditionally have used the pen as a kind of metaphorical penis with which they maintain partriarchal authority (5–8).

Lacan emphasizes that gender is a matter of positioning and that biology influences gender difference at a secondary level. At this level, the female for whom a sense of self has not been so tied to a reproductive organ is more likely to have less investment in *méconnaissance* than does her male counterpart. Her *jouissance* is more likely to be addressed to the Other, and her investment in the phallus will be directed less toward covering up an inherent lack-in-being than toward striving for wholeness in the sexual union. Since her wholeness is always dependent on an other rather than on an associative link between her self and her sex, the femininely positioned subject is able to strive for a unity beyond the sexual unity, for a "Oneness" which Lacan links to the Other. This Other position—a feminine one—is more closely based on bodily narcissism than is a masculine one, since the female is often less identified with the signifier of difference than is the male and retains more fluid ego and body boundaries. To go beyond the biological, then, is not to bypass or negate the real of body experience. But to go *through* that experience toward the Other from which it is derived means incorporating body and beyond-body through Eros, from which stems woman's sexuality. For Lacan, as Ragland-Sullivan emphasizes, Eros may well be mixed with Thanatos, and so can never be purely sexual. That is, words, myths, and all other manifestations of language tinge Eros with "alienation" effects which, for Lacan, strive toward death. The paradoxical mingling of a unity-seeking sexuality and the alienating function of language is that which Nin's concept of the feminine subject position takes into account.

For Nin, feminine creativity stems from love, which she sees as the unifying element between all people and all art, an element distinguished from what she calls "man's abstractions" (2:233) and to which she refers throughout the diaries as the intellectual systems with which man separates himself from others. Nin sees man's separateness contrasting with woman's need for unity. That is, Nin says, man creates a world of ideas out of a need to become separate and to dominate, a need which I see as maintained by Lacan's *méconnaissance*. By March 1937 Nin sees herself becoming "completely divorced from man's world of ideas" (2:188) as she concentrates on *"being* the womb" (2:188). Her diary becomes her "struggle against the scientific intellectual inventions of man" (2:203). She writes, "Ideas are a separating element. Love is a communion with others. Mental worlds are isolators. Love makes one embrace all races, the whole world, all forms of creation. The artist really seeks a universal language, and artists from all parts of the world can understand each other" (2:101). Nin's conception of intellectual systems of thought as masculine also makes sense from a Lacanian perspective. Since *connaissance* lies on the side of fiction for Lacan, the pleasure the ego derives from a belief in the "cunning of reason" (*Ecrits* 308) is a function of pretense, or repression. Feminine *jouissance*, on the other hand, deals with "a *jouissance* of the body which is . . . *beyond the phallus"* (*Feminine Sexuality* 145), beyond the function of pretense. This means, as I take it, that it does not stop at the Other, but quests for "truth," for *savoir*. Since *savoir* cannot be attained through the intellect, Lacan distinguishes between knowing and experiencing: "There is a *jouissance* proper to [woman] and of which she herself may know nothing, except that she experiences it" (*Feminine Sexuality* 145).[2] As in Nin's system, *connaissance*, or the ego's knowledge of the systems it creates to maintain the illusion of unity (such as the positive sciences), is seen as masculine. Nin places unconscious knowledge or "truth"—*savoir*—on the side of the feminine, and it is this with which Lacan also credits the mystics as well as certain other males.

Nin's striving for unities, fundamental to what she sees as the feminine position, may be considered in terms of Eros, which she embraces as the cornerstone of feminine creativity. For Lacan, too, Eros—"the thing called love, since we too must call it by the name under which it has echoed across the centuries" (*Feminine Sexuality* 139)—is closely linked to femininity. As I understand Lacan to be saying, it is through Eros, the unifying element, that the feminine addresses its demand to the *"something of One."*

Since this "something" is akin to God in Lacan's theory, his showing the correlation between femininity and mysticism is particularly relevant to Nin's depiction of feminine creativity. For Lacan, the feminine as well as the mystic understands God, not with an intellectual knowledge but with what may be considered an intuitive or experiential type of knowledge, which is linked to the feminine *jouissance* of being. Thus Lacan writes that the "many people who compliment [me] for having managed to establish . . . that God does not exist" (*Feminine Sexuality* 140) are those that understand "intellectually." This is what I think Lacan means by saying, "Unfortunately they understand, and what they understand is a little hasty" (140). Lacan's objective, rather than to show that God does not exist, is to say "in what he exists" (141); in my interpretation, "God" exists for Lacan in and *as* the relation between the gender identity one adopts as symbolic position and one's relation to desire and law. This position depends on *jouissance* of the body on the side of the man, and of a more global *jouissance* for the woman. A *jouissance* of "the supreme Being, that is of God" (*Feminine Sexuality* 142) is on the side of the woman.

In a section of her diary labelled "Summer, 1937" Nin emphasizes the woman writer's relation to God. The following passage from this section is perhaps one of her strongest statements about gender differences as played out in the field of creativity:

> As to all that nonsense Henry [Miller] and Larry [Durrell] talked about, the necessity of "I am God" in order to create (I suppose they mean "I am God, I am not a woman"). Woman never had direct communication with God anyway, but only through man, the priest. She never created directly except through man, was never able to create as a woman. But what neither Larry nor

Henry understands is that woman's creation far from being like man's must be exactly like her creation of children, that it must come out of her own blood, englobed by her womb, nourished with her own milk. It must be a human creation, of flesh, it must be different from man's abstractions. As to this "I am God," which makes creation an act of solitude and pride, this image of God confused woman. (Man too, because he thinks God did it all alone, and he thinks he did it all alone. . . .)

Woman does not forget she needs the fecundator, she does not forget that everything that is born of her is planted in her. If she forgets this she is lost. What will be marvelous to contemplate will not be her solitude but this image of woman being visited at night by man and the marvelous things she will give birth to in the morning. God alone, creating, may be a beautiful spectacle. I don't know. Man's objectivity may be an imitation of this God so detached from us and human emotion. But a woman alone creating is not a beautiful spectacle. The woman was born mother, mistress, wife, sister, she was born to represent union, communion, communication, she was born to give birth to life, and not to insanity. It is man's separateness, his so-called objectivity, which has made him lose contact, and then his reason. Woman was born to *be* the connecting link between man and his human self. . . .

I do not delude myself as man does, that I create in proud isolation. . . . Woman is not deluded. She must create without these proud delusions of man. . . . She must create that unity which man first destroyed by his proud consciousness. (2:233-34)

Nin thus formulates gender differences according to the way one relates to oneself as creator in relation to the Creator; by understanding "God" in Lacan's terms, we can see this relation as relation itself. He writes, "In loving God it is ourselves we love, and by first loving ourselves . . . we render to God the appropriate homage" (*Feminine Sexuality* 142). The feminine position is that which takes the Other into account whereas the masculine position can only love a self divorced from unconscious "truth."

In my interpretation, Nin supposes her male colleagues to take on the identity of proud and independent God because she sees them in the masculine position, adopting through *méconnaissance* an illusion of autonomy. In other words, the masculine renounces its dependence through the construction and maintenance of an illusory unity whereas the feminine, for Nin, is based on recognition of dependence on the "fecundator," which may be likened to what Lacan calls the Other. When Lacan says that "man has no chance of enjoying the body of the woman, in other words of making love" (*Feminine Sexuality* 143), I take him to mean that because he represses his dependence on the Other as source of unconscious desire and invests in a genital sense of autonomy, his *jouissance* stops at the body and does not "go beyond." The masculine is "encumbered" (147) by the symbolic phallus which is given an imaginary privilege as "real" penis for its representation of the image of presence, which corresponds to the mirror-stage child's identification with the illusion of a bodily *Gestalt*. Just as the subject embraces this image as denial of primordial fragmentation, an image which is perpetuated through the social dialect, Nin's masculine creator denies dependence on any other/Other and conceives himself as *tout*. I take Nin's statement that "woman never had direct communication with God anyway, but only through man, the priest" to mean that woman, as part of the social dialect through which she is alienated, is a signifier which for Lacan "can never reach its sexual partner, which is the Other, except by way of mediation" (*Feminine Sexuality* 151). Within the social dialect, naming renders woman feminine from a masculine perspective.

Thus Lacan opposes significance, whose motive is *jouissance* of the body, to God (*Feminine Sexuality* 142). In other words, signification is proper to alienation whose reality *méconnaissance* denies. Nin's concept of femininity as involving remembrance of the fecundator is illuminated by Lacan's idea of God as "he who comes" (146). And it is the feminine position to experience this orgasm of God's—to experience, but not to know.

In summary, Nin uses biological mothering as a metaphor for feminine creativity, seeing her literary works as coming "out of her own blood, englobed by her womb." A work of literature is for Nin a creation of flesh, with which she contrasts those of "man's abstractions." I have argued that a Lacanian concept of metaphor, because it involves the real of bodily experience in the interrelations between language and a subject's reality, illuminates this link between biological and metaphorical reproduction—the word made flesh. Nin's creation from flesh may be seen as the effort to give body to desire, which for the feminine is closely linked to corporal issues. Mothering, as I have shown, may be seen as a specific way of relating to others and the Other, as a relation to desire and law which allows one to create artistic unities through a retained awareness of the subject's inherent lack.

Seen as a matter of positioning rather than primarily of biology, the feminine has been shown to exist on the side of unconscious "truth" rather than on the side of *connaissance;* whereas the masculine defends against awareness of a lack-in-being by identifying with the symbolic phallus as the image of illusory presence, the feminine identity retains an openness toward the Other characterized by relational ability, fluidity, and a lack of ego rigidity. A way of experiencing more than knowing, femininity for Nin as well as for Lacan involves the acceptance of dependence on the Other, for which Nin uses God as metaphor. Nin's metaphorical equation of God as the fecundator in feminine reproduction shows the feminine identity as relational and experiential, a way of being which Lacan compares to the mystic; he describes both as having as a *jouissance* which goes beyond. That is, feminine *jouissance* is a *jouissance* of the body and of the *parole* which goes beyond the phallus as image of presence, an idea with which I have linked the materiality of language in order to show the creative function of the Symbolic. Because the feminine strikes a position away from the signifier of law even while existing in and as a function of both it and desire, "mothering" may be seen at the crossing of Nin and Lacan as the feminine position per se. This is not an idealization of a normative wholeness maintained through identification with the phallus, but a relation to the Other as source of unconscious desire through which Nin's "life, hope and creation" revolve as interwoven elements of a fluid and dynamic subjectivity.

Notes

1. I am greatly and gratefully indebted to Professor Ragland-Sullivan whose teachings and guidance have enabled me to think and to speak about Lacan. Where I have not cited a page number from her book, I have based my statement on her lectures during seminars entitled "Lacan" (spring 1987) and "Psychoanalysis and Feminism" (fall 1987) at the University of Florida.

2. Lacan adds that not all women experience it, reiterating his view that gender is a matter of positioning rather than primarily of biology.

Works Cited

Gilbert, Sandra M., and Susan Gubar. *The Madwoman in the Attic: The Woman Writer and the Nineteenth-Century Literary Imagination*. New Haven, Conn.: Yale UP, 1979.

Lacan, Jacques. *Ecrits: A Selection*. Ed. and trans. Alan Sheridan. New York: Norton, 1977.

——. *Feminine Sexuality: Jacques Lacan and the école freudienne*. Trans. Jacqueline Rose. Ed. Juliet Mitchell and Jacqueline Rose. London: Norton, 1985.

Nin, Anaïs. *The Diary of Anaïs Nin.* Ed. Gunther Stuhlmann. 7 vols. New York: Harcourt, 1966–80.

Ragland-Sullivan, Ellie. *Jacques Lacan and the Philosophy of Psychoanalysis.* Urbana: U of Illinois P, 1986.

Rich, Adrienne. *On Lies, Secrets, and Silence.* New York: Norton, 1979.

The Go-Between Child:
Supplementing the Lack

Virginia L. Blum

Jacques Lacan observes that "in the case of the speaking being the relation between the sexes does not take place" ("God" 138). Heterosexuality strives to make two into one, denying the intersubjective "relational" experience; furthermore, what there is to speak of is phallocentric, premised only on the male position. There is no relation because only one sex is articulated and a relation necessarily denotes more than one.

Then what of the child produced by this "union," this nonrelation? Typically obscure, Lacan philosophizes that *"There is something of One,"* which he goes on to explain "is set forth in [Freud's] concept of Eros, defined as a fusion making one out of two, that is of Eros seen as the gradual tendency to make one out of a vast multitude" ("God" 138). Yet isn't the "something" derived from the two-become-one very specifically (literally) the child-representative of the sexual fantasy? Isn't the child in fact installed in the space fantasy has veiled, a space that is paradoxically disavowed? We might say that like Aphrodite, the child springs from the oceanic landscape of love where identities merge and dissolve, the very desubjectifying condition of love engendering love's subject.

The child is supplementary in the sense that it adds to the sexual relation; a third party joins the parental couple. Yet, in an ironic twist the "supplement" subtracts as well, in a single stroke effacing both itself and the duality of the parents. Even though the child appears as an emblem of the parental unity, it is an emblem that has to be cast out from the sexual scene the moment it appears. This is because the child necessarily reveals the very space of difference it is bound to mystify. In other words, its unifying function belies the insuperable gap it traverses.

If the idea of the sexual relation is founded upon a gross deception, so then is the child proceeding from a relation that never occurred. We know from what Freud tells us of the sexual theories of children that they originally think the baby is born from the cloaca, like feces, and that the female child grows up to imagine she will give birth to her own penis. In short, the child is never just that. Rather, it is inevitably the product of a series of equations founded upon distortions. Because of its position vis-à-vis human sexuality, the child can never *be* any more than the unspeakable sexual relation.

If the child is the representative of the longed-for "fusion" of the sexes, then the child in turn figures the duplicity of its own referentiality. Either it plays its role as feces, meaning that, since both sexes are equipped with an anus, it can be produced from either—or it supplies the missing penis to the woman who, as a result, becomes—what? Just like a man. Or finally, and more familiarly, the child represents the wished-for convergence of man and woman into a single undifferentiated sex, because the child is the mark of the denial of sexual difference.

But when I tell you that the child plays the phallus par excellence, what can you think? Especially when one considers that this very phallus is what Lacan designates as marking the place of sexual difference. But recall Lacan's insistence that the phallus can only play its role as veiled ("Phallus" 82). Like the snake-infested Medusa's head, the phallus manifests the opposite of what it disguises—castrated genitals. Thus, if the phallus rises up in the place where the sexes diverge, it only to mystify the other of phallocentrism (the woman without a penis), whereby it negates sexual differentiation, proclaiming its decree: there is no sexual relation; there is only something of One. There is only the child who is born to traverse the renounced gap between the sexes, destined at once to figure and supplement the censored space of difference. The child is fated to be the go-between.

Children in literature frequently are installed in go-between positions, be it between classes, races, generations, good and evil, nature and civilization. Whatever the operative metaphor, however, the child is always, radically, the sexual go-between, with the other triangles merely displacing and reformulating the Oedipal.[1] The child cannot help but allude to the parental partners, the very word "child" articulating the terms of its production.

L. P. Hartley's novel, *The Go-Between*, presents us with the prototypical go-between child in that he overtly functions as a sexual liaison. In presenting a psychoanalytic reading of this text, I hope somewhat to sidestep the perils of cementing characters and motifs into inflexible psychoanalytic categories. Rather, I would like to attempt an intertextual approach in which the role of the psychoanalytic subject illuminates the text and the fictional protagonist in turn addresses the ramifications of our psychology.

In brief, *The Go-Between* is narrated by a sixty-year-old bibliographer who turns to his childhood diary to recover the "truth" of his life. For the month preceding his thirteenth birthday, Leo Colston, renowned at his prep school for his occult code- and spell-making talents, is a guest at the country estate of a school friend's wealthy family. During his stay, Leo acts as a messenger between his friend's older sister, Marian, and her lower-class lover, Ted Burgess, a tenant farmer. The culmination of his go-between activity is to witness the pair fornicating on the ground in an outhouse.

The Oedipal triangle is immediately apparent, with Marian in the position of mother, Ted as father, and Leo as the child traumatized by the primal scene, the future anterior of his own conception.[2] Leo identifies the various members of his newfound world with the gods of the zodiac. Marian plays the Virgin while Ted is Aquarius, the Water-Bearer, and the Viscount Trimingham, Marian's fiancé (and another father figure), is associated with Sagittarius. Leo himself is pronounced Mercury by Trimingham, who is the first of the group to employ Leo as a messenger. The child revels in his membership in the zodiacal community and initially appreciates his role as their envoy.

The zodiacal identifications represent Leo's attempt to master the Oedipal positions, the only means whereby he can determine his own location in the symbolic register of language. Thus Leo would like people and things to remain inflexibly fixed in their respective functions— and classes. Being middle-class himself, the very in-betweenness of his status is dependent upon the opposition of rich to poor (a political variation on the masculine/feminine opposition).[3] From the moment Leo recognizes the actual nature of Marian's relationship with the tenant farmer, he wants it to cease. Rather, he would prefer Marian to be with Lord Trimingham, a more apposite class connection. Leo explains that "order would have been restored: social order, universal order" (Hartley 261).

Nevertheless, Leo's reassuring demarcations threaten to disintegrate around him. Despite his efforts, the masculine/feminine oppositions shift and interlace as intractably as the classes. Ted, imaged as the virile organ itself, is also the Water-Bearer and, in addition to the phallic emblems, is surrounded by feminine amniotic water imagery. Leo's first sight of Ted is diving into the lake, a moment at which the phallic and the feminine seem to converge. As a member of the lower class, Ted is perceived as somehow feminine, perhaps because he is closer to nature, less civilized. Leo remarks that he knew it was acceptable to shed tears in front of a man of Ted's class. Moreover, it is Ted who maternally tends to Leo's injured knee; later Marian will re-bandage the wound. In many ways, Ted's alliance with Marian is more identifying than oppositional which for Leo must seem to be an egregious failure on the part of the sexual constellation. Trimingham, called the Archer because of his association with war, is grotesquely disfigured, figuratively castrated. Yet, while the zodiacal Archer is a considerably more "phallic" figure than the Water-Bearer, Ted is Marian's sexual partner; with Trimingham, there seems to be no question of sex. In fact, the child Marian eventually bears to Trimingham, who becomes her husband, is Ted's.

Marian as the Virgin, although ostensibly equated with the mother, is also sexually ambiguous, both phallic and "not all." The Virgin (in her Mary-an persona) is self-impregnating, a phallic mother, whose other is the whore, phallicized in that her body carries the phantoms of other men's penises. Originally, Leo imagines that Marian is a kind of phallic mother, nevertheless at the same time recognizing that she wants something. As we can see, the sexual coding is less reliable than Leo would like. Both men and the woman are alternately feminized and phallicized, a vivid replication of Leo's own slippage as the symbol that conditions the sexuality it obfuscates.

It is in the sexual slippage that we find the kernel of Leo's ambiguous role and self-image—the split between the child of twelve and the adolescent of thirteen. The child is a willing participant in the sexual fantasy of "Oneness." As Leo admits, "I volunteered to fill the gap" (155). The adolescent, however, is struggling to locate himself as an identity in contradistinction to the sexual partners. Leo's initial childhood eagerness to "fill the gap" turns into his desperation to define and separate. It is important here to distinguish between the imaginary order Leo craves and the social discursive order he is about to enter. Leo imagines a "real" constellation apart from what is symbolically constructed by language.[4]

Leo is Mercury, "the messenger of the gods," as Trimingham explains (90). It is Mercury's Greek counterpart, Hermes, however, who becomes relevant to our project.[5] Hermes is a phallic god, bearing the caduceus.

He is related to the phallic herm which rises from the intersections of roads, the very herm to which Lacan alludes in "The Meaning of the Phallus" (80). Like the herm, the phallus stands at what Edward Casey and J. Melvin Woody have described as "the intersection of the natural and signifying" (106), or more specifically, at the place where sex is alienated into discourse and men and women are divided according to the presence and absence of the penis.

One could say that on a superficial level, Leo is analogous to the very penis connecting the sexual partners, the human organ that literally unites them. The text indicates that before Leo's arrival on the scene, Ted and Marian's meetings were rare and, furthermore, that they had not yet consummated their relationship. Leo is the "inter" of their discourse, both sexual and verbal, bearing the love letters that determine future sexual assignations. The terrain between the hall and the farm, rich and poor, woman and man, is collapsed in the person of their courier, the very mediating child who paradoxically yearns for the taxonomies he throws into question.

If Leo is really no more than a penis—a signifier of the phallus that plays a literal intersecting role—he imagines himself a phallus, what Lacan has described as "an abstract, heroic, unique phallus, devoted to the service of a lady" (*Four Concepts* 39). Early on, he wants to *be* the phallus for the mother (Marian). In reference to his "duties as Mercury," he tells us that "I felt I was doing for Marian something that no one else could" (110). Later, he wants to *have* the object of her desire: "Deep down I wanted what Marian wanted," the possession of which would make him desirable as the purveyor of the phallus (148). Recall that the phallus obfuscates the castration (sexual division) for which it stands, just as Leo's four-mile journey between Marian and Ted is intended to dissolve the space it measures. Leo's situation is as self-negating as that of the phallus he both enacts and subserves.

Hermes is also the patron of hermeneutics, the art of interpreting symbolism, a requisite skill for both the young Leo in his attempt to negotiate the wonders of the adult constellation, and the aged Leo who rakes the diary of his past in search of clues. Nonetheless, just as young Leo repeatedly misinterprets adult codes, old Leo finds it impossible to decipher the child's code in which a portion of his diary is inscribed. In other words, Leo's childhood voice does not entirely transcend the generational divide—the bridge flung across the gap is only makeshift, in its very construction half-disguising, half-exposing its insufficiency. Like the sexual go-between, the bridge is only just that, supplementary.

It appears that Leo is no more successful in his role of Mercury (no more a one-to-one equation) than the adults in their zodiacal configurations. As I remarked earlier, Leo requires what he imagines to be the safety of human beings captivated by allegory. What he denies is *symbolic* potential or indeterminacy. Paradoxically, at school, he was touted as "a master of language" and experienced the ecstasy of having his own special language circulated for several days (15). To have the phallus is to be the subject presumed to know, to master the appropriation of nature by language. Yet, if within the scene of childhood, Leo wields authority, his situation in the adult world is a different story altogether. He is excluded from the code contained within the letters he delivers. " 'You wouldn't understand it' "(90), Ted Burgess points out when Leo suggests he transmit a message orally. As far as Leo is concerned, this would be a literal revelation of the letter. Leo doesn't mind, though, because, as he explains, "I liked giving and receiving information. . . . I didn't resent or feel aggrieved because I couldn't understand it. I was the smallest of the planets, and if I carried messages between them and I couldn't always understand, that was in order, too: they were something in a foreign language—star talk" (98). The message seems like "star talk," as long as the sexual couple remains celestial.

From the moment the Marian/Ted relationship is dashed to the mundane level of what Leo calls "spooning," Leo begins to resent his outsider, spectating position. Because spooning is a familiar word linked to some vague ideas of physical contact, he assumes that he has cracked what he hitherto imagined to be an impenetrable "foreign" code. What is most interesting is that the very relationship he believes he has interpretively mastered in fact remains inaccessible to his field of knowledge, a situation which precisely parallels Lacan's description of the universal human dilemma of acceding to knowledge through language. Like Leo, the human subject invariably stands "outside" the code, always bears rather than creates the language by which he or she is constituted. Leo's plight is then the general one in which the child-subject tries to come to terms with his relationship to discourse, the very inclusion in which is invariably exclusive as well. What Leo comes to resent is the fact that he seems to be at once inside (between sender and addressee—the locus of the message itself) and outside in that he never seems to be himself either the sender or addressee. According to Lacan, however, "It is from the place of the Other that his [the subject's] message is emitted" ("Phallus" 80). Hence, although Leo fantasizes becoming the source of the message, because of the very constitutive nature of language, the individual subject can never really create his own messages. Nor can he, as the text indicates, directly receive the message that returns to the Other. What sends and receives is always the Other, never ultimately the subject who is "subjected" as the Other's go-between. Further, the unequivocal Oedipal nature of the triangular Marian/Ted/Leo interaction is precisely the brand of unconscious material that the Other articulates. Hence, Leo's frustration at being marginalized reflects the world of speaking beings caught in the space between consciousness and the other scene. Unfortunately for Leo, it takes fifty years for him to recognize his childhood oppression by the message as illustrative of the human condition. He claims that subsequently his motto became " 'Once a go-between, never a go-between' " (295), as he clearly failed to come to terms with the inevitable. His resolution in the epilogue to convey one last message for Marian (to her grandson) suggests Leo's renunciation of his fantasy, his final belated capitulation to the symbolic order.

What Leo perhaps minds most about the sexual relationship between Marian and Ted is the diminution entailed in his descent from messenger of the gods to mere sex organ. When Ted and Marian coerce Leo into continuing on as what they jokingly term their "postman" (120), Leo resolves to become an "editor" instead (134). As long as Leo delivers the messages intact, he remains undifferentiated from the message he bears. It is in the effort to become more than the message that Leo is driven to alter its contents. The last message Leo delivers to Marian is the hour Ted expects her, a time Leo alters by a fatal half hour, during which Marian's mother catches them in the act. It is this very gap between 6:00 and 6:30 around which all of the lovers' hopes and plans disintegrate—the gap hitherto filled by Leo himself. Earlier, Leo imagined that the gap in time would serve to alert the couple to the social discrepancy between them, the transgression of which has disturbed Leo considerably. His zodiacal system has been set awry by the insertion of the patently non-godlike Ted Burgess. Leo assumes that, as a result of his misinformation, a scene will ensue in which Marian will take note of Ted's social inferiority. What seems to be most distressing to Leo is the lovers' repudiation of social law, and social law as rooted in the prohibition of incest.

If we read this as an Oedipal story in which the paternal interdiction of incest is established, Leo's alarm becomes understandable. Edward Casey and Melvin Woody write that "the incest taboo is only the nexus at which these two dimensions of human existence, the natural and the signifying, most conspicuously intersect" (107). Recall that the post that marks that very nexus of animal sexuality and human law is the herm, the phallic bar, and Leo Colston is the *"post*man" whose function is utterly dependent upon obeisance to the law he signifies. Ted Burgess is the man of nature, who looks out of place in clothes to Leo, engaging with Marian in a purely carnal (anticulture) affair. But it is Ted with whom Leo identifies most nearly, as he frequently admits, even going so far as to suggest that as a result of Ted's suicide, Leo died as well. Leo projects his incestuous feelings in relation to his substitute-mother, Marian, on to the Marian/Ted relationship. Therefore, as we can see, his virulent response to their social transgression is merely a brand of paranoid projection of his own carnality vis-à-vis the "mother." His wish to destroy the relationship evidences the repression of his incestuous impulses in order to assume his castrated (socialized) position in the Oedipal arena. Yet the Marian/Ted relationship is no more than a mask. Both Leo and the text appropriately crush the apparent incestuous liaison while legitimizing the more nearly incestuous social endogamy of Marian's alliance with Trimingham.

To an extent, the novel describes the penultimate incest fantasy in that the child precedes the sexual coupling, a conjunction which amazingly depends on the child's intercession. In this way the child can become the cause of its own creation; it is "incestuously" incorporated into the very parental sexual activity from which it is subsequently excluded. This model can be reversed, however, from the point of view of the adult participant. One could speculate that the literary go-between indicates to what degree we imagine the child preexists its own conception. If, via a series of displacements, the child has come to represent the fantasy of fusion, it is in conjunction with the construction of this fantasy that the child comes into mythical being. The birth of the child is coincidental with conception or, more mystifying still, to conceive *of* the child is to conceive the child. What is most disorienting in all this is that the question of origins exceeds the question and instead becomes asymptotic. Wordsworth's fond assertion that the child is father to the man suddenly seems to be a grotesque evocation of a chain of genealogical distortions.

One reading of Hartley's novel is as the prenatal figure of the child culminating in its own conception during the traumatic primal scene encounter in the outhouse. It is at this juncture that the go-between is superannuated. The "two bodies moving like one" seem to have closed the gap of desire (290), and Leo is abruptly deferred from the space between to the periphery of the union. It is a death-evoking scene in more ways than one. Certainly, Leo's self-aggrandizement as the phallus is blasted. No longer the "linchpin" he imagined (225), he sees himself where he used to "be"—representing the unconquerable space between the bodies that can only move as or "like" one—but always irremediably *two*. And in that epiphanic glance, the child must necessarily (traumatically) come to terms with his own mythical status—he is compelled to see where he is *not*, where he never was, now that he has been relegated to a position outside of a space he never filled.

Death is portended in other ways as well, in the act of sexed reproduction, the death blow to human immortality. Leo's earlier denial that Marian would "spoon" echoes every child's protest. To be the product of sexuality implies flesh-bound mortality to the child who dreams of spontaneous and incorporeal generation. Thus, in witnessing his own conception, Leo apprehends the lineaments of his destiny—in the dust of the outhouse, where culture recedes back into nature.

What the child resonates most significantly is generational future. Leo observes: "[T]here was a picture of a lady and a gentleman bicycling gaily along a country road, looking at me and at the future with surprised but pleased and confident expressions" (191). Freud himself was preoccupied with the question of a transcendent future through procreation and, in relation to the current topic, it is worth considering at this point his dream of the bridge-children in *The Interpretation of Dreams:*

> At last we came to a small wooden house with an open window at one end. Here the guide set me down, and laid two planks, which stood in readiness, on the window-sill so as to bridge the chasm which had to be crossed from the window. Now I grew really alarmed about my legs. Instead of the expected crossing, I saw two grown-up men lying upon benches which were fixed on the walls of the hut, and something like two sleeping children next to them; as though not the planks but the children were intended to make the crossing possible. (429)

Recalling his descent into an Etruscan grave containing two adult skeletons, Freud interprets the hut as his grave. He goes on to observe, in reference to the children, that "perhaps my children will achieve what has been denied to their father . . . a fresh allusion to the strange romance in which the identity of a character is preserved through a series of generations . . . " (430). In the beginning of the dream, Freud watches his pelvis and legs being dissected, which suggests a kind of castration (even though Freud never says as much), an operation from which he miraculously recovers, although considerably weakened. If we follow the dream to its logical conclusion, then the deterioration of his legs becomes associated with death (the ultimate castration), and only his children, phallically depicted as planks, can continue the journey—in short, live. For one's legs to fail, to be unable to carry on, or to be mortal, is to be castrated. Via the plank-stiffened bridge-children, Freud dreams that he can transcend the grave and circumnavigate castration. If we were to reduce this dream to a single wish, it might be: I wish my children could be for me the phallus.

In "The Meaning of the Phallus," Lacan writes of the phallus: "By virtue of its turgidity, it is the image of the vital flow as it is transmitted in generation" (82). Thus the phallus as emblematized by the child is generational immortality as well, the indefatigable progress of man as mankind. If Leo represents the "future" of society, he is also the "future" of the sexual couple, what they hope to "be" when they become one—a child. It is noteworthy that the sexual act Leo witnesses is probably the consummation of what was until then only a flirtation. Furthermore, since it is the only time the couple has intercourse, what Leo witnesses is the moment of conception itself. In a sense, he cannot help but be present for this decisive event, because he stands for (and in for) the contact of bodies. As "future," then, the fantasmatic child is annihilated into the past (the real child) in the very instant that the "future" is fulfilled.

In the epilogue, the older Leo explains that he "missed that experience [of war], along with many others, spooning among them" (294). As the child "pivot" of the illusions of the sexual relation (246), Leo has been petrified in conjunction with the simultaneous fulfillment and evaporation of the illusions, thereafter incapable of assuming a subjectivity apart from being the support of a fantasmatic system. Interestingly, the sexual relation has lost its appeal, its mystique having vanished for Leo when he glimpsed the trace of impossibility in the culmination of the sexual experience. Leo confesses that he aspired to be a writer but, apparently lacking sufficient drive, instead became a bibliographer; the creativity of writing being too intimately linked with a sexuality he has disavowed. Leo has been de-sexed, and, when one considers the circumstances, what else could happen to the child who was expected to collapse sexual difference? The de-sexed progeny of the sexual relation becomes the concretization of the drive to reduce two into one, to eliminate sex altogether. Being neither on the side of the man or the woman, Leo ends up outside sex, the inevitable result of a sex-repudiating fusion.

Hartley emphasizes that this summer is in many respects a turning point for Leo. In his pubertal passage from twelve to thirteen, he is at the same time introduced into the rarefied world of the wealthy and the mysteries of adult sexuality. He is also, crucially, progressing from the childhood realm of magic to the adult system of reality and its attendant social laws. About the day of his thirteenth birthday, Leo elaborates:

> Now that I was thirteen, I was under an obligation to look reality in the face. . . . Looking back on my actions since I came to Brandham, I condemned them all; they seemed the actions of another person. . . . All the time at Brandham I had been another little boy, and the grown-ups had aided and abetted me in this; it was a great deal their fault. They like to think of a little boy as a little boy, corresponding to their idea of what a little boy should be—as a representative of little boyhood—not a Leo or a Marcus. (272)

Clearly, Leo is trying to outgrow the go-between position and achieve a subjectivity in contradistinction to the "terms of another person" (257) and representationality in general. It is in the assertion of a separate identity that Leo is thwarted by Marian, who is disinclined to release him from his job as her Cupid. As a child, inhabitant of the imaginary zodiac, Leo is happy to unite the sexual couple and function for them as the signifier of the relation. As an adult, however, Leo renounces this role. It is Marian's backward tug that fixates Leo at the junction of the social and the fantasmatic, the adult and the child, the symbolic and the imaginary. He cannot go to war (which Leo associates with manhood), nor can he write, a procreative act.

Hitherto trapped in a world in which words are real, Leo regards language as inherently deadly. He believes that his spells literally have maimed two boys at school and killed Ted Burgess. The messages he bears as well are more real to Leo than the sexual relation they advance. Thus he imagines that "by removing myself [as go-between] I had removed the danger" (225).

Marian asks Leo to tell her estranged grandson that "there's no spell or curse except an unloving heart. You know that, don't you?" (310). Of course, to date this was just what Leo did not know. Fixated as he has been for the past fifty years at the stage where the child becomes *more than* the figure for the adult relation, Leo has hovered in the imaginary (we might even say psychotic) register where spells are real, not symbolic, and the word is absolutely identified with its referent. Because Marian captivated him, it is only fitting that it is Marian who finally, albeit unwittingly, releases him into the symbolic register. Hence the novel-product of Leo's final transcendence. The princess-cum-witch has broken the stultifying spell, and, as a result, Leo becomes a message-bearing adult—who knows that his message is only language.

The "One" we seek, of course, is that originary experience of the mother/child symbiotic union which we expect the heterosexual relation to replicate. The one is the plenitude of the mother as the uncastrated Other; and the one is the omnipotent child as well who, in its conjunction with the mother creates himself as he is in her. Therefore, the space trod by the go-between child is fundamentally the breach between the mother and himself, having become, in his ejection from the symbiotic landscape, the figure of his own dislocation and division. The adult idealizes in the child his own former omnipotence at the same time that he blames the child for the tragic rupture his image revivifies. The child, in turn, repeats the story as he has heard it narrated.

As we can see, one of the most perplexing aspects of Leo's role in the text is the confusion between the fantasmatic child and the actual child, in other words, the child from the point of view of the adult and the child as he constructs himself. More perplexing still, we must determine to what extent the child's point of view is premised on the adult. Hence, as reader, one is constantly shifting between the question of what Leo wants and is as a character and what is projected on to Leo as an idea. We can recognize this very indecision manifested in the adult Leo's relationship with his child self. Alternately, he installs himself in the child's point of view and outside of the child whom he then metaphorizes as peremptorily as the sexual couple.

Readers, at any given moment, find themselves on the side of the child or the adult, reversals which replicate the textual ambivalence. Thus, in the act of reading, one cannot help but experience the universal internal bisection. Like the literalized argument that transpires between old and young Leo, in which old Leo chastises the misdemeanors of the child, the child in literature precipitates an analogous split in the reader. We are compelled helplessly, interminably, to go between.

Notes

1. Huck Finn and Little Lord Fauntleroy are examples of literary children who on the surface seem to be "going between" black and white, and aristocratic and middle class/British and American, respectively. But Jim is clearly identified with the maternal function and Cedric reconciles the father's side to the mother's.

2. *The Go-Between* is quite self-conscious of the Oedipal story it presents. Leo goes so

far as to think of Marian as his "substitute mother," and it is Marian's lover, Ted, who offers to unfold for Leo the mysteries of "spooning," assuming the father's role and cementing the triangular relationship between Ted, Marian, and the child who is their message-bearing liaison. Yet Ted turns out to be a false father who will not fulfill the promise he made/showed. Another triangle is formed in terms of Lord Trimingham, Marian, and Leo. And, underlying the first two triangles is Leo's "real" parental scene including his real mother and his dead father. On a superficial level, we might conclude that Leo is seeking a father to replace the deceased and a mother in the form of a young woman who can function as a more appropriate object of displaced sexual passion. But Marian is in many ways a more masculine figure than her male partners, and the triumvirate of fathers in the text all fail miserably in the paternal function. The real father has abdicated altogether by dying, while Trimingham is "castrated," and Ted, who first suppresses the truth of generation, the discourse of the sexual relation it is the father's function to supervise and transmit, takes his own life. Hence we have a text overpopulated with dead fathers and a central female character who plays the mother like a man. In a sense *The Go-Between* has at once too many parents and no parents at all, the overabundance signifying the underlying absence. Beneath the sturdy edifice of the Oedipal structure, might we find the absence of any family system whatsoever? And isn't the story of the child longing for the parent of the opposite sex and fearing the retribution of the same-sex parent yet another fiction installed in the space of desire that gives a form to what is formless and a name to nothing? The Oedipus complex itself becomes the story of how classic psychoanalysis recapitulates the very unary structure it professes to elucidate. Lacan elaborates a "quaternary system" in place of the Freudian triangle which incorporates a distinction between the real and symbolic parent. "The Neurotic's Individual Myth," *The Psychoanalytic Quarterly* 48 (1979): 422.

3. Consider furthermore the reversal inherent in Marian's and Ted's social positions in that the woman is allied with wealth and social power while the man is installed in the inferior, lower-class role—yet another disorienting, "improper" rearrangement of the categories Leo must assimilate.

4. What often becomes confusing in the text, however, is the distinction between useful and destructive forms of organization, an issue that would be worth treating at further length.

5. Consider the connection between the hermaphroditic product of the hermes/Aphrodite liaison and the child as in some sense a displacement of the hermaphroditic urge—to be the "whole" Aristophanic man/woman.

Works Cited

Casey, Edward S., and J. Melvin Woody. "Hegel, Heidegger, Lacan: The Dialectic of Desire." *Interpreting Lacan.* Ed. Joseph H. Smith and William Kerrigan. New Haven: Yale UP, 1983.

Freud, Sigmund. *The Interpretation of Dreams. The Basic Writings of Sigmund Freud.* Ed. and trans. A. A. Brill. New York: Modern Library, 1938.

Hartley, L[esley] P[oles]. *The Go-Between.* New York: Stein and Day, 1953.

Lacan, Jacques. *Feminine Sexuality: Jacques Lacan and the école freudienne.*

Trans. Jacqueline Rose. Ed. Juliet Mitchell and Jacqueline Rose. New York: Norton, 1985.

————. *The Four Fundamental Concepts of Psycho-Analysis.* Trans. Alan Sheridan. Ed. Jacques-Alain Miller. New York: Norton, 1978.

————. "God and the *Jouissance* of the Woman." *Feminine Sexuality* 137–48.

————. "A Love Letter." *Feminine Sexuality* 149–61.

————. "The Meaning of the Phallus." *Feminine Sexuality* 74–85.

Gastro-exorcism: J.-K. Huysmans and the Anatomy of Conversion

Carol A. Mossman

The Catholic church made a prestigious conversion in the case of J.-K. Huysmans. In his 1903 preface to *A rebours* (1884), the converted author attempts to explain, as much to himself as to his readers, the curiously monkish tastes of the novel's neurotic hero, des Esseintes, who is nothing if not a dyed-in-the-wool hedonist bent on exploring the limits of sensual experience. Far from repudiating this earlier product of an "un-Christian" phase, as one might have expected him to do, Huysmans maintains that "all the novels which I have written since *A rebours* are contained in embryonic form in that book" (Preface, *A rebours* 50).[1]

Thus a continuity is postulated throughout the work in spite of a radical shift in state of mind occurring somewhere within the span. Nonetheless it is a troubled continuity, one which is (to use the phraseology of conversion) not without lapses: "I understand . . . up to a certain point," proffers Huysmans, "what happened between the year 1891 and the year 1895, between *Là-bas* and *En route*, but nothing at all about what happened between 1884 and 1891, between *A rebours* and *Là-bas*" (*A rebours* 58).

How, then, might one account for Huysmans's celebrated passage from the profane to the mystical, for that shift which is merely apparent since *A rebours* is an embryonic form of all future creations? Referring to des Esseintes, Huysmans advances the following: "It seems in fact that the neuroses open up fissures in the soul through which the Spirit of Evil penetrates" (51). The conversion which took place at an indeterminate point in the erstwhile naturalist's career was already manifest in some form in the illness which is the subject of *A rebours.* Looking backward in 1903, Huysmans affirms a kinship between mind and soul, between the self-divisive attacks of neurosis and infiltrations diabolical.

One is tempted to wonder whether this soul, evidently prone to fracture and highly vulnerable to exterior forces, can be situated in some specific locus, as Descartes had placed it, for instance, in the pineal gland? By way of response, we can turn to the final sentence of *Là-bas,* the second way station cited by Huysmans in his spiritual itinerary. There the misanthropic protagonist Durtal, having finished his novel on satanist Gilles de Rais, muses on the future awaiting the offspring of what he views as an abject modernity, devoid of spiritual values. These children "will do as their fathers and mothers . . . they will fill their guts and empty out their souls through the lower abdomen!" (282). [2]

The soul, it would seem, must be sought somewhere in the digestive tract whence it apparently runs the unorthodox risk of being flushed out. It follows from this that spiritual therapy might best be envisaged in terms of containment or retention, an inference borne out, indeed, by the obvious attraction which reclusion and claustration exercise over many of Huysmans's characters, and which the monastic temptation exercised over Huysmans himself (Baldick 267–89). In *En route,* the third and final stage of the itinerary, Durtal (again the novel's protagonist) explains that his conversion occurred in a manner redolent of the digestive process: "For God acts as He pleases. . . . [The method] he used in my case . . . was something analogous to a stomach digesting without my feeling it" (32).

Clearly, then, the continuity which joins the sacred to the profane is alimentary in nature. However, the profile of conversion is by no means a simple one. Overlaying the gastroreligious fundament and infusing it to a rather remarkable extent are two alternate systems which seek to explain disorders, be they religious or digestive: neuropathology and demonology. Throughout these three key works which Huysmans named as milestones on his personal road to Damascus, the discourses of the divine, the demonic, the digestive, and the neurotic intertwine. The depiction of salvation and the resultant state of grace is problematic, to say the least. In this study, I shall argue that for J.-K. Huysmans, good, evil, and insanity cohabit the self-same space in the body.

In May 1884 Huysmans wrote to Emile Zola explaining his struggle writing a novel which featured a single character, with no love interest— in short, a book lacking traditional narrative structure. If the master was later to chastise his "disciple" for overturning the naturalist canon in his

novel, *A rebours,* an entire generation would find that it spoke directly to
their sensibilities. For it was perhaps the first novel to draw on a genre
which, however appreciated, had not yet crossed over into the French
literary camp: the case history. It is well known that Huysmans based the
narrative progression of *A rebours* on the etiology of "nervosisme" as
elaborated by Bouchut in his 1877 edition of *Du nervosisme aigu et
chronique et des maladies nerveuses* (Huysmans, *Lettres* 103). This is the
documentary aspect of the novel through which its links to naturalism
are retained.[3]

Françoise Gaillard has brilliantly argued that the very scrupulousness
with which Huysmans adheres to Bouchut's narrative gives the lie to the
medical myth by exposing the gaps in a doctrine which fails to establish
convincing links between the cause (heredity) and the disease itself
(90–94). I shall return to this point later insofar as it relates to Huysmans's own diversion from the neuropathological and his conversion to
another mode of explanation.

Meanwhile, it is perversion which prevails in *A rebours. Webster's
New International Dictionary* defines "perversion" as a "deviation from
the right, true or regular course . . . as, to *pervert* the order of nature,"
and it is certain that *A rebours* flaunts the unnatural, including the
pathological, with perverse relishment. Nor, it has been observed, does
des Esseintes seem to want to seek a cure to his malady. (Gaillard goes so
far as to say that illness is the essence of the character.) This indulgence
can doubtless be ascribed to the fact that what the exaltation of neurosis
secures, at the expense of all that is "normal" and "natural," is access to
privileged zones of the mind open to the irrational, the suprasensible,
the unconscious, and the demonic. It thus comes as no surprise that this
aesthetic of pathology should take as its principal devices of expression
dreams, involuntary memory, and hallucinatory descriptions of paint-
ings, all activated through the senses and set against a Baudelairean
metaphysical backdrop of correspondences.

Central, then, to Huysmans's aesthetic is communication with a
beyond lying, vaguely, *là-bas.* However, there is a disturbing aspect to
this contact, for in order to move in and out of these zones of revelation,
there must be passage points. Victor Brombert has demonstrated the
Huysmansian hero's unending quest for hermetic reclusion (149–70).
Perhaps equally revealing, I would suggest, is the corollary to this penchant for sequestration—the terror of leakage. Therein lies the anguish
and the interest of this writer's universe. For it stands to reason that try as
one may, a perfect sealing off can never be achieved: madness can always

seep in through some crack (*A rebours*), or "le Démon" can penetrate through one of the soul's fissures (*Là-bas*), and, more disquieting still, grace always runs the risk of escaping through the bowels ("they will empty out their souls through the lower abdomen").

As we shall see, throughout Huysmans's works, the dread of puncture and penetration translates into a discourse which is riddled with holes, scars, orifices, and wounds being sutured up. Yet as fear-inspiring as the prospect of invasion seems to be, the anxiety of penetration is, at the very least, an equivocal one. After all, it seems only fair that the "Divinity" should have an equal right of access to the soul as "le Malin." Indeed, the conversion/digestion operated in *En route* began with an aperture: "Christ opened, little by little, the shuttered lodging of his [Durtal's] soul, and light came streaming in" (cited by Baldick; 200). Neoplatonic metaphors aside, in Huysmans's novels the struggle of madness versus sanity, of possession versus grace is won or lost in the openings.

With these various equivalences provisionally set forth, let me examine *A rebours* in greater detail. It begins, as a nineteenth-century case history should, with the genealogy of the family des Esseintes, the underlying assumption being that the young Duke Jean's nervous malady has been transmitted to him hereditarily. The hereditary solution, forged into literary doctrine by Zola, enjoyed the credibility of the evolving community of neurologists, as was pointed out earlier. Not only had Bouchut grounded his nosology of "nervosisme" in heredity (see Gaillard), but it also provided Charcot, Huysmans's celebrated medical contemporary, with the theoretical base for his own more systematic study of the neuroses. (Charcot's Tuesday Lessons almost invariably began by tracing the hereditary pathological "antecedents" of his patients; 41, 46, 56, 58.)

Thus the gallery of ancestral portraits exhibited at the beginning of *A rebours* as a mode of scientific explanation of des Esseintes's physical and mental degeneration is true to genre. Striking, however, is the fact that on closer scrutiny, one notices that Jean des Esseintes's most direct "racial" forebear, if such it can be called, is none other than a hole: "a hole existed in the lineage of this race" (62). This interruption of the family chain is itself subsequently interrupted and patched over by the insertion of one "mysterious" head which "was a suture between the past and the present" (62). If the missing link has been restored, the gap in the family tree has merely been filled in. As a weak spot, it still bodes a potential for rupture.

Clearly, the "mysterious other" with the "ambiguous expression" who is associated with openings is to be regarded as des Esseintes's most direct hereditary influence. It is with some interest, then, that we perceive this ancestor's relation to orificial irregularity as being *double*, since his one most noteworthy function in life lay in serving as one of Henri III's celebrated minions. Through the discourse of heredity and neuropathology, one is returned to the bottom end of the alimentary canal.

It is scarcely a matter of returning to the repressed, however, because it is precisely in terms of gastric dysfunction which the progress of des Esseintes's neurosis is measured. He begins his "refined Thebaid" with modest, mild menus suited to a stomach which, in the past, had already proven itself rebellious. Des Esseintes, like any human being, must bodily take in nourishment from the exterior. This limited dependence on nature and the outside world finds its parallel at the plot level, since the erudite recluse is still able to derive spiritual nourishment from books.

As des Esseintes's health deteriorates, the reader is treated to a succession of essays on the virtues of artifice, Latin authors of the Decadent period, the significance of gemstones through history, and the art of Moreau and Redon, to name a few. The delirious description of the "erudite hysterias" captured in the Salome painting marks a crucial point in the evolution of des Esseintes's illness, for following it, the protagonist ceases to draw on the outside world for sustenance: "He lived off himself, took nourishment from his own substance, like a sluggish animal nestled in his hole for the winter . . . " (122). The hibernal period of feeding off one's reserves cannot go on indefinitely; sooner or later des Esseintes, whose intellectual and gastrointestinal systems are no longer digesting material, is bound to become an empty shell, incapable either of ingesting at one end or producing at the other. But the greatest danger resides in the fact that the vacating of this internal space renders it vulnerable to assault, all the more so because access to the mind/stomach can always be gained through an aperture.

In fact, that is precisely what does happen at this point in the narrative. The hollowed-out des Esseintes relinquishes all control over his environment and becomes a passive receiver, submitting to the vagaries of uncontrollable exterior forces: solitude "guided a stream of dreams to which he submitted passively without even trying to escape them" (122). "Morbid" symptoms appear (127) as des Esseintes is assailed by thoughts of "le Démon" and by "the madness of magic, black masses, sabbaths, possessions and exorcism . . . " (128). And it is as if these thoughts of the demonic, relishing that vacuum which nature is said to abhor, have penetrated through some crack into des Esseintes's stomach regions. In spite of the sick man's attempt to evict the alien pressures through "vain and urgent efforts," his belly bloats ("il gonflait"), and no manner of effort can exorcize the "gaseous heartburn" from the vulnerable region (131).

When des Esseintes realizes that his stomach is temporarily dysfunctional, he turns to the outside world to divert his attention. He purchases ornamental plants which, assembled together "as in a hospital," form a forest of gaping, syphilitic apertures. Although the collection is primarily genital in character (as has often been noted), at least two of these floral monstrosities represent the alimentary openings. In fact, the cypripedium orchids even combine madness and digestion. As if "imagined by a demented inventor," they resemble human tongues "as one sees these rendered in the illustrations of works treating disorders of the throat and mouth . . . " (135). The nidularium fungi, on the other hand, display "raw and gaping fundaments" (135). The promenade through the forest of scar tissue masquerading as plants gives way to the famous nightmare, a sort of allegory of the ravages of Syphilis, in which Huysmans's misogyny is very much in evidence.

It is one of those remarkable conjunctures of science and literature that, writing in Paris one year before Freud was to embark upon his decisive course of study under Charcot in that very city, Huysmans should give us a masterpiece which focuses nearly its entire attention on the divagations of the unconscious mind. In fact, certain of these oneiric meanderings so clearly constitute a system, having deep structures, a syntax, and so on, that they virtually beckon for interpretation. Nor has that beck gone unheeded by critics, particularly in the case of the nightmare. Charles Bernheimer, for instance, sees in these dream sequences appearing throughout Huysmans's works a textual site which privileges the articulation of psychoconstructs: "These dream narratives open up onto a fantasy space and allow Huysmans complete freedom . . . to recreate his personal obsessions" (105). I would like to examine two other such episodes, less explicitly unconscious since they both take place in des Esseintes's waking life, which demonstrate the extent to which the gastrointestinal discourse presides over the narrative structure and the unconscious psychological content of *A rebours.*

When des Esseintes's illness progresses to the point where he begins to hallucinate smells and wonders if he might not be "under the influence of one of those possessions that they exorcized in the Middle Ages" (161), he determines to take a trip to London. Every reader of the novel knows that the voyage remains an imaginary one, since the would-be traveller contents himself, Baedecker in hand, with an excursion into a pub and, later, an English eating establishment. Another victory of mind over matter is proclaimed. Or so it would seem. Yet nothing is more physical than des Esseintes's visit to the Bodega which takes on all the allegorical flavor of a descent into the human belly. The pub into which des Esseintes slips is described as a "belly decorated in crenellated wood" (168).

Making his way further into this medieval abdomen, our hero pursues his architectural observations, noting that in "the lower abdomen" of the building there is a "hole connected to a pipe" (168). Will des Esseintes be flushed out of this clearly rectal nether exit, just as the souls of the plebeian children were imagined to do in *Là-bas?* No, instead, des Esseintes watches the operations of this bowel with a fascination that suggests he is observing the functioning of his own poor stopped-up organism, which at this point, it will be recalled, will receive almost no foreign matter. The "explosive sodas" (169) which the bartender is opening are redolent of that "gaseous heartburn" which agitates his own digesting machine.

At length, the general ambiance combined with the sight of a "cigar planted in the hairy hole of [the] mouth" of one client, has a relaxing effect on des Esseintes, who surrenders himself to "a certain softening" (170). Evidently the quest in this journey to the center of the organism has been therapeutic in nature. With the gastric juices stirred into movement, des Esseintes is subsequently able to consume a hearty meal for the first time in months.

One of the most intriguing aspects of *A rebours* is not only that it stages a series of forays into the beyond, but also that these take place at different levels of unconsciousness. The more lucid episodes, such as the descent into the abdominal cavity, can be read as allegories. It is, in fact, probably no accident that the decor of this journey is medieval, and it is by reading this episode in terms of genre that one is led to conclude that what is at issue is a quest, albeit one whose goal ("a certain softening") can hardly be called lofty. Interpretation takes place at a fairly rational level through substitution of whole blocks of the narrative. The syntax of the tale thus remains intact. By comparison, the syphilis nightmare operates according to a more complex logic in which the smooth seams of allegory are occasionally torn through by occurrences of signifiers felt to be out of place. Reading through a generic screen will not satisfactorily decode this episode.

Let me turn to another of those texts which seems to articulate unconscious desires, this time at the level of the daydream. I am referring to
des Esseintes's memory of his visit to the dentist. Proustian *avant la lettre*, the act of recollecting is triggered by the "music" which des Esseintes
composes on his mouth organ through various blends of arcane liqueurs.
From the palate to the tooth, the associational device linking the two
experiences is thus the mouth. But here it is worth interjecting that with
Huysmans, there is more to the mouth than meets the eye. For at its
simplest, the mouth merely represents a point of access into the alimentary canal and is, as such, interchangeable with the anus. (In fact, des
Esseintes's ultimate triumph over nature at the end of the novel results
from precisely this reversal, as will be seen.) Actually, the anal/buccal
permutation was already suggested in the pub adventure when des Esseintes, at his ease in the nether extreme of abdomen-pub, had noted the
man with an (excremental) cigar "planted in the hairy hole of [the]
mouth."

That one orifice can stand for another is nowhere more clear than
during the hero's visit to the terrible Doctor Gatonax.[4] The dentist's
extraction of the troublesome tooth takes on the aura of a forcible and
painful penetration. When, at first, "having stuck an enormous index
finger into his mouth" (102), only half the tooth is recovered, the practitioner renews his assault: "The man . . . again flung himself upon
him [des Esseintes] as if he wanted to plunge his arm to the far end of the
abdomen . . . " (102). And the result of the penetration through this
equivocal mouth into the "abdomen" most often associated with the
bowel is that des Esseintes feels bestialized: he "began . . . to kick and
squeal like an animal being killed" (102). Just as a sense of relief came to
des Esseintes in his therapeutic journey into his own internalia, here the
grisly experience leaves him, a trifle oddly, "happy, feeling ten years
younger" (103).

Des Esseintes's terrifying encounter with the dentist and the operation
which the latter performs is further linked to the discourse of neuropathology. Somehow the penetration of an orifice entails the advent of
madness. The suffering protagonist exhibits behavior "similar to a
madman's." On the threshold of the office "a horrible fear overcame
him" (102), and during the scene, his reason deserts him.

If forcing an opening of the "mouth" is related to the puncture of the
rational mind, the last-recourse visit to the dentist also takes on the al-
lure of a degrading visit to a low-class brothel: "He decided to go to the
first one he came upon, to a vulgar tooth-puller." These sorts "know

how to extract, with unmatched speed, the most tenacious stumps; they are open early in the morning and one is not kept waiting" (101).[5] By this time one suspects that a discourse which allies a vocabulary of mental alienation to a passive sexuality operated upon by a male dentist will probably also insist on those orifices which point both to digestion and the demonic. In fact, the text is quite explicit to the effect that vulgar practitioners of this ilk "know how to extirpate" and not how to "fill cavities and seal up holes" (101). Their function is thus to exorcize, to vacate, and not to heal. It will be seen that terms relating to healing through blocking the apertures (the word "panser" occurs with persistence in Huysmans's prose) constitute references to divine operations. Leaks in the bottom are more the Devil's handiwork.

Now it is very much to our point that the various excursions into the realm of the unconscious are initiated in a similar manner, namely when des Esseintes has somehow come into contact with that exterior he so dreads. The terrifying remembrance of the visit to the dentist, for instance, is preceded by des Esseintes's opening the window: "This abrupt passage with no transition from torrid heat to a wintry chill had taken its toll on him . . . " (99). The syphilis nightmare was similarly inspired: "The *passage* from the outside air to the warmth of his dwelling, from his static, reclusive life to the mobility of a liberated existence had been too abrupt . . . soon he fell prey to the somber *madness* of a nightmare" (138; emphasis added). His ventures into the English bookstore and the Bodega are marked by identical assaults perpetrated by an inclement Mother Nature. In all these cases, ravings, deliria, and pure dementia are felt to be the results of invasions wrought by an exterior which has managed to force itself into the hero's mind through a "passage."

As des Esseintes's health begins to decline more and more rapidly, his throat becomes obstructed (195). At length, he is reduced to digesting food outside his body with a "sustenteur" and then ingesting it: "He drank a spoonful of muddy, salty juice deposited at the bottom of a pot. Then he felt a warm presence descend like a velvety caress" (204). The coprophagic tenor of this ingestion finds its "unnatural" echo in the final phase of his illness which des Esseintes sees as his ultimate triumph over nature: his feeding through enemas. Nature has at last been turned upside down, one orifice replacing another: "[D]es Esseintes could not help secretly congratulating himself on the event which was the crowning triumph . . . of the life he had contrived for himself . . . nourishment thus absorbed was surely the last aberration of the natural that could be committed" (230–31). Exultant and carrying the inversion of nature to its extreme, des Esseintes regales this "strange palate" (231) with liquified three-course "meals."

Earlier it was suggested that the dramas of Huysmans's plots are played out in the apertures. It is this final joke on Mother Nature in *A rebours* which signals that the narrative—and des Esseintes's life—have reached, quite literally, an impasse, for with the orificial inversion, no future writing can be produced, no material excreted. Surely it can be no coincidence that the moment of organic shutdown is also that of des Esseintes's celebrated prayer (addressee unknown) imploring that an unbeliever be shown the faith. Nor is it coincidental that the formulation of this plea should betray an anguish at the thought that faith, even if arrived at, can always leak out: des Esseintes "would have liked to have forced himself to possess faith . . . to have been able to secure it to his soul with clamps . . . "(237). *A rebours* comes to rest unresolved, and its final dilemma can be formulated (as one might by now have suspected) in alimentary terms: therapy of an exorcistic nature can indeed be effected in the lower gastrointestinal zones (the mouth having been sealed off); however, it is within the logic of this gastrotheology that faith can make its exit through the same passages.

Durtal, the hero of *Là-bas*, takes over where des Esseintes left off. Early in this novel, which explores the relationship of satanism to insanity, Durtal also expresses a desire to believe. Unfortunately, muses he, what is wanting is "a naked soul and his was obstructed with filth, soaking in the concentrated juices of old guano" (41). This view of the soul as cesspool, a repository of fecal matter, besides being related to neurosis as we saw in *A rebours,* is intimately linked to the notion of erotic visitation of incubi and succubi, a topic which the novel explores in considerable detail. For not only is this brand of diabolic possession frankly sexual, but it includes one element which distinguishes it from the "natural." Gévingey, the astrologer and one of the work's several occultists, informs Durtal: "You must know that the member of the incubus splits and penetrates both the openings at the same time" (149).

Thus it is that the Devil gains a rear access to the soul, and it is not hard to imagine that Durtal's soul is a cesspool for the good reason that it harbors the "Demon." What is troubling in this theology *par derrière* is that the divine soul, that is, the state of grace, can also be evacuated from below as was noted earlier. This suggests an uneasy equivalence of God and Devil, of good and evil, which, in fact, is entirely consistent with Huysmans's own beliefs. Inasmuch as both partake of the supernatural, both may penetrate by the same entrances. (In this connection one thinks immediately of Freud's analysis of Chief Justice Schreber who, in one phase of his illness, assumed a passive sexual position vis-à-vis divine penetration.)

Huysmans's remark to the effect that nothing much occurred in matters of religious conversion between *A rebours* (1884) and *Là-bas* (1891) is not entirely accurate. True, the preoccupations of the two novels remain similar, but in the interim separating them an important inversion has nonetheless been operated. The discourse of neuropathology, dominant in *A rebours*, has become explicitly subservient to the theme of thaumaturgy in *Là-bas*. This coup de théâtre is crucial because no longer will mental illness be accorded the status of prime cause, but rather it will be invoked as a *manifestation* of the occult, indeed much as it was in the Middle Ages. The genre to which *Là-bas* adheres is still that of the case history since one of the two principal narratives is a clinical discussion of the pathological Gilles de Rais complete with documentary evidence. Now, however, it has become a matter of diagnosing the ills of the spirit. In this way, in the seven-year gap which separates these novels, the two-headed monster of materialism and positivism has been vanquished. Henceforth in Huysmans's work, the spiritual will reign.

Of course the irony of this shift lies in the fact that neuropathology now assumes an adversarial posture. And the proponent of this scientific mode of explanation in *Là-bas* is none other than Doctor Charcot in person. Now, what Huysmans finds repugnant in the discipline which was then emergent at the Salpêtrière Hospital is Charcot's reduction of demonic presence to mere symptoms of hysteria. In *Là-bas*, des Hermies, the doctor who has lost his medical faith through contact with the "Inexplicable," declares that the notion of hysteria is secondary and in itself explains nothing: "Yes, without doubt Charcot is good at pinpointing the phases of the attack . . . he finds the hysterogenic zones and, by adroitly manipulating the ovaries, can slow down or speed up the crises, but . . . as for knowing their sources and causes, as for curing them— that's another matter!" (153).

There is some truth to this Pascalian sulk. Like Bouchut before him, Charcot does establish a nosology of hysteria, but he fails to explain it except in terms of heredity. It will, in fact, take Freud to remove the neuroses from the materialist arena through postulation of an unconscious.[6] Meanwhile, as Gaillard observes apropos of *A rebours:* "Just as a photograph at the moment of development, it [the fiction] will reveal, in the very processes through which it takes form, that which it does not suspect itself of knowing: *medicine's blind spots"* (93). If Huysmans has unwittingly uncovered and displayed the holes in the neuropathologi-cal edifice (and Charcot's caustic remarks against des Esseintes-like crea-tures [37, 201] seem to bear out Gaillard's argument), then perhaps this text worked similar unconscious magic on its own author, by turning him away—perverting him—from his old patterns of predilection.

A satisfactory cause of hysteria thus lacking, at least for the time being, Huysmans is free to turn the tables on science as he had earlier done on nature in *A rebours,* in a movement from perversion toward conversion. Madness becomes a mere symptom of diabolic presence which is now promoted to the status of prime mover. Victims of possession, advances des Hermies of *Là-bas,* "end up mad. The insane asylums are overflowing with them. The doctors, even most of the priests do not understand the causes of their dementia . . . " (148). If all of science remains powerless to determine the true cause of the disorder, as does most of the religious community, Huysmans has left himself one critical loophole: mysti-cism. The Church may be the "hospital of souls" (*En route* 1: 43), but Durtal diagnoses his own ill as (inevitably) "dyspepsia of the soul" (1: 68), and his case of digestion/conversion requires more esoteric atten-tions which can only be dispensed at a Trappist monastery.

After sniffing about the robes of the Church for two novels already, it is hardly surprising that the Huysmansian protagonist balks consider-ably at such a dire solution. Urging—indeed almost forcing—Durtal to come to this decision is the good priest Gévresin, who exhibits monastic tendencies himself. What is remarkable is that the act of persuasion which takes place against Durtal's will resembles des Esseintes's encoun-ter with the dentist to an uncanny degree. Gévresin, "hitherto so discreet, suddenly flung himself on Durtal's being and *opened it violently.* . . . And Durtal . . . agreed that the priest was right and that he had to *stop up* the pus of his senses and expiate for . . . their abominable desires; their *decayed* tastes [goûts cariés]; and he was overcome by an intense, irrational fear (1: 227; emphasis added).

Reading across these two texts which define each pole of the author's conversion, one does indeed find the continuity which he proclaimed in the 1903 preface to *A rebours.* The forcible sodomy performed by the dentist on des Esseintes ("the man . . . flung himself upon him [des Esseintes] as if he wanted to plunge his arm to the far end of the abdo-men") is repeated here in the same terms. The rape perpetrated by Gévresin may well be a spiritual one, but it is wise to bear in mind what I have been at pains to demonstrate: namely, that at all times the Huysmansian discourse equates dyspepsia, mental pathology, and disorders of the soul. In Huysmans's case, it is abundantly clear that the body's stigmata are irremedially branded onto the representation of the soul, or, perhaps more accurately, the text of the flesh is inscribed forever in the language of the soul.

The two quotations above indicate that both des Esseintes and Durtal have been forcibly penetrated for therapeutic purposes. At this point, however, important differences between the twin operations emerge. The dentist, it will be recalled, was but a vulgar practitioner. Thus his function—limited to ridding the organism of an undesirable presence— could be termed exorcistic in nature. He lacked the ability to "fill the cavities and seal up the holes," and, anyhow, at that stage on life's way, the Huysmansian hero has no intention of rendering his stomach/ mind/soul hermetic because it is precisely the access to an elsewhere which he holds dear and on which his art depends. In contrast, the Durtal of *En route* has acquiesced to the idea ("convenait") that the cavities must be filled if conversion is to take place. It has become apparent that sealing the apertures is the only guarantee against the Devil.

Unfortunately the horns of the Devil are also the horns of a dilemma. It has been seen that good and evil penetrate the body in identical ways, often rectally. (The privileging of one alimentary aperture seems to carry with it a closing off of the other: in *A rebours*, des Esseintes rarely speaks, and at last, his mouth becomes useless for feeding purposes, while the miracles of *En route* can only be accomplished under a Trappist rule of silence.) How is one to know which supernatural power has penetrated, which words "emanate from God and not from our imagination or even from the Devil" (1: 173)? The evil Demon, brushed aside by Descartes in a similar formulation of the problem, is not so easily dispatched by Huysmans, who realizes full well that "from lofty Mysticism to frustrated Satanism, there is but one step. In the beyond, everything touches" (*Là-bas* 73). Furthermore, divine invasion as Durtal experiences it is not unequivocably pleasurable: "It must be admitted that it is most disturbing to feel that infusion of an invisible being into one's being, and to know that it could nearly evict you, if it so chose, from the domain of your own person" (*En route* 1: 253).

The dilemma alluded to earlier is the following: openings permit supernatural penetration, although one can never be sure of the identity of the occupying force, but closing the holes could entail sealing in Satan and thus the soul's perpetual annexation by the Devil. Besides making the state of grace uncomfortably analogous to a state of constipation,

: ●

Huysmans's peculiar representation of religion in gastrointestinal terms has led him to a theological impasse.

Indeed, in the course of these three key works, J.-K. Huysmans has ensnared himself in a web of his own spinning. The contrapuntal play of discourses in *A rebours* (neurological, digestive, and demonic) is reinforced and embroidered upon in *Là-bas*. With devilish force and by dint of accumulated metaphor, the text turns against its maker in *En route,* which spends many an anguished page wrestling with the Demon. The final solution—something of a *truquage*—lies outside, in the doctrine of mystical substitution.

Ironically enough, for Huysmans, the author of interiors if ever there was one, no help can be sought from within. Mystical substitution allows the expulsion of diabolic influence from weaker souls by projecting it onto consenting "victims" who compose certain contemplative orders such as the Poor Clares. The Poor Clare, weak of body but staid of soul, thus serves as a decoy, substituting herself for the intended victim of the attack. As Gévresin explains in *En route,* "They draw the demonic fluid upon themselves" (1: 78), and Durtal benefits from their intercession during his own arduous conversion.

The Huysmansian gastrointestinal representation of soul may strike one as idiosyncratic, if not downright obscene. Yet it is important to realize that this highly personal *vision du monde* poses the larger problem of man's linguistic relation to the divine. In what language, code, or system of signs, through which incantations, prayers, or ritual acts can the sacred by grasped from out of the profane? Yea—how can the discourse of mysticism *not* be forged out of the flesh forever to bear its imprint? From Huysmans's case we stand to learn that all language, however exalted, is grounded in the body.

Notes

1. All translations from the French are my own.

2. Huysmans exhibits a decided penchant for ending with the end. "Sac au dos," his *Les Soirées de Médan* contribution, finishes with its main character sighing in the watery bliss of his very own *cabinet.*

3. In fact, the symptoms afflicting the faded and jaded des Esseintes who has declared war on nature, "cette vieille radoteuse," are those of the classic neurasthenic: passivity, loss of sexual desire, inability to do intellectual work, and dyspepsia (Charcot 128, 203).

4. It is worth noting that the names of the few characters invoked in *A rebours* are also signifiers of the gastrointestinal thematic. "Miss Urania" certainly suggests the nether openings which, it has become increasingly clear, are privileged to the exclusion of the

mouth. Although the ventriloquist is never mentioned by name, the name of her function is important. The synonym for "ventriloquism" (speaking belly) is "gastromancy," the practice through which divine or satanic presence becomes articulated through some mortal's stomach. Converging in this term are the gastrointestinal and demonic themes. As for the dentist, the leap from "Gatonax" to "Gastronax" is not a very great one.

5. This visit to a low-class dentist is not without similarities to Durtal's former visits to a brothel in *Là-bas:* "When the stable doors of his senses opened," he would take "the disgusting herd of his sin to slaughterhouses where the butchers of love would finish it off in one blow . . . " (108).

6. It was perhaps inevitable that Freud should have been interested in the phenomenon of possession. His 1923 investigation titled *A Seventeenth-Century Demonological Neurosis* intersects in some ways with Huysmans's case inasmuch as it treats, among other things, the prevalence of gold and fecal matter in connection with the Devil.

Works Cited

Baldick, Robert. *The Life of J.-K. Huysmans.* Oxford: Clarendon, 1955.

Bernheimer, Charles. "L'Exorbitant textuel: castration et sublimation chez Huysmans." *Romantisme* 45 (1984): 105–13.

Brombert, Victor. "Huysmans: The Prison House of Decadence." *The Romantic Prison: The French Tradition.* Princeton: Princeton UP, 1978. 149–70.

Charcot, Jean-Martin. *Leçons sur l'hystérie virile.* Paris: S.F.I.E.D., 1984.

Freud, Sigmund. *A Seventeenth-Century Demonological Neurosis.* 1923. Vol. 19 of *The Standard Edition of the Complete Psychological Works of Sigmund Freud.* Ed. and trans. James Strachey. 24 vols. London: Hogarth, 1953–74.

Gaillard, Françoise. "Le Discours médical pris au piège du récit." *Etudes françaises* 19 (1983): 81–95.

Huysmans, Joris-Karl. *A rebours.* Paris: Garnier-Flammarion, 1978.

———. *En route.* N.d. Vol. 13 of *Oeuvres complètes de J.-K. Huysmans.* Ed. Charles Grolleau. 18 vols. 1928–34. (Volume 13 is actually two volumes. All references herein are to the first volume.)

———. *Là-bas.* Paris: Garnier-Flammarion, 1978.

———. *Lettres inédites à Emile Zola.* Geneva: Droz, 1953.

Zola, Emile. *Les Soirées de Médan.* Paris: Charpentier, 1926.

"We have been a little insane about the truth": Poetics and Psychotic Experience

Nancy Blake

"A poem," writes Laura Riding in her preface to *The Poems of Laura Riding,* "is an uncovering of truth of so fundamental and general a kind that no other word besides poetry is adequate except truth. Knowledge implies specialized fields of exploration and discovery; it would be inexact to call poetry a kind of knowledge" (xviii). This opposition between poetry and rationality is also expressed by Wallace Stevens when he says: "The poem must resist the intelligence / Almost successfully" (*Collected Poems* 350).

The focus of this paper will be the problematical relationship between truth, in its various guises, and anxiety as expressed in certain poetic contexts. Defining anxiety, however, is no easy matter; what we call anxiety is precisely a fear of the unnamable. Questioning the effect of the poetic as it intersects with anxiety necessitates an examination of the relationship between naming and poetry, and of the role of negativity, of saying without putting into "so many words." For the analyst, this fear without a name is, of course, a screen for the fear of death. The study of anxiety in poetry would eventually lead us to several hypotheses concerning the psychological structure of melancholia, but that would also be another paper.

In this essay, I want first to look at Wallace Steven's "Thirteen Ways of Looking at a Blackbird." Is this poem a lesson—as so often in modernism—which leads the reader to abandon his passive position, forcing him to give form to the text, transforming words into fiction?

Does Stevens expect me to invent the string that will make of these thirteen pearls a necklace? Or, is the poem a paradigm of the discontinuous where no unifying thread is to be sought?

The poem as a whole will not be explicated here. In particular, the underlying suggestion that the obscure object hidden behind the fixation on the blackbird is death itself will remain, for the moment, implicit. Stevens says everything that he has to say. That is, he says nothing, but demonstrates the relationship which is always the basis of his poetics, the relationship between the observer and the observed.

> Among twenty snowy mountains,
> The only moving thing
> Was the eye of the blackbird. (92)

In this first stanza, the blackbird is at the same time seen and seer. As the thing seen, the blackbird provides perspective, focus, proportion. The blackbird defines the value of the vision. As seeing/seer, on the other hand, the blackbird acts upon the vision of the observer. No one is the master of the visual, for seeing is not a stasis. The moving eye of the blackbird introduces change, uncertainty, even chance, that which is unseeable.

Wallace Stevens (1879–1955) always referred to himself as a romantic poet. It is possible, moreover, that the biography of a poet is always a literary biography, that it is never life, but only literature which creates literature. Chomsky has observed that knowing how to speak a language implies knowing many things without having lived or learned them. No poet speaks a new language. As far as Stevens's language is concerned, the major echoes are those of Wordsworth, Shelley, Keats, Emerson, and Walt Whitman. It would be possible to study any number of Stevens's poems as examples of a romantic *krisis*—that is, of the crisis or default of poetic vision. The romantic poem often expresses a doubt which arises as to the validity of the poet as visionary, for to be a visionary is to be capable of a response to the world. It is, on the contrary, the disappearance of an interior vision which forms the subject of Stevens's "The Snow Man," as of Coleridge's "Dejection: an Ode." "Thirteen Ways of Looking at a Blackbird," as a study of disjunction, also seems typical of the romantic crisis in another way: *krisis* which gives us "crisis" as well as "critical" comes from the root *krinein*, to separate, to decide, to choose. Much of the difficulty of Stevens's poetry is an effect of this effort to "analyze" perception. For Stevens, analysis retains its etymological force as the process of breaking down an illusory unity in order to examine components.

First of all, then, I would like to examine a typically romantic attitude toward poetic praxis. The romantic would define the poetic as opposed to the intellectual; that is to say, from the point of view of the poetic, reason appears as a defense mechanism. One of the first aspects of this refusal of the logical apparatus, which will from now on be compromised, is a confusion of the former opposition between the subject and the object in the enunciative act.

In order to begin this discussion on an analytical, as opposed to a philosophical basis, let us consider an example of this confusion drawn from clinical data rather than from literature. One day, as I was leaving the meeting room at the psychiatric hospital where group therapy meetings are held, I met a patient who had not attended the session. As usual in such cases, I greeted him and reminded him of the time of our next meeting the following week. All smiles, he assured me, "I will come, if I am memorable." In this phrase is expressed the essence of psychoanalytic transference. Transference, in the analytic sense, is the instability of the place from which one speaks. In the phrase of this psychotic patient, what value can be assigned to the personal pronoun? My patient said, in effect, "I will come if I remember you and you remember me." In the analytic situation, the position occupied by the subject, as opposed to the object, is, in the words of a contemporary biological attempt to describe the structure of the living, "far from equilibrium." Life is lack of balance, uncertainty, contradiction; only death is stable.

That a schizophrenic patient expresses his belief that he is spoken by another is, of course, typical of his symptom. That the poet speaks of himself as carried away by the force of his own creation is also probably not unexpected. Yet, if the poetry of Wallace Stevens has something to teach us, that something is contained in what Stevens called "a dissociated abundance of being, / More definite for what she is— / Because she is disembodied." This quality belongs to the imaginary woman of a poem, and in this quality resides the only possibility of encounter, in Stevens's words: "the taciturn and yet indifferent, / Invisibly clear, the only love" (*Collected Poems* 445).

Who is seeing what? "Thirteen Ways of Looking at a Blackbird" evacuates the self, as we saw a moment ago in the confusion between seer and the object seen. In "Inhibitions, Symptoms and Anxiety" (1926), Freud affirms that the ego is the seat of anxiety. He goes on to repeat his differentiation between the ego as unifying function as opposed to the fragmentary nature of the id. "Thirteen Ways of Looking at a Blackbird," in the first volume published by Stevens, presents a version of what I call the poetics of depersonalization. We can now consider another well-known Stevens poem, "The Snow Man," in order to take a look at another side of this phenomenon.

The depersonalization of "The Snow Man" can be seen, at least as far as this study is concerned, as a glimpse of what Lacan has called the "truth of the true" (*le vrai du vrai*). For the self is fiction.

> For the listener, who listens in the snow,
> And, nothing himself, beholds
> Nothing that is not there and the nothing that is. (10)

Elsewhere Stevens speaks of the "white of ultimate intellect," while the title of this poem itself contains a possible play on words: *It' sNo Man.* The negative vision of the poem looks at the other side of human subjectivity: the "nothing" of the poem excludes the eye which always sees itself in what it is looking at. Anthropocentrism is human, of course, and to see the winter landscape as a metaphor for human distress would permit a narcissistic recognition satisfactory for the understanding of both the experience and the poem. However, this narcissistic palliative is impossible as "The Snow Man" recognizes that this pastime is part of the human imaginary structure. The truth of poetry, the truth that Stevens gets a glimpse of in this text, lies not in language, but in the individual's separation from the world. As William Faulkner put it, the word is "just a shape to fill a lack" (136).

It is this experience of depersonalization that the moderns tell us about (I am thinking of certain poems by Stevens here, but Marianne Moore and William Carlos Williams could also provide examples). Depersonalization, in the psychiatric sense, appears first of all through a series of subtle changes which primarily affect spatial awareness and the sonar landscape that helps to condition spatial perception. Take, for example, the cry of a bird, which belongs both to the realm of objective reality and to inner perception. A beginning of anxiety is experienced when the phenomenon, which is understood as both exterior and interior, resists interpretation. Depersonalization becomes evident in cases of momentary psychotic states when a modification of perception is experienced in which a message seems to be transmitted. The message has a content which remains obscure, a content which the subject hardly dares to take seriously because of its extreme banality. The psychotic experience of Freud's Chief Justice Schreber and of other less famous patients has often led them to conclude that the voices they heard were stupid. How, for example, can one tell of the emotion, which seems at the same time entirely natural and yet strange, which one feels at nightfall hearing the cry of a solitary blackbird perched on a rooftop? For one brief moment, the bird's cry seems to convey an extraordinary meaning, something forgotten but on the point of returning to consciousness. But, very quickly, everything returns to normal, becomes self-evident and thus empty of any hidden meaning. The experience just described, in its banality, is typical of the unnamable. Because this type of experience cannot be put into words, because it is outside of intersubjectivity, it opens the door to unconscious anxiety. This is the experience which Henry James fictionalizes in *The Turn of the Screw* in which the governess-narrator, unable to assign meaning to the rooks cawing as they circle the castle tower at dusk, is obliged to "see" the possibility of interpretation in a hallucinatory vision of the ghost of Peter Quint.

Turning now to question the problematical relationship between truth and poetry, one may remember Stevens's "The Poems of Our Climate." The "poems," in the plural, speak of multiplicity. But who is speaking? A good number of poems, like this one, are written in the first person plural, *we*. We converse, but also speak between, through, speech is mixture, impurity. Dialectics is consciousness in its fundamental unhappiness, in its impossible distance from its object and itself. Yet Hegel believed that man's fate was to create his happiness out of this unhappy consciousness through the joy of the exercise itself. It is this faculty which permits the mind to perceive its own movement, the movements of objects, and the reflections of these movements.

From these various movements, Stevens derives the images which haunt his work: snow and the ideal of whiteness. These images clearly owe something to the continental influence of Mallarmé, yet, for the New England poet, the "mind of winter" ("The Snow Man") was indelibly a factor of his native land. White is the nonhuman, whereas the human is only at home in the "composed," the composite, the impure: "the imperfect is our paradise." That this is a "bitterness" does not prevent imperfection from constituting a source of delight. Our delight "lies," that is, resides, but it also tells an *untruth* ("The Poems of Our Climate," *Collected Poems* 193). The unitary nature of truth makes it unsuitable for human consumption.

There is something in the solitary position of the speaker of "The Poems of Our Climate" that is typically romantic. Stevens, however, is a "late-comer" (Heidegger 17). Unlike Wordsworth and Shelley for whom the suffering of solitude was proof of nobility, Stevens, as modern, can never suggest nobility without irony. The sublime, then, for Stevens, is double: there is a false sublime which is personal, affective, and which belongs to the realm of mortal beauty. Especially in the poetry of the end of his life, however, Stevens pursues the sublime in imperfection, in the tragic: this is the elegiac dimension which includes "a new knowledge of reality" (*Collected Poems* 534).

One example of fortunate imperfection would be color. All color is mixture, betweenness, degree rather than absolute. Stevens is a painter with words. His father, in an early letter, referred to his "power to paint pictures in words" (*Letters* 14). Color, is however, the negation of oneness: "It was something to see that their white was different" (*Collected Poems* 312). Unlike his great rival, T. S. Eliot, who needs few colors and uses them in reference to an allegorical system, Stevens has no basis upon which to found a system; he lacks a dogma in which color could occupy a place. The world of sense perception is at the origin of his thought, and perception is ambiguous. Color then has a double focus. It is both the effect of light coming from the outside and an imaginary discovery, an element in an interior vision. Light as an absolute would mean the absence of color and this absence—white—would be, for Stevens, a metaphor for death, whether physical or imaginary, while for Eliot it could point to the desire for transcendence.

If the paradise of perfection is impossible, the world must be created. Originally the word *cosmos* meant "order." Originally poetry and myth were one, and their function was to found this necessary order. Perhaps this is the point of departure for the title of Stevens's second volume of verses, *Ideas of Order*. Note again that the idea is plural. The title is taken up by one of Stevens best-known poems which proclaims, "She sang beyond the genius of the sea."

> It was her voice that made
> The sky acutest at its vanishing.
> She measured to the hour its solitude.
> She was the single artificer of the world
> In which she sang. And when she sang, the sea,
> Whatever self it had, became the self
> That was her song, for she was the maker. Then we,
> As we beheld her striding there alone,
> Knew that there never was a world for her
> Except the one she sang and, singing, made.
> "The Idea of Order at Key West" (*Collected Poems* 129–30)

Who sings the world into being in "The Idea of Order at Key West"? In Genesis, Adam names creation; Stevens, like all the American romantics, was interested in the possibility of a new world. Yet, here there is more at stake than the simple substitution of a feminine persona for the father of mankind. Woman, in our civilization, is a basis for exchange, and the poem proposes a type of creation that is not unilateral. Artistic creation is reciprocity. If the singer creates, so, too, she is created by her world.

The problem of what we can know about the creative force often comes up in Stevens's correspondence. Toward the end of "The Man with the Blue Guitar," is found the phrase, "You are yourself." To this the poet comments, "Being oneself being so not as one really is but as one of the jocular procreations of the dark, of space. The point of the poem is, not that this can be done, but that, if done, it is the key to poetry . . . " (*Letters* 364).

I have used the term depersonalization to designate an anxiety typical of the romantic position and which evokes a lack of being (Lacan's *manque à être*). Being is used to name that which coincides with itself. Yet the poem is experienced as a double, a copy of reality. Freud could discover in the possibility of sublimation the superiority of man as speaking animal. The modernist poet, on the other hand, can accept no substitutes. The poem, as Stevens tells us time and again, provokes a war with reality and does so on the only ground available, that of reality. That is why art must always fail.

Still, if creation does take place, it is only at the moment of the song that the world is put into order. The reciprocity of the creative act is inscribed in a sovereign temporality. At the moment I pronounce the words "I speak," I cannot be accused of compromise. The speaker is identical with the spoken: " . . . there never was a world for her / Except the one she sang and singing made." Who is speaking? This question comes back several times in the course of the poem. It is voiced by the narrative "we."

> Whose spirit is this? we said, because we knew
> It was the spirit that we sought and knew
> That we should ask this often as she sang.

The poet is the mouthpiece: she sings "a tune beyond us, yet ourselves" (*Collected Poems* 165). The fact that artistic activity is valued, that it resembles omnipotence, must not blind us to its counterphobic function. Poetry is really a matter of losing perspective. For a short time, at least, the subject is intimately identified with the Other, so that the experience of self is altered and even seems at times to give way to an alien self.

In "Landscape with Boat," for example, Stevens practices a poetics of the moment, a language in which each phrase is both starting point and conclusion. Instead of a composition with a reassuring solidity, where each element has its place and its function as support for the whole, Stevens writes a poem in which each image can only repeat the coming into being of the moment and its ellipsis.

As the poet questions the value of logical categories, such as the differentiation between subject and object, he inaugurates an attitude of laisser faire. For the romantics, this attitude conjured up the image of the aeolian harp and of the poetic voice as a passivity. For the poet of modernism, the attitude is one of acceptance of a copresence in which his poetic voice no longer belongs to a Self:

> He never supposed
> That he might be truth, himself, or part of it,
> .   .   .   .
> He never supposed divine
> Things might not look divine, nor that if nothing
> Was divine then all things were, the world itself,
> And that if nothing was the truth, then all
> Things were the truth, the world itself was the truth.
> (*Collected Poems* 242)

If we listen carefully to the examples of poetic truth given here, we can draw several conclusions. Poetic creation abolishes the poles of causality, ruins the categories of subject and object, active and passive: the singer exists in her song; the artist exists in the work of art, and the work has its origin in the artist. Everyday temporality is therefore reversed in the reciprocity of the relationship. In order to put this discovery into words, Stevens reaches for the boundaries of his language: the place "Where was it one first heard of the truth? The the" (*Collected Poems* 203).

The stuttering conclusion to this poem may suggest a limit to language. Originally, poetry and myth were one. There is a cliché in the literary tradition which consists in pretending that language can master time, that literature can situate itself outside of the world in order to talk about the world. The work of art is seen as prophecy or history, and literature travels across time, backwards and forwards, with the mission of revealing the substance of time itself, visible and eternal. Perhaps the modern poet, then, as Stevens imagines him, defeats this cliché. He is modest, for he works only in the momentary. "I am thinking of aesthetics as the equivalent of *apercus,* which seems to have been the original meaning. I don't know what would happen if anybody tried to systematize the subject, but I haven't tried" (*Letters* 469).

We are in the habit of thinking of modernity in terms of a break with tradition, the words *rupture* or *divorce* come back often since there seems to be a loss of unity between speaker and spoken. Since Mallarmé, we have known that the word is the manifest inexistence of that which it designates: presence in language is paid for with absence in the world. One of the conclusions to be drawn here is that the message of modern poetry is closer to Lacanian theory than to ego psychology. The possibility of reinforcing a vacillating ego would be equivalent, then, to reinforcing the illusion. The "subject" of poetics is not the ego, for the ego is fictional; it is not the Self which is speaking through poetry. Nor is language as a pure reflection the subject of poetics. For Stevens (and others like him), poetry elaborates a *space:* the place of being.

The "I speak" of poetry would constitute, then, a negativity for the "I think" of traditional philosophy. The latter permitted the hypothetical existence of the *I.* The former, on the other hand, erases this existence in order to reveal its mask.

"Tea at the Palaz of Hoon" (1912), which first appeared in tandem with "The Snow Man," in *Poetry* presents an example of this questioning of Being. Hoon expresses the masquerade of appearances as the authenticity of the self. Like the Snow Man, he is identified with his world. Unlike the mind of winter, Hoon gives birth to his world (*Collected Poems* 65).

> I was the world in which I walked, and what I saw
> Or heard or felt came not but from myself;
> And there I found myself more truly and more strange.

The task of the past was to understand the concept of truth; the task of modernity is to understand fiction. This is one more conclusion which can be drawn from Stevens's long theoretical poem with its Heideggerian title: "Notes Toward a Supreme Fiction." The disappearance of the gods which Hölderlin announced as a source of possibilities yet to come, the emptiness of the heavens in which Stevens constructs his poetic space as potential, these are founded upon the impossibility of truth in language. To encounter this negativity is to come to terms with the absence of the illusion of the self which we call psychosis; it is to accept the fact that

> . . . these images, these reverberations,
> And others, make certain how being
> Includes death and the imagination.
> *(Collected Poems* 444)

Works Cited

Faulkner, William. *As I Lay Dying.* New York: Jonathan Cape & Harrison Smith, 1930.

Freud, Sigmund. "Inhibitions, Symptoms and Anxiety." *The Standard Edition of the Complete Psychological Works of Sigmund Freud.* 24 vols. Ed. and trans. James Strachey. London: Hogarth, 1953–74. 20: 75–175.

Heidegger, Martin. *Poetry, Language, Thought.* Trans. Albert Hofstadter. New York: Harper and Row, 1971.

Riding, Laura. Preface. *The Poems of Laura Riding.* Manchester: Carcanet New Press, 1938.

Stevens, Wallace. *The Collected Poems of Wallace Stevens.* New York: Knopf, 1955.

_____. *The Letters of Wallace Stevens.* Ed. Holly Stevens. New York: Knopf, 1966.

_____. *The Necessary Angel: Essays on Reality and the Imagination.* New York: Vintage Books, 1951.

Kingston's *The Woman Warrior:*
The Object of Autobiographical
Relations

Elise Miller

Autobiographies—narratives defined by the need to assert, "I am"—can tell us a great deal about the aggression required to claim our existence and the dangers of defining our identity and of celebrating our separateness from others. Maxine Hong Kingston's *The Woman Warrior* (1977) is no exception. Indeed, her unconventional text, structured largely around the third-person point of view, reveals something most autobiographies obfuscate: that the process of composing an autobiography inevitably entails a regression to one's earliest stages of development. The autobiography is thus a reenactment of infantile modes of being in and relating to the world. The unusual structure of *The Woman Warrior* reflects Kingston's interest in fantasy, dreams, and unconscious memories, and more importantly, reveals, as Margaret Mahler states, that an "old, partially unresolved sense of self-identity and of body boundaries, or old conflicts over separation and separateness, can be reactivated (or can remain peripherally or even centrally active) at any or all stages of life" (4–5).[1]

Kingston divides her autobiography into five discrete sections. The first four are devoted to the stories of important female figures in Kingston's life. In the first chapter, "No Name Woman," Kingston's aunt (and the black sheep of the family) bears a child out of wedlock in China and then kills herself and her newborn. The second story remains in China to retell the myth of Fa Mu Lan, a famous Chinese heroine. The middle talk-story narrates Kingston's mother's education as a doctor and later immigration to the United States. Kingston's other aunt, Moon

Orchid, is the subject of the fourth section, which traces her immigration, her failure to assimilate, and finally, her nervous breakdown. It is not until the last section that Kingston discovers the first person point of view, which she uses to document her girlhood years in California.

The Woman Warrior has been seen as a feminist exploration of a woman's efforts to discover her identity and especially to disentangle her sense of self from the significant women around her. Kingston's text has also been read as a commentary on the cultural dislocations experienced by Asian-Americans.[2] What I hope to show is that alongside Kingston's conscious political intentions is a more powerful struggle, a struggle every person—and every author of an autobiography—experiences. Our infantile battles for power and boundaries, our primitive grief over separations and abandonments, our earliest efforts to tolerate fragmentation and dislocation must, I believe, predate and predetermine any later alienation Kingston felt as a woman or as an Asian-American. Instead of challenging feminist or cross-cultural readings, I will thus complement them with a psychological approach that underlines how the pieces of Kingston's story evoke different aspects of infantile development and experience. At the same time, I will suggest how the ideas of D. W. Winnicott, Melanie Klein, and Margaret Mahler can facilitate an understanding of the ways in which an autobiography is a reenactment of the writer's earliest object relations.[3] These primitive experiences of ego—rendered accessible via the writer's fantasies—are as intimately connected to an adult's discovery and enjoyment of a self in the act of writing as they are in life and in therapy.

The Woman Warrior, subtitled "Memoirs of a Girlhood Among Ghosts," is a working through of many ghosts: the ghosts of her parents, the ghosts from China, and, even more profoundly, the ghost of her earliest self—the traces of her most primitive experience of boundaries, mergings, separations. *The Woman Warrior* is a palimpsest: every conscious and adult search for definition and identity resonates with a prior yearning for differentiation, a past hunger for a sense of self, bounded by a stable, real world. Kingston's conscious and current explorations of the boundaries between America and China and between her self and her mother are repetitions of these primitive conflicts and fantasies.[4]

The Woman Warrior begins with Kingston's mother's statement: " 'You must not tell anyone . . . what I am about to tell you' " (4). By beginning with Brave Orchid's admonition, Kingston reveals that her text is the stuff of stolen secrets, betrayed confidences, and surreptitious intentions, and she also prepares us for the ubiquitous presence of Brave

Orchid, who will be the source and nemesis of her daughter's identity. From the very beginning, we see that Kingston's search for self takes place in the context of the mother (or of other women who take the place of the mother). In remembering these m/others, Kingston can uncover forgotten or never known aspects of Brave Orchid and of her self.

The first object within Kingston's memory is Brave Orchid's sister-in-law, No Name Woman. Brave Orchid's version of No Name Woman's life resonates for Kingston, who finds in No Name Woman an aspect of herself, and who intuits in her aunt's predicament an allegory for her own autobiographical quest. No Name Woman symbolizes the glories and dangers of having a self. In No Name Woman's crime, Kingston finds a symbol of autonomy and distinctiveness. She watches while "at the mirror my aunt combed individuality into her bob" (10). Through No Name Woman's suicide, Kingston symbolically murders her own adult self. And through the birth of the illegitimate infant, Kingston is reborn into the fantasized, literary self that exists within the autobiographical space. Kingston, in a sense, returns to her origins, to a pre-Oedipal time, a time before selves and names. When her aunt immediately murders the newborn, Kingston signals the start of her own revision of origins and reveals her fears about the risks and insecurities of identity.

Like No Name Woman and her child, Kingston's self at this point in the text has no name, no place, no definition. Like the newborn's, Kingston's new identity is hypothetical, symbolic, projected. And it will remain so throughout the autobiography, because for Kingston the very quest for identity throws every aspect of the self into question. The quest erases boundaries, challenges definitions, and leaves Kingston, as writer, in an undifferentiated state, structured only by the boundaries of the autobiographical text and task. Thus, the image of the baby conveys the tentativeness, the creativeness, the malleability of identity, and is typical of the ways characters throughout the text are described, transformed, renamed, reborn, replaced, recreated. Not only does Kingston infuse her narrative with the fragile quality of the infantile self, but she also suggests that identity is *always* ephemeral, illusory, fictional.

Kingston needs to breathe life into her aunt, needs to make her real as a way of affirming her own autobiographical powers. To Brave Orchid's bareboned account of No Name Woman, Kingston must add imaginative speculations through "perhaps" and "she may have been." By moving past Brave Orchid's literal and moralistic version, Kingston gives No Name Woman motives, moods, quirks, and flaws. In this way Kingston reenacts No Name Woman's sin of "acting as if she could have a private life, secret and apart from them" (14). By giving her aunt a distinctive self, a rich inner world, Kingston can disavow the fact that while selves can be imagined and formed, they can just as easily be distorted and destroyed. By merging, in fantasy, with No Name Woman, Kingston can challenge namelessness, thwart self-lessness.

Though No Name Woman nurtures Kingston's identity, she also threatens it, and in doing so, she epitomizes the paradox of identification—the dangers, especially for women, inherent in mirrored and reflected selves. Identity is explored as a form of mirroring throughout *The Woman Warrior*. Identity, for Kingston, is always being speculated about and is always specular. Indeed, for most of the text, Kingston is present only as a projection or reflection. In a sense, she is in pieces. Eschewing the conventional autobiographical first-person report, Kingston informs her text not as actor, but as witness and as third-person narrator of the stories of women who function as fragments of Kingston's self, as displaced versions of Kingston's "I," as alienated pieces of Kingston's potential identity. In the same way that a mother functions simultaneously as the other and as part of the infant's ego, so these female figures are both merged with and alienated from Kingston's autobiographical self. They exist as transitional objects, neither subjects nor objects.

Kingston thus creates and sustains a self through these specular relationships, but she also exemplifies the radical decentering and otherness of the human subject. Conscious of her self only in these alienated fragments, Kingston recalls what Lacan describes as the "first months of life" when the infant recognizes itself in the mother and thus *"out there* as a unified whole in contrast to" its own "fragmented and chaotic jumble of impulses and sensations." These simultaneous recognitions of self and object *"split* the subject in the moment of his own specular capture" and thus establish what Lacan sees and Kingston vividly dramatizes as the essential dual nature of identity (in Evans 394–95).[5] Kingston's identifications with figures like No Name Woman are thus simultaneously comforting and fragmenting. These symbiotic bonds are remnants of the "complete" self experienced during infancy, a self that seemed more true, perfect, or whole because not yet distinguished from m/other. By inhabiting these symbiotic states, by remaining in her hall of mirrors, Kingston can forestall, as the infant does, the tragedy of differentiation.

Though Kingston understands the tentativeness of the "I" and the dangers of merging, she uses chapter 2, "White Tigers," to revisit a crucial phase of infant development, a time when the infant enjoys intoxicating experiences of power and autonomy.[6] In this chapter, Kingston borrows from fantasy and myth to tell the tale of Fa Mu Lan, the famous Chinese woman warrior who leaves her family to live with a strange, elderly couple who teaches her the ways of magic, good and evil, and war. Fa Mu Lan employs her skills to free China from an evil tyrant. She marries her childhood sweetheart, gives birth during battle, and later lives out her life as a great heroine. Fa Mu Lan's life branches into Kingston's by means of Chinese folklore, dreams, and fantasies. Eventually myth and daydream merge, and Kingston becomes Fa Mu Lan. This flight of fancy takes Kingston to ancient China and, more importantly, to a time when the infant—suspended between symbiosis and autonomy—could be said to have the best of two worlds.

During what is often called the omnipotent phase, reality continually converges with—indeed serves—fantasy. Through magical thinking and play, the infant experiments with boundaries between self and object, between desire and reality.[7] As Fa Mu Lan, Kingston can create a fantasy world with new parents ("There at the bottom of the gourd were my mother and father scanning the sky, which was where I was"), new enemies, new saviors (27). Fa Mu Lan's powerful tutors teach her "dragon ways": "After five years my body became so strong that I could control even the dilations of the pupils inside my irises. I could copy owls and bats. . . . After six years the deer let me run beside them. I could jump twenty feet into the air from a standstill, leaping like a monkey over the hut. Every creature has a hiding skill and a fighting skill a warrior can use" (28).[8]

Fa Mu Lan practices her magic with an aim: to rid China of an evil tyrant whose soldiers pillage villages, rape women, and kidnap young men. Fa Mu Lan's ancient China is a world where good and bad are markedly divorced. She has learned to recognize evil in any form: "I watched powerful men count their money, and starving men count theirs. When bandits brought their share of raids home, I waited until they took off their masks so I would know the villagers who stole from their neighbors. I studied the generals' faces, their rank-stalks quivering at the backs of their heads" (36). Kingston watches Fa Mu Lan's heroic zeal with admiration, since she too must exercise strong powers of discrimination. Kingston reports that Fa Mu Lan's army "brought order wherever we went," and she celebrates Fa Mu Lan's ability to defend good and destroy evil (44). The many passages recording Fa Mu Lan's battles are a way for Kingston to play with primitive, infantile modes of organizing the world.[9] They might also be a way for Kingston to play out in fantasy the destruction of her mother. Though Brave Orchid is absent from this tale, she haunts its margins as the object against whom Kingston often violently defends and defines herself. While Fa Mu Lan "cut off his leg with one sword swipe," "slashed him across the face and on the second stroke cut off his head," Kingston recreates the violent and primitive drama between infant and mother (49). "In his aggressive fantasies," Melanie Klein explains, "he wishes to bite up and to tear up his mother and her breasts, and to destroy her in other ways" (in Segal 35).[10] In the psyche of the primitive, fragile ego, an experience of frustration or envy can unleash all the infant's destructive tendencies, an experience Kingston repeatedly recalls in her journey back to her origins.

By the end of the chapter, Kingston has moved beyond her idealization of Fa Mu Lan and has transcended the compulsion to play out infantile aggressions. She is ready to confront her mother, the focus of the next and central chapter of *The Woman Warrior*. This transition supports Klein's thesis that fantasies of destruction are always accompanied by "omnipotent fantasies of a restoring kind." After having bitten, torn, and swallowed the evil emperor/mother, Kingston can fantasize that she "is putting the bits together again and repairing her" (Klein, *Love, Guilt and Reparation* 61). Fa Mu Lan offered Kingston the vicarious experience of manipulating and annihilating m/other; and through the very act of writing, Kingston can repair and return to her mother.[11] By the end of "White Tigers," Kingston has learned that aggression accommodates love and reparation, that good and bad coexist. Kingston has worked through a symbiosis with Brave Orchid as well as the need to depict her as monster and enemy of the self. With the aid of Fa Mu Lan, Kingston's trial by fire prepares her to confront the source and nemesis of her identity—her mother.

Like the mother during the symbiotic phase, Brave Orchid has been too big, too threatening, too important to acknowledge as a separate entity. She can emerge only after Kingston has internalized and integrated the lessons of No Name Woman and Fa Mu Lan. And Brave Orchid emerges in full force—at the center of the text and in a chapter called "Shaman." In this chapter, Kingston relinquishes Fa Mu Lan's first-person point of view and narrates her mother's education at To Keung School of Midwifery, her return to her home village to practice medicine, and her immigration to the America where her ignorance of English forced her to work as a tomato-picker and laundress.

For most of this chapter Brave Orchid is, as the title suggests, larger than life. Her every aspect is exaggerated: "My mother may have been afraid, but she would be a dragoness ('my totem, your totem'). She could make herself not weak. During danger she fanned out her dragon claws and riffled her red sequin scales and unfolded her coiling green stripes. Like the dragons living in temple eaves, my mother looked down on plain people who were lonely and afraid" (79). Kingston carefully approaches the mother dragoness, watching, listening, hungry for the secrets of Brave Orchid's power and identity. This process is fraught with ambivalence. The infant's "wish for reunion with the love object and his fear of engulfment by it" translates into intense ambivalence toward the mother, an emotional state that pervades this chapter (Mahler 77). Like the toddler in the midst of rapprochement, Kingston takes bold steps toward autonomy, only to regress back to less differentiated states of being. In this way, "Shaman" recapitulates the central dilemmas of *The Woman Warrior* and of infancy: the longing for symbiotic union as it competes with a desire for an independent, separate self.

Kingston must learn to tolerate the paradoxes of identification, that process of surrendering the self in admiration of the other. Kingston knows that she could become devoured by her curiosity, swallowed up in endless speculations about Brave Orchid. As she recalls how "my mother funnelled China into our ears," Kingston notes: "Before we can leave our parents, they stuff our heads like the suitcases which they jam-pack with homemade underwear" (89). "Shaman" dramatizes Kingston's alternations between loving and emulating Brave Orchid, on the one hand, and on the other, striving to disentangle herself from her mother's efforts to merge with, to create her daughter in her image.[12] Kingston complains: "She pries open my head and my fists and crams into them responsibility for time, responsibility for intervening oceans" (126). Brave Orchid even invades Kingston's dreams: "My mother has given me pictures to dream, nightmare babies that recur" (101).

Her "mother's monkey story" becomes a metaphor for the way Kingston experiences Brave Orchid as constantly penetrating her, violating her, literally picking at her brain. Kingston tried not to listen, but then "the monkey words would unsettle me; a curtain flapped loose inside my brain":

> "Do you know what people in China eat when they have money?" my mother began. "They buy into a monkey feast. The eaters sit around a thick wood table with a hole in the middle. Boys bring in the monkey at the end of a pole. Its neck is in a collar at the end of the pole, and it is screaming. Its hands are

tied behind it. They clamp the monkey into the table; the whole table fits like another collar around its neck. Using a surgeon's saw, the cooks cut a clean line in a circle at the top of its head. To loosen the bone, they tap with a tiny hammer and wedge here and there with a silver pick. Then the old woman reaches out her hand to the monkey's face and up to its scalp, where she tufts some hairs and lifts off the lid of the skull. The eaters spoon out the brains." (107)

Kingston is the monkey in this scene. When she heard the story, she said, "I have wanted to say, 'Stop it. Stop it,' but not once can I say 'Stop it.' " Her need for Brave Orchid keeps her vulnerable to her intrusions, open to her invasions, yet she must find a way to be with Brave Orchid without being destroyed by her, to take in Brave Orchid without being devoured by her.[13]

Brave Orchid's story of the Sitting Ghost dramatizes the power of these primitive agonies and reveals their persistence in the adult or artistic consciousness. Like the suffocating mother of the infant's fantasies, the Sitting Ghost is intent on absorbing Brave Orchid's very identity, "As if feeding on her very thoughts." Its heavy, suffocating presence threatens to annihilate her being. Brave Orchid survives the night with her self intact. In response to the ghost's devouring engulfment, Brave Orchid keeps thinking and talking—asserting her presence, insisting her right to be. Kingston has another explanation for her mother's triumph: "My mother could contend against the hairy beasts whether flesh or ghost because she could eat them, and she could not-eat them on days when good people fast" (108). When Brave Orchid advises, " 'If it tastes good, it's bad for you. . . . If it tastes bad, it's good for you,' " she summarizes the essential capacity to discriminate, to take in the good and expel the bad—a crucial skill when one must continually risk merging with the m/other in the process of developing a self. A bad object is dangerous only when it is external. The Chinese, who believe that "all heroes are bold toward food," know this. Eight pages of "Shaman" are devoted to talk-stories that prove this. These tales explain the Chinese tendency to waste no food, to eat "scorpions, snakes, cockroaches, worms, slugs, beetles, and crickets." "Big eaters win," and they do so because they are able to eat and therefore master any ghost or enemy (105).

No wonder Kingston is horrified by Brave Orchid's story of the "child born without an anus . . . left in the outhouse so the family would not have to hear it cry." Kingston cannot escape the image of the baby, "sobbing, heaving, as if it were trying to defecate" (101). The "holeless baby" evokes in Kingston a very primitive fear, an infantile anxiety that the world will invade and annihilate, and shows that the holeless baby story parallels the one about the Sitting Ghost, for both dramatize the anxieties around merging: the loss of self or the fear that the self can become so permeable, so penetrable that it will take in good and bad without being able to expel the poisonous or undesirable. Kingston's preoccupation with eating, defecation, incorporation, and expulsion in this section indicates the unconscious dimensions and primitive traces of her efforts to sort out "what's just my childhood, just my imagination, just my family, just movies, just living" (5-6).

The end of "Shaman" illustrates Kingston's evolution along these lines. Here, Kingston shows that the capacity to distinguish good and bad also includes an awareness of the difference between fantasy and reality. Brave Orchid enters the sleeping Kingston's bedroom: "That night she was a sad bear; a great sheep in a wool shawl. She recently took to wearing shawls and granny glasses. American fashions." Brave Orchid mistakes cold pills for LSD, and appears lonely, even senile (though she still gives Kingston migraines). As Kingston's beacon in the world of reality, Brave Orchid no longer has to be powerful shaman or heroic physician. Kingston is able to absorb Brave Orchid's lessons because she has allowed herself to get close to her mother and, in doing so, is able to see her mother for what she really is. Brave Orchid's transition from fantastic internal object to real person marks Kingston's own autobiographical transformations. As Kingston grows up, Brave Orchid grows smaller, weaker, more fallible.[14] Brave Orchid's transformation from idealized good object to real mother signals Kingston's transition from fantasy to reality.

I have argued that the progression of Kingston's chapters represents successive stages of infant development. With each chapter, Kingston moves from rebirth to symbiosis to omnipotence, and in "Shaman," to the ambivalent swings between merging and differentiation. But with every step forward, Kingston also regresses, gaining ground only to lose it in nostalgic gestures toward earlier, simpler states of being—hence her oscillation between woman warriors or shaman mothers and feeble women in tattered shawls, and hence her conflict between oral fixations and mature perceptions. This pattern persists in the last two chapters, where Kingston continues to vascillate between poignant yearnings for symbiosis and clear celebrations of autonomy.

In "At the Western Palace," Kingston traces the story of her Aunt Moon Orchid's immigration to America and eventual psychotic breakdown. At the time of this tale, Brave Orchid is 68, yet she is full of energetic and grandiose plans for Moon Orchid's liberation and Americanization. Kingston's comic portrayal of Brave Orchid's pushy plans and absurd aspirations for Moon Orchid cuts Brave Orchid down to size and thus reminds Kingston of the underside to Brave Orchid's dragoness/shaman aspects. But Kingston's detachment from Brave Orchid in this chapter affects Kingston, as well as the shape of the autobiography, profoundly, for her alienation from Brave Orchid places Kingston literally beside or outside of herself. The few times Kingston is present in this chapter, she speaks of herself in third person: "There was indeed an oldest girl who was absent-minded and messy. She had an American name that sounded like 'Ink' in Chinese" (152). Kingston's distance from Brave Orchid is powerfully decentering. And it is precisely such a displacement of self that becomes the theme of "At the Western Palace."

Like No Name Woman, Fa Mu Lan, and Brave Orchid, Moon Orchid functions as a version of Kingston's ego. Like Brave Orchid and Moon Orchid, "two old women with faces like mirrors," Kingston and Moon Orchid mirror each other. Kingston often portrays their similarities comically. When Moon Orchid first arrives, she is fascinated by Brave Orchid's children and is intent on "testing what kinds of minds they had, raised away from civilization." Moon Orchid studies these "sweet wild animals" who were raised in the "wilderness" and who "smelled like milk," and like an author, she narrates their activities aloud (137, 155). Like Kingston, Moon Orchid is the detached observer, articulating and recording the family for posterity. By making fun of Moon Orchid, Kingston can caricature her own art, her own compulsion to understand and report. She can detach herself from the autobiographical task and enjoy the playful aspects of its process. Moon Orchid's childlike wonder and amusing game recall a time when play provided our first lessons in self, separation, and symbol-formation. Around the infant—and, I would add, within the boundaries of an autobiography—is what Winnicott calls the "potential space," an intermediate area "between me-extensions and the not-me. This potential space is at the interplay between there being nothing but me and there being objects and phenomena outside omnipotent control" (*Playing and Reality* 100).[15]

Writing an autobiography is also a transitional activity. As a psychological and historical document, the autobiography exists in that twilight between fantasy and reality, subject and object. Within the potential space of Kingston's autobiography are many transitional objects—words, m/others, food, feces, swords, etc.—that function as extensions or parts of Kingston's self. Through these transitional objects, Kingston plays with merging and separating in order to separate out me from not-me. Within this potential space, real people are converted to play-things or hypothetical entities in a manner that replicates the infant's playful development of identity. Everything and everybody within the autobiography has a role in her re-creation of self. The autobiography becomes a place where neither subjects nor objects can be truly said to exist, or where they exist in confusion, in transition. It is out of this space inhabited by projections and fragments of m/other and fantasies of the primitive self that Kingston uncovers the "I."

Moon Orchid plays a crucial role in Kingston's transitional space. In one sense, their connection is reminiscent of Kingston's relationship to No Name Woman. In contrast to Brave Orchid's enviable traits and threatening powers, Moon Orchid seems to function as a negative, or at best comic model—a symbol of homelessness, self-lessness, and finally, madness. Her immigration becomes for Kingston a metaphor for her own quest for identity. Though Kingston portrays Moon Orchid's fail-ure to assimilate in humorous terms, she knows that being without a home, family, or country is like being without a self. As Kingston watches Moon Orchid leave her home and attachments, she sees a nightmare version of her own efforts to separate her self from home and family. If "Shaman" records the nightmare of merging and symbiosis, "At the Western Palace" explores the horror of utter isolation, of a kind of separation or aloneness that destroys the self.

In the end, Moon Orchid cannot adapt. She cannot find a place, a definition, a Self. She goes mad; her immigration becomes a metaphor for the dangers of ruptured attachments and displaced selves. Kingston's mother explains the nature of Moon Orchid's madness: "Moon Orchid had misplaced herself, her spirit (her 'attention,' Brave Orchid called it) scattered all over the world" (181). Moon Orchid loses her self, her mind, but she discovers a home at a California mental asylum. Here, as Moon Orchid tells her visitors, " 'No one ever leaves. . . . We are all women here. . . . We speak the same language, the very same' " (185). Moon Orchid reacts to her nightmare dislocation by reverting to narcissistic origins, to a pre-Oedipal world of mothers and daughters, of sameness and symbiosis. Moon Orchid returns to a state of being Kingston ideal-izes and is attempting to escape. Through Moon Orchid, Kingston can fantasize about the bliss of the symbiotic union, the wholeness and per-fection of the self prior to differentiation, the comfort of merging and mirroring. And through Moon Orchid, Kingston can finally relinquish her longing for these origins and prepare for an experience of self that is neither suffocatingly dependent nor psychotically isolated.[16]

Moon Orchid's fate undermines our desire to read *The Woman Warrior* as a chronological, developmental progression from self-lessness to mature identity. The location of her story speaks, instead, to the circular, the regressive elements of identity formation, and argues that a quest for women warriors and shamans must also include a recognition of weakness and madness. Kingston's attachment to Moon Orchid suggests that development is never linear, and that identity—unpredictable, unlocatable, unnameable—must always establish a relationship to madness. Moon Orchid reminds Kingston of the fragility of identity, but her presence in the text also proves that Kingston is now ready to tolerate the instabilities of the self.

In the transition from "At the Western Palace" to "A Song for a Barbarian Reed Pipe," Kingston shifts from a third- to a first-person point of view. After four chapters, Kingston is now ready to claim the autobiographical "I," and she does so with a vengeance. This chapter is filled with talk-stories that replay, rehearse, and resolve the symbiosis-separation dilemma that has haunted her quest. For ten pages, Kingston confesses her gruesome efforts to terrorize a silent Chinese girl into talking. In this scene that parallels Brave Orchid's efforts to Americanize Moon Orchid, Kingston assumes her mother's position and proceeds to bully the girl into talking and thus having a self. The more Kingston screams, the more silent the girl becomes; the more Kingston slaps and pinches, the more passive and malleable the girl (" 'I thought I could put my thumb on her nose and push it' "). Kingston shouts to the nightmare version of herself: " 'You're such a nothing. . . . And you, you are a plant. . . . If you don't talk, you can't have a personality. . . . You've got to let people know you have a personality and a brain' " (204–10).

Some form of this voiceless, shapeless, self-less girl has haunted *The Woman Warrior*. She is the symbol of the infant self not yet differentiated from m/other. She is the emblem of that tentative, transitional self fantasized within the potential space of the autobiography. She hid within the Sitting Ghost and soothed Moon Orchid's isolated self. Once the ghost of Kingston's self, she is now shaped and determined by Kingston. "Song" is the story of Kingston's triumph over her ghosts—the ghost of the self-less girl, of the woman with no name, of brave Fa Mu

Lan, of mad Moon Orchid, and finally, of her mother. In this chapter, Kingston is able to take back her projected selves, to synthesize her fragments, to unify her dispersed pieces of being.

In one of the last talk-stories of the autobiography, Kingston integrates the fears of Moon Orchid with the courage of Fa Mu Lan to play out one last battle with her mother: "I had grown inside me a list of over 200 things that I had to tell my mother so that she would know the true things about me and to stop the pain in my throat." With this recitation of past crimes, Kingston believes that if "only I could let my mother know the list, she—and the world—would become more like me, and I would never be alone again" (230). With this glance backward to Moon Orchid's solution of self-lessness, Kingston proceeds to speak, but when she is finished, she feels misunderstood and utterly alone. Instead of producing a bond with her mother, the list merely irritates Brave Orchid; Kingston speculates, "I had probably interrupted her in the middle of her own quiet time . . . my mother's time to ride off with the people in her own mind" (233). At this lonely moment, Kingston is, in fact, closest to Brave Orchid. Because of this experience of her essential separateness and difference, Kingston is able to have true empathy into her mother's mind, true insight into her mother's otherness. With this vision of her real mother—separate but equal—Kingston can transcend the tendencies toward narcissism and splitting and acknowledge the differences between self and other, fantasy and reality, America and China, etc. In that moment, Kingston becomes the author of her existence: "And suddenly I got very confused and lonely because I was at that moment telling her my list, and in the telling, it grew. No higher listener. No listener but myself" (237). The listeners or audience of Kingston's autobiographical process—Brave Orchid, Kingston's readers—fade in importance as she confronts her own separateness, her own authority. Kingston can no longer experience Brave Orchid as the source or audience of her existence because, in this moment, Kingston becomes her own mother, her own witness, her own author. In this moment, she finds a self and a voice for that self, knowing that the "throat pain always returns, though, unless I tell what I really think" (239).

Most of the talk-stories in *The Woman Warrior* were Brave Orchid's, but in the end, Kingston has the last word—almost. Having found her self, her voice, she can now share the last tale with Brave Orchid: "Here is a story my mother told me, not when I was young, but recently, when I told her I also talk-story. The beginning is hers, the ending, mine" (240). Brave Orchid tells how her grandmother saved the family from murderous thieves by insisting they attend the opera. The tale ends happily with the moral that "our family was immune from harm as long as they went to plays." Kingston's story is also about mothers, families, and art. This tale, told from the third-person point of view, is about Ts'ai-Yen, "a poetess born in A.D. 175," who is captured by barbarian soldiers. "During her 12-year stay with the barbarians, she had two children" and wrote countless songs "about China and her family there. Her words seemed to be Chinese, but the barbarians understood their sadness and anger. Sometimes they thought they could catch barbarian phrases about forever wandering" (243).

Ts'ai-Yen's life is a testament to creativity, to integration, and to the unifying powers of art, yet in telling the tale, Kingston is once again dislocated, decentered. She abandons the first-person point of view, enjoyed so briefly in this final chapter, and leaves us with the poet's message about forever wandering. Perhaps her search for the "I" must continue. Or perhaps, as Winnicott has said: "The self is not really to be found in what is made out of products of body or mind, however valuable these constructs may be in terms of beauty, skill, and impact. If the artist (in whatever medium) is searching for the self, then it can be said that in all probability there is already some failure for that artist in the field of general creative living. The finished creation never heals the underlying lack of sense of self" (*Playing and Reality* 54–55).

Kingston's ending has been read as a celebration of artistic identity or as a recognition of the power of translation, the ability to bridge differences between cultures and races. But I suggest that such interpretations show that, as readers, we need to see a search for self completed; we require realization, resolution, wholeness. That need—derived from our own incomplete selves and unfinished processes—explains our interest in autobiographies and perhaps our discomfort with Kingston's ending. As Kingston knows and her readers suspect, the autobiography can neither manufacture a self nor obfuscate its absence. The autobiography can merely testify that, when attempting to understand or speak about the self, one stands, indeed, on dangerous ground.

Notes

1. In *The Reproduction of Mothering*, Nancy Chodorow argues that a woman regresses while mothering, and by unconsciously reexperiencing her own infantile needs and early object relations, she can care for those of her baby. Perhaps, writing an autobiography can

be seen as a process of (re)mothering oneself, and a process that entails a regression. Or alternately, perhaps the need to construct an autobiography is itself a sign of regression.

2. Although Kingston is an active member of a community of Asian-American writers, she once stated in an interview, "Sexism more than racism hurt me" (Pfaff 4).

3. Otto Kernberg defines object relations theory as the "study of the nature and origin of interpersonal relations and of the nature and origin of intrapsychic structures deriving from, fixating, modifying, and reactivating past internalized relations with others in the context of present interpersonal relations. . . . [V]ery primitive, distorted object-images certainly continue to exist in the unconscious mind" (56). Obviously, every autobiography will resonate with these unconscious characteristics to different degrees.

4. The importance of these early and largely unconscious dimensions of experience are acknowledged in Kingston's own account of her writing process: "I feel that I have two methods of writing. . . . One of them is tapping the sources of creativity, in order to get down to the id of the self or the subconscious. . . . I don't have a controlled way of going about that. . . . By sitting down and writing, writing crazy, writing anything, single-space, fast—that's the way that that works. Often it turns out to be just a reminder, about how something felt." Of this rough draft, Kingston states, "It has to be reworked" (Pfaff 15).

5. It is important to note that every object relationship involves the tendency to identify (become like) the object. In *A Structural Study of Autobiography* (37–38), Jeffrey Mehlman explains: "For every relationship with another is plagued by the tendency to narcissistic identification, to crowding the other out or letting oneself be crowded out by him." The more primitive the ego, the greater the tendency to identify.

6. According to Margaret Mahler, after physical birth the infant experiences a "psychological birth" that involves an evolution from symbiosis (the beginning of differentiation from the mother), to practicing (complete absorption in newfound physical and emotional autonomy), to rapprochement (an ambivalent rehearsal of independence and fearful flights back to mother), and finally, the development of object constancy (stabilization of the subject/object separation). If "No Name Woman," with its fixation on mothers and infants, recalls the symbiotic phase, "White Tigers" can be seen as an allegory of the practicing phase.

7. In *Collected Papers: Through Pediatrics to Psycho-analysis* Winnicott states: "In the most primitive state, which may be retained in illness, and to which regression may occur, the object (person or part-person) behaves according to magical laws, i.e., it exists when desired, it approaches when approached, it hurts when hurt. . . . In fantasy things work by magic: there are no breaks on fantasy and love and hate cause alarming effects" (146).

8. Such passages suggest the palpable presence of primitive fantasy, recalled or re-created, throughout this text, a narrative in which internal and external landscapes become blurred, where Kingston's wishes and nightmares convert history, where her constant projections and internalizations create dizzying demarcations. Fantasy, Meredith Skura explains, interacts with a literary text insofar as it "adds depth by evoking the unconscious remnants of infantile experience." A text can thus bear the marks of "a whole way of seeing the world," a "kaleidoscope of images and scenes," "clusters which do not distinguish person, place, or time." Fantasy, "a primitive form of organizing all internal and external experience," is for Skura the true building block of the imagination and is "shaped by all aspects of early experience—not only instinctual, but cognitive, perceptual, social" (73–74, 77–78).

9. Fa Mu Lan's ethical world view is reminiscent of one of the achievements of the early

ego—splitting. According to Melanie Klein, "It is splitting which allows the ego to emerge out of chaos and to order its experiences. . . . It is the basis of what is later to become the faculty of discrimination, the origin of which is the differentiation between good and bad." Early on, the baby develops a relationship to two different mothers/breasts: the good one, confirmed by "gratifying experiences of love and feeding," and the bad one, reinforced by "real experiences of deprivation and pain." At first, the infant must split, as Fa Mu Lan does, these objects and separate its feelings, "trying to retain good feelings and introject good objects, whilst expelling bad objects and projecting bad feelings" (26).

10. According to Winnicott, this battle persists throughout childhood and adolescence. He believes that "growing up means taking the parents' place. *It really does.* In the unconscious fantasy, growing up is inherently an aggressive act" (*Playing and Reality* 144).

11. One might view the writing of an autobiography as an act of reparation for Kingston's infantile aggressions for her mother. Kingston sublimates these destructive tendencies and offers a form of reparation in this text, which is aimed at reconstructing Brave Orchid and reuniting mother and daughter.

12. One can speculate that fears about merging and engulfment would be found more frequently in women's rather than men's autobiographies. Since the symbiotic union is less easily relinquished by daughters, female autobiographies might reveal more elements from these primitive stages of development as well as more focus on the mother. For more on the differences between women's and men's autobiographies, see Estelle Jelinek's *Women's Autobiography* (Bloomington: Indiana UP, 1980).

13. If the infant is forced to react to or deal with the environment before s/he has developed emotional and psychological integrity, the infant will become decentered, dispersed. Winnicott explains: "The alternative to being is reacting, and reacting interrupts being and annihilates. Being and annihilation are the two alternatives." If the infant is not sheltered from environmental impingements, s/he will risk experiencing one of the "primitive agonies": (1) going to pieces; (2) falling forever; (3) having no relation to the body; (4) having no orientation; (5) complete isolation because of there being no means of communication (*The Maturational Processes and the Facilitating Environment* 46).

14. Klein claims that when "the parents are actually seen, admitted to be seen, in a more realistic light, idealization is diminished and tolerance can come about" (*Narrative of a Child Analysis* 51).

15. This potential space is central to the infant's transition from an undifferentiated state (normal autism) to its recognition and acknowledgment of m/other. Winnicott sees this potential space as filled with transitional activities/objects, "transitional" because the infant does not yet distinguish itself from other, and therefore subject from object. Through play, which takes place in this overlap of inner and outer, fantasy and reality, the infant does not yet distinguish its self from other, and therefore subject from object. growing sense that m/other exists as a separate being, the infant discovers symbols or activities (blankets, thumb, etc.) that stand for the breast or mother. This primitive capacity for symbol formation helps the infant tolerate the mother's increasing absences so central to their eventual separation. Winnicott claims that the infant's ability to symbolically substitute the transitional object for mother belongs "to the realm of illusion," and "throughout life is retained in the intense experiencing that belongs to the arts and to religion and to imaginative living, and to creative scientific work" (*Playing and Reality* 108).

16. Such scenes exemplify Kingston's constant efforts to replay, remake, and thus resolve earlier conflicts, especially with her mother. A number of analysts (Lowenstein, Kris,

Loewald, Greenson, Rangell) have developed the theory that early traumas produce in us grim unconscious beliefs about the world, our parents, our relationships. Alongside of these pathological beliefs is an unconscious wish for mastery, an unconscious desire to overcome problems generated by these beliefs. One might see the autobiography as a vehicle for replaying and mastering early conflicts.

Works Cited

Chodorow, Nancy. *The Reproduction of Mothering*. Berkeley: U of California P, 1978.

Evans, Martha Noel. "Introduction to Jacques Lacan's Lecture: The Neurotic's Individual Myth." *The Psychoanalytic Quarterly* 48 (1979): 386–404.

Kernberg, Otto. *Object Relations Theory and Clinical Psychoanalysis*. New York: Jason Aronson, 1976.

Kingston, Maxine Hong. *The Woman Warrior*. New York: Vintage Books, 1977.

Klein, Melanie. *Love, Guilt and Reparation and Other Works*. 1921–45. New York: Delacorte, 1975.

———. *Narrative of a Child Analysis*. New York: Dell, 1961.

Mahler, Margaret. *The Psychological Birth of the Human Infant*. New York: Basic, 1975.

Mehlman, Jeffrey. *A Structural Study of Autobiography*. Ithaca, N.Y.: Cornell UP, 1974.

Pfaff, Timothy. "Writing Out the Storm." *California Monthly* (Oct. 1979): 4–14.

Segal, Hanna. *Introduction to the Work of Melanie Klein*. London: Hogarth, 1973.

Skura, Meredith. *The Literary Use of the Psychoanalytic Process*. New Haven, Conn.: Yale UP, 1981.

Winnicott, D. W. *Boundary and Space*. Ed. Madeline Davis and David Walbridge. New York: Brunner/Mazel, 1981.

———. "The Child and the Family." 1966. In *Boundary and Space*.

———. *Collected Papers: Through Pediatrics To Psycho-analysis*. In *Boundary and Space*.

———. *The Maturational Processes and the Facilitating Environment*. In *Boundary and Space*.

———. *Playing and Reality*. London: Tavistock, 1971.

Infanticide and Object Loss in
Jude the Obscure

Jeffrey Berman

Little Father Time's suicide in *Jude the Obscure* (1895) is the turning point of a novel demonstrating the spirit of cruelty that pervades nature and society. As if the boy's suicide is not terrible enough, Hardy has him hang his younger half-brother and half-sister, the three children suspended pathetically from closet hooks. Located near Father Time's body is a note with the victim's last words: *"Done because we are too menny"* (405). The suicide letter reveals the boy's belief that his father, Jude Fawley, and stepmother, Sue Bridehead, would be better off without the children, who only add to the couple's woes in a Malthusian world. Jude sees his son's suicide as symbolic of an impending universal death wish, and he mournfully reassures Sue that she could not have averted the tragedy. "It was in his nature to do it. The doctor says there are such boys springing up amongst us—boys of a sort unknown in the last generation—the outcome of new views of life." These boys, adds Jude, see all the terrors of life before they are strong enough to resist them. "He says it is the beginning of the coming universal wish not to live. He's an advanced man, the doctor: but he can give no consolation to—" (406).

Curiously, although no subject is more important to society than the growth and nurture of its children, the double murder and suicide in *Jude the Obscure* have elicited virtually no literary commentary—a scholarly neglect confirming Father Time's judgment that the world would be better off without the children. The dearth of criticism is more surprising in light of the fact that the violent deaths of the three children represent, as Ian Gregor notes, the "most terrible scene in Hardy's fic-

tion, indeed it might be reasonably argued in English fiction" (22).[1]
Nearly all readers have agreed with Irving Howe's authoritative conclusion that the suicide is aesthetically botched, "botched not in conception
but in execution: it was a genuine insight to present the little boy as one
of those who were losing the will to live, but a failure in tact to burden
him with so much philosophical weight" (145–46). Yet Howe consigns
this observation to a parenthesis, and Hardy's critics have condemned
Father Time's suicide without investigating the underlying causes.

There are, admittedly, several objections that may be raised to a psychological interpretation of the double murder and suicide. Father Time
is clearly an allegorical, not a realistic character. Few literary children
have appeared so relentlessly morbid and fatalistic, and his melodra-
matic entrance and exit strain credibility. To take seriously his fears and
vulnerability may strike some readers as misplaced critical attention.
Does it matter how Hardy disposes of the three shadowy children, two of
whom are neither named nor described? Despite these criticisms, *Jude
the Obscure* remains one of the most psychologically rich novels in our
language, as the published criticism confirms.[2] However artistically
contrived Father Time's suicide may be, it reveals many of the characteristics of real-life suicides. More importantly, Father Time's actions fore-
shadow the murderous impulses culminating in Sue's grim return to her
former husband, Richard Phillotson, and Jude's own suicide. Father
Time is not biologically related to Sue, but he is the true heir to the
gloomy philosophy of his father and adoptive mother. Although Jude
and Sue attribute his death to his "incurably sad nature," it is also possible to view the suicide as a logical result of a series of narcissistic injuries
involving defective parenting. This is a more disturbing interpretation
of Father Time's actions as it implicates the parents in the children's
deaths.

To be sure, from the beginning of the novel Hardy seems to be indict-
ing nature, specifically, the brutality of a scheme in which the living are
condemned to inevitable death. Nature itself appears to be a defective
parent, allowing one species to survive, temporarily, at the expense of
another. An early incident, young Jude's identification with a flock of
rooks scavenging for food, evokes Hardy's pessimistic naturalism.
"They seemed, like himself, to be living in a world which did not want
them" (11). Instead of scaring away the birds to prevent them from devouring the produce destined for human consumption, as Father Trou-
tham has paid him to do, the compassionate youth allows them to feed
off the land. He is swiftly punished for the act. The narrator remarks

upon the "flaw in the terrestrial scheme, by which what was good for God's birds was bad for God's gardener" (13). To be alive is to be victimized, the novel suggests, and the Tennysonian belief in nature "red in tooth and claw" pervades Wessex. Jude cannot walk across a pasture without thinking about the coupled earthworms waiting to be crushed on the damp ground. "Nature's logic was too horrid for him to care for. That mercy towards one set of creatures was cruelty toward another sickened his sense of harmony" (15).

Although the narrator ascribes these gloomy thoughts to Jude's "weakness of character," reflective of an unusually sensitive disposition, the other major figures in the story echo the awareness of injustice. Jude's dismay during the pig-killing scene with Arabella foreshadows Sue's horror at the thought of pigeons intended for Sunday dinner. "O why should Nature's law be mutual butchery!" she exclaims (371). Phillotson similarly observes to Arabella that "cruelty is the law pervading all nature and society; and we can't get out of it if we would!" (384). *Jude the Obscure* "fluctuates between two opposing views of 'nature,' " Robert B. Heilman notes, "between a romantic naturalism . . . and the pessimistic aftermath of scientific naturalism" (9). Not only does there seem to be a fundamental defect in the universe, but nature itself, including the mystery of sexual instinct and procreation, perpetuates suffering and death.

To demonstrate the unfortunate consequences of nature, Hardy introduces Little Father Time into the novel. He is the accidental product of the ill-fated marriage between Jude and Arabella. Born eight months after Arabella left England for Australia, the boy spends his early years with her. Arabella hands over the unwanted child to her parents, who in turn decide they no longer wish to be "encumbered" with him. Arabella then turns him over to Jude. Symptomatic of Father Time's past treatment is the fact that he was never christened, because, he explains, "if I died in damnation, 'twould save the expense of a Christian funeral" (337). His mother and grandparents name him "Little Father Time" because of his aged appearance. He is, the narrator states, "Age masquerading as Juvenility, and doing it so badly that his real self showed through crevices" (332). Sue observes that his face is like the tragic mask of Melpomene, the muse of tragedy. A younger and more extreme portrait of Jude, Father Time is obsessed with death and indignant over the inevitable termination of life. His response to flowers seems almost pathological, especially coming from a child. "I should like the flowers very very much, if I didn't keep on thinking they'd be all withered in a few days!" (358). By the same logic he might have concluded that the flowers' fragility compels us to admire their beauty and vitality. The lively exchange in *Sons and Lovers* on how to pick flowers is missing from *Jude the Obscure*. Unlike Jude, Father Time makes no effort to escape his surroundings or to pursue a better life; for this reason he remains pathetic, not tragic, defeated too easily and quickly.

Jude agrees to accept his newly discovered son, telling Sue: "I don't like to leave the unfortunate little fellow to neglect. Just think of his life in a Lambeth pothouse, and all its evil influences, with a parent who doesn't want him, and has, indeed, hardly seen him, and a stepfather who doesn't know him" (330). Jude obviously recognizes that a child's healthy development depends upon loving parents and a friendly environment. Sue intuitively empathizes with Father Time's situation, and she is moved to tears when he calls her "mother." She is distressed, however, by Father Time's physical resemblance to Arabella, which causes Jude to exclaim, "Jealous little Sue!" (335). Sue evidently wishes that Father Time resembled only his father, not his mother. Significantly, Jude earlier expresses a similar wish. Contemplating the marriage between Sue and Phillotson, Jude "projected his mind into the future, and saw her with children more or less in her own likeness around her" (212). The consolation is denied Jude and all such dreamers, the narrator wryly observes, by the "wilfulness of nature." Yet ironically, Father Time in no way resembles his biological mother: temperamentally, he eerily resembles Sue. A number of years pass, with Father Time bringing unexpected joy into his parents' lives. Even though Jude and Sue live together without marrying, consequently suffering social ostracism, they are portrayed as loving, conscientious parents. Jude's decision to move elsewhere for employment prompts Sue to reaffirm her allegiance to Father Time. "But whatever we do, wherever we go, you won't take him away from me, Jude dear? I could not let him go now! The cloud upon his young mind makes him so pathetic to me; I do hope to lift it some day!" (361). Jude reassures her that the family will remain intact.

The crucial scene preceding the children's deaths takes place in Part Sixth, ii, in which Sue and Father Time are talking in a cheerless room of a lodging house from which they have just been evicted. Opposite the lodging house stands Sarcophagus College, whose outer walls "threw their four centuries of gloom, bigotry, and decay into the little room she occupied" (401). Despondent over the loss of lodgings and Jude's declining prospects for employment, Sue mirrors this gloom to Father Time. When he asks her if he can do anything to help the family, she replies:

"No! All is trouble, adversity and suffering!" (402). As the dialogue continues, it becomes increasingly clear that Sue's despair exacerbates the boy's innately melancholy temperament:

> "Father went away to give us children room, didn't he?"
> "Partly."
> "It would be better to be out o' the world than in it, wouldn't it?"
> "It would almost, dear."
> "'Tis because of us children, too, isn't it, that you can't get a good lodging?"
> "Well—people do object to children sometimes."
> "Then if children make so much trouble, why do people have 'em?"
> "O—because it is a law of nature."
> "But we don't ask to be born?"
> "No indeed." (402)

Father Time's questions imply that he and the other two children are responsible for the family's desperate situation. Instead of heeding the child's cry for help and restoring his wounded self-esteem, Sue validates his worst fears. She repeatedly misses the opportunity to allay his suspicion of being unwanted and unloved. In the next line he expresses the fear of becoming a burden to his family, a fear intensified by the fact that Sue is not his biological mother, therefore, under no obligation to care for him. "I oughtn't to have come to 'ee—that's the real truth! I troubled 'em in Australia, and I trouble folk here. I wish I hadn't been born!" Here is the perfect moment for Sue to reassure him that he is indeed loved by his parents, and that if they didn't want him, they never would have consented to adopt him. With luck and determination, she might have added, their lives will improve. What the boy is seeking, of course, is the reassurance any child would expect in a frightening situation. However allegorical Father Time's role may be in the novel, during this scene he acts and talks like a scared child. The reader responds to him as if he is fully human, deserving of sympathy. Father Time requires neither increased despair nor false consolation but hope. He certainly does not need to hear that unwanted children are responsible for their parents' suffering. Yet how does Sue respond to his wish never to have been born? "You couldn't help it, my dear."

Sue's empathic failure triggers Father Time's inner violence, and his statements become increasingly frantic. "I think that whenever children be born that are not wanted they should be killed directly, before their souls come to 'em, and not allowed to grow big and walk about!" (402).

These unwanted children are Father Time and his two siblings. He contemplates infanticide here because he realizes that his parents would be better off without him. Sue does nothing to diminish his despair because it coincides with her own point of view. "Sue did not reply" to the boy's accusations, the narrator tells us, since she was "doubtfully pondering how to treat this too reflective child" (402). Father Time is too reflective, but that is not the main point here. His thinking remains morbid, obsessional, and frighteningly simplistic in its solution to suffering. Mary Jacobus refers to Sue's "mistaken honesty" in telling Father Time that another child is on the way (319),[3] but Sue's real mistake lies in her failure to understand her child's needs. Sue mistakes Father Time's pessimism for profundity, resolves silently to be "honest and candid" with him, as if he were a mature adult rather than a terrified child, and then informs him that she is pregnant again. The information predictably drives him into a frenzy. The dialogue closes with the distracted boy vowing that "if we children was gone there'd be no trouble at all!" Sue's answer "Don't think that, dear" (403), tacitly confirms his reasoning. The next time she sees him, he and the other two children are hanging from their necks. Devastated by the sight, Sue prematurely goes into labor and suffers a miscarriage.

Jude and Sue adopt Father Time to avoid exposing him to further parental neglect, yet, as the final dialogue between mother and son suggests, it would be hard to imagine a more chilling family environment for the child. Although the novel implies that suicide runs in families, like a defective gene passed from one doomed generation to another, a more plausible explanation lies in environmental and interactional causes. Sue remains only partly aware of this. She reads Father Time's suicide letter and breaks down, convinced that their previous conversation has triggered his violence. Sue and Jude plausibly conjecture that upon waking from sleep, Father Time was unable to find his mother and, fearing abandonment, committed the double murder and suicide. Sue accepts responsibility for Father Time's actions, but her explanations mitigate her complicity in the boy's suicide. Perhaps she should have told him all of the "facts of life" or none of them, as she says. Nevertheless, the disclosure of the pregnancy is less wounding to Father Time's self-esteem than her failure to convince him that he is wanted and loved.[4] By projecting her morbidity onto Father Time and confirming his infanticidal fantasies, Sue has effectively placed a noose around his neck. Father Time's inability to enjoy flowers because they will be withered in a few days has its counterpart in Sue's rationalization of the children's deaths. "It is best, perhaps, that they should be gone.—Yes—I see it is! Better that they should be plucked fresh than stay to wither away miserably!" (409). Jude remains characteristically supportive, agreeing that what has happened is probably for the best. "Some say that the elders should rejoice when their children die in infancy" (409). Jude certainly does not rejoice at the children's deaths, yet he remains unaware of how his statements here and elsewhere mirror the self-destructive philosophy that has victimized the Fawleys. Even the attending physician's interpretation of Father Time's suicide—"the beginning of the coming universal wish not to live"—contains a subtle rationalization; for if nothing could have been done to prevent the three deaths, no one is to blame for the tragedy.

Psychoanalytically, Sue's empathic failure is striking. Her inconsistency of love and self-distraction overwhelm Father Time, as they later do Jude. In Kohutian terms, the defective maternal mirroring represents Father Time's final narcissistic injury.[5] By treating Father Time as a selfobject, an extension of herself, Sue acts out her own unresolved inner conflicts. Moreover, by reinforcing Father Time's suspicion that all children are monstrous, she repeats Victor Frankenstein's abandonment of the Creature. Sue is the very opposite of the healthy mirroring mother Alice Miller writes about in *Prisoners of Childhood:* "If a child is lucky enough to grow up with a mirroring mother, who allows herself to be cathected narcissistically, who is at the child's disposal—that is, a mother who allows herself to be 'made use of' as a function of the child's narcissistic development, as Mahler (1968) says—then a healthy self-feeling can gradually develop in the growing child" (32). The issue is not whether Sue is the "perfect" mother but the "good-enough" mother who can prepare her children for the vicissitudes of life. In suggesting that Sue is implicated in her children's deaths, however, we raise other questions. In what way is Sue's abandonment of Father Time symptomatic of other conflicts in her life? Why does she forsake Jude, the man she loves, for Phillotson, whom she does not love? How does she enact the roles of both Narcissus and Echo? These questions inevitably lead us to Sue Bridehead, Hardy's most enigmatic heroine.

Sue's contradictions are dazzling. Intellectually liberated but emotionally repressed, she claims to reject the church's outmoded teachings but then embraces reactionary dogma. Refined and ethereal—Jude calls her a "phantasmal, bodiless, creature" with hardly any "animal passion" in her (312)—she arouses men only to reject them. Torn between the conflicting claims of the body and mind, she sacrifices the integrity of both in a futile quest for self-absolution. Intent upon breaking men's hearts, she resembles Estella in *Great Expectations,* though unlike Dickens's frosty heroine, Sue is filled with remorse. The pattern of her behavior suggests defiance, guilt, self-punishment, and abject submission. "There was no limit to the strange and unnecessary penances which Sue would meekly undertake when in a contrite mood" (322). Early in the story she buys two plaster statuettes of Venus and Apollo, symbolic of her attraction to classical beauty and wisdom, respectively; but when the landlady asks her to identify the objects, she dissembles, claiming they are casts of St. Peter and Mary Magdalene. She cannot tell the truth to Jude, not even after the landlady has spitefully shattered the pagan objects.

What are the origins of Sue's conflicts? To answer this question, the psychological critic must carefully examine her childhood in an effort to reconstruct her past. Unfortunately, the novelist passes over this period, as Albert J. Guerard points out. "The origin of Sue's epicene reticence lies somewhere in her childhood, of which Hardy tells us almost nothing; the origin of her moral masochism lies there also" (109). Hardy gives us an important clue, though, about Sue's history before her introduction into the story—her "friendly intimacy" with a Christminster undergraduate. Sue accepted his invitation to live with him in London, but when she arrived there and realized his intentions, she made a counterproposal—to live with him in a sexless union. Sue's relationship with the Christminster undergraduate remains ambiguous. Was she aware of the sexual implications of his invitation to live with him, for example, and if so, for what reasons did she decline a passionate romance? Several possibilities come to mind: fear of pregnancy, wish for a platonic relationship, threat of social ostracism. The friends shared a sitting room for fifteen months until he was taken ill and forced to go abroad. Although the shadowy episode represents part of Sue's struggle to emancipate herself from repressive social conventions, she blames herself for the undergraduate's death. It remains unclear whether Sue actually intended to hurt him; in narrating the student's account of their relationship, Sue seems to accept both his version of reality and his censure. "He said I was breaking his heart by holding out against him so long at such close quarters; he could never have believed it of woman. I might play that game once too often, he said. He came home merely to die. His death caused a terrible remorse in me for my cruelty—though I hope he died of consumption and not of me entirely" (177–78).

We have no way to authenticate what actually happened between Sue and the Christminster undergraduate, but we can analyze the transference implications of Sue's narrating style. Just as patients' stories in psychoanalysis repeat the themes and conflict of their past, so do fictional characters' narrating styles represent "memorializations of their unresolved pasts" (Olinick and Tracy 320). When Sue expresses the hope that the student "died of consumption and not of me entirely," she seems to acknowledge the strength of her power over others. In characterizing the young man as a victim of love, Sue depicts herself as a victimizer, the person who controlled and determined the outcome of their relationship. Sue feels remorse for her cruelty, but she also feels satisfaction over her power, even though in hurting others she hurts herself. Jude is understandably horrified by Sue's story, provoking her to say, with a "contralto note of tragedy" in her voice: "I wouldn't have told you if I had known!" (178). But Sue unconsciously knows how Jude will react to her story. Like Estella, who repeatedly warns Pip that she will break his heart if he becomes romantically involved with her, Sue forewarns Jude about the dangers of intimacy with her—a heeding Jude perilously disregards.

Sue's relationship with Phillotson and Jude appear to be replays of the unhappy union with the Christminster undergraduate. Phillotson is a hardworking schoolteacher whose name evokes his conventional social views and stolid character. Eighteen years older than Sue, he is clearly a father figure to her, a fact which troubles his rival, Jude. Despite the temperamental and age differences between teacher and student, they enter into a chilling marriage and wisely agree to separate when the failure becomes apparent. After the deaths of the three children, Sue inexplicably returns to Phillotson and remarries him. As Mrs. Edlin observes at the end, "Weddings be funerals a' b'lieve nowadays" (481).

Sue marries Phillotson largely to seek revenge on Jude, whom she incorrectly believes has betrayed her. The engagement and marriage to Phillotson follow Jude's disclosure of his imprudent marriage to Arabella. As if to hurt Jude further, Sue asks him to give her away at the wedding. She even teases him by calling him "father," the term for the man who gives away the bride. The rejected suitor represses his response to the word: "Jude could have said 'Phillotson's age entitles him to be called that!' But he would not annoy her by such a cheap retort" (206). During a morning walk Sue and Jude find themselves in front of the church where the scheduled marriage is to take place. She holds Jude's arm "almost as if she loved him," and they stroll down the nave as if they are married. Sue defends her provocative behavior by saying that she likes "to do things like this." Shortly before the wedding ceremony Jude reflects on Sue's unconscious cruelty toward him, concluding that "possibly she would go on inflicting such pains again and again and grieving for the sufferer again and again, in all her colossal inconsistency" (210).

Sue's wish to captivate men has both Oedipal and pre-Oedipal implications. By marrying Phillotson, Sue may hope to repair the troubled relationship with her own father. By calling Jude "father," Sue invests the same complicated symbolism onto him. But if Sue sees Phillotson and Jude as variations of Oedipus, she seems to view herself as a female Narcissus, exerting fatal attraction over men. "I should shock you by letting you know how I give way to my impulses, and how much I feel that I shouldn't have been provided with attractiveness unless it were meant to be exercised! Some women's love of being loved is insatiable; and so, often, is their love of loving" (245). Sue's language implies here, and the novel bears out, a pattern of infatuation that contains within it the seeds of its own inevitable disillusionment and failure. She later expands upon the reasons for her marriage to Phillotson. "But sometimes a woman's *love of being loved* gets the better of her conscience, and though she is agonized at the thought of treating a man cruelly, she encourages him to love her while she doesn't love him at all. Then, when she sees him suffering, her remorse sets in, and she does what she can to repair the wrong" (290). Like Narcissus, Sue seems to be in love with the unobtainable, the elusive, the spectral; like other narcissistic lovers, she proceeds from idealization to devaluation. Sue is also an Echo, denying her own independence and free will. Toward the end of the novel Sue admits to Jude that she began her relationship with him in the "selfish and cruel wish" to make his heart ache for her. "I did not exactly flirt with you; but that inborn craving which undermines some women's morals almost more than unbridled passion—the craving to attract and captivate, regardless of the injury it may do the man—was in me; and when I found I had caught you, I was frightened" (426). Although Sue has grown to love Jude and experience happiness with him, she abruptly abandons him, causing anguish to both of them. "And now you add to your cruelty by leaving me!" Jude says, to which she replies: "Ah—yes! The further I flounder, the more harm I do!" (426).

Significantly, Sue's need to be loved by men has little to do with the wish for sexual gratification. She is so horrified at the possibility of intercourse with her husband that she throws herself out of the bedroom window when he accidentally enters her room. Jude calls her return to

Phillotson, with whom she has never had sexual relations, a "fanatic prostitution" (436). She returns to her former husband presumably to punish herself and Jude for their nonconformist behavior. The "wickedness" of her feelings at the end of the novel is the same self-revulsion she experiences scarcely eight weeks into her first marriage to Phillotson. Denying there is anything wrong with her marriage, she delivers to Jude one of the most revealing speeches in the book:

> "But it is not as you think!—there is nothing wrong except my own wickedness, I suppose you'd call it—a repugnance on my part, for a reason I cannot disclose, and what would not be admitted as one by the world in general! . . . What tortures me so much is the necessity of being responsive to this man whenever he wishes, good as he is morally!—the dreadful contract to feel in a particular way in a matter whose essence is its voluntariness! . . . I wish he would beat me, or be faithless to me, or do some open thing that I could talk about as a justification for feeling as I do! But he does nothing, except that he has grown a little cold since he has found out how I feel. That's why he didn't come to the funeral. . . . O, I am very miserable—I don't know what to do! . . . Don't come near me, Jude, because you mustn't. Don't—don't!" (255–56).

To interpret the meaning of Sue's speech, we may apply the interpretive tools of ego psychology, the second phase of the psychoanalytic movement.[6] Sue's speech reveals a multitude of defenses gone awry. The middle sentences confirm the need for outside intervention she denies in the beginning and end. Indeed, Sue's cry for help anticipates Father Time's appeal for assistance preceding his suicide. Through displacement, Phillotson becomes the hated object, a projection screen for Sue's inner conflicts. Phillotson is not a brutal man; when he releases her from marriage, he shows admirable selflessness. Sue's first marriage to Phillotson may be attributed in part to naiveté and inexperience, but her second marriage suggests an unconscious need to continue her self-punishment. Sue's sexual surrender takes on the appearance of the "fanatic prostitution" Jude has sadly prophesied.

In remarrying Phillotson, Sue chooses to act out rather than analyze her conflicts. Unable to divorce herself from the institution of marriage she no longer believes in, she falls back upon martyrdom. Yet even as she punishes herself by returning to a husband she has never loved, she abandons the lover who has remained devoted to her. Sue occupies a dual role in the novel, Phillotson's victim and Jude's victimizer. In terms of ego psychology she identifies with the aggressor—a process, Anna

Freud remarks, in which passive is converted to active: "By impersonating the aggressor, assuming his attributes or imitating his aggression, the child transforms himself from the person threatened into the person who makes the threat" (113). Ironically, Sue invokes an unsound social code to rationalize an unhealthy psychological situation. The repressive institution of marriage—repressive to Hardy because its rigidity did not allow a relationship to be dissolvable as soon as it became a cruelty to either party—legitimizes her self-punishment.[7] Sue's second marriage thus becomes a more sinister replay of her first marriage, an example of a repetition-compulsion principle that dominates *Jude the Obscure.*

Hardy's novel, in fact, anticipates by twenty-five years Freud's *Beyond the Pleasure Principle* (1920). In this speculative and far-reaching book Freud defines the repetition-compulsion principle as "something that seems more primitive, more elementary, more instinctual than the pleasure principle which it over-rides" (18: 23).[8] Freud linked the repetition-compulsion principle to a metaphysical death instinct, "*an urge inherent in organic life to restore an earlier state of things* which the living entity has been obliged to abandon under the pressure of external disturbing forces" (36). Freud viewed the death instinct as inherent in life, outside of environmental, familial, or interactional influences—not unlike Jude's interpretation of Father Time's suicide as a defect in nature. Although most analysts have abandoned the death instinct as empirically unprovable, the repetition-compulsion principle has rich clinical implications, including the need to repeat traumatic experiences for the purpose of mastery. Repetitions may be creative or destructive, depending upon whether they result in working through or acting out conflicts. The compulsion to repeat may be seen in many actions; Robert Stoller suggests that perversion, for example, represents the reliving of sexual trauma in order to convert passive into active, pain into pleasure, defeat into victory: "But the need to do it again—unendingly, eternally again in the same manner—comes from one's inability to get completely rid of the danger, the trauma" (6). The implication of Freud's repetition-compulsion principle is that, to paraphrase the philosopher Santayana, those who do not remember the past are condemned to relive it, a theme that governs the world of *Jude the Obscure.*

Jude and Sue both act out the marital conflicts of their parents' broken marriages. Sue's family background is almost identical to Jude's, her first cousin. In endowing them with similar family backgrounds, Hardy intimates their unity of character. "They seem to be one person split in two!" Phillotson remarks (276), miffed at his failure to understand them.

To this extent they resemble Catherine and Heathcliff in *Wuthering Heights*, who also evoke incestuous love. The products of broken marriages, Jude and Sue have lost one or both parents at an early age, and are raised by indifferent caretakers. According to Arabella, Jude's father ill-used his wife in the same way that Jude's father's sister (Sue's mother) ill-used her husband. Both marriages are ill-fated. After Jude becomes involved with Arabella, his great-aunt, Drusilla Fawley, informs him that his parents never got along with each other, parting company when he was a baby. Jude's mother, continues Arabella, later committed suicide by drowning. Drusilla makes no effort to soften this terrible revelation to Jude or to understand its impact upon him. Drusilla's empathic failure repeats his mother's earlier rejection of him and foreshadows Sue's rejection of Father Time. After hearing the details of his mother's death, Jude attempts suicide in almost the identical way by walking out on a frozen pond. The cracking ice manages to sustain his weight, temporarily thwarting his wish for self-annihilation.

Hardy does not elaborate on the reasons for Jude's half-serious suicide attempt, but the painful repetition of the past cannot be ignored. As with most suicide attempts, including Father Time's, the motivation is complex and overdetermined. Jude's attempt to repeat his mother's suicide is unmistakable, recalling John Bowlby's observations about the relationship between maternal loss and children who later commit suicide. Jude's suicide attempt suggests a wish for reunion with the lost mother, a desire for revenge, a need to punish himself for harboring murderous feelings toward the dead person, and a feeling that life is not worth living. Both Jude and Father Time attempt or commit suicide following maternal loss; both are mirror images of each other, portraits of the same abandoned child. Jude internalizes his grief, preferring masochism to sadism. After his mother's death, Jude is raised by a father about whom he never speaks, not even after he has grown up and himself become a father. This is one of the many conspicuous instances in the novel concerning absent parents. After his father's death, Jude is taken in by his great-aunt, who makes it clear to him that he would have been better off dead, like his parents. "It would ha' been a blessing if Goddy-mighty had took thee too, wi' thy mother and father, poor useless boy!" (8–9).

Against a background of parental loss, Jude grows up to be a compassionate and idealistic man. Nothing in his family history accounts for his remarkable sensitivity, and for a time it seems as if he has escaped his past. His willingness to adopt Father Time demonstrates his generosity of spirit, and he remains devoted to his wife and children. Jude is a better parent to his newly discovered son than presumably his own parents were to him. Nevertheless, Jude is absent when Father Time most needs him, during the moments preceding the suicide. Although Jude's role in Father Time's death is more ambiguous than Sue's, he readily accepts the inevitability of his son's loss.

Sue's background reveals a similar pattern of parental loss. According to Drusilla, Sue's father offended his wife early in the marriage, and the latter "so disliked living with him afterwards that she went away to London with her little maid" (81). We never discover the length of time Sue lives with her mother in London or the circumstances of their life. Sue is then brought up by her father to hate her mother's family. Like Eustacia Vye in *The Return of the Native,* another motherless daughter raised by a remote male guardian, Sue grows up to reject conventional society. Yet her rebellion, like Eustacia's, is unsuccessful. It is scarcely possible to reconcile Sue's defiance as a twelve-year-old girl, boldly exhibiting her body as she wades into a pond, with her later inability to be touched by her husband. Sue's craving for conformity culminates in her sexual surrender to Phillotson. Notwithstanding the suicides of Father Time and Jude, Sue's remarriage is perhaps the most repellent action in the novel. She returns to her former husband to reestablish an unhealthy bond in which self-debasement is a necessary precondition for survival. *Jude the Obscure* reflects a closed system in which loveless marriages, restrictive social conventions, and unmerciful superegos thwart the possibility of a fulfilling life.

Sue's pattern of defiance followed by blind submission suggests, clinically, the child's ambivalence toward the parents: the rejection of the mother, the original love object, followed by the need to recover the lost unity of infancy. Sue and Jude return to the wrong marital partners, of course, and the attempt toward reparation is doomed. From an object relations point of view,[9] Sue and Jude's inner world is precarious and unstable. Each returns to a despised marital partner, suggesting the child's inability to separate from an ambivalent love object. Phillotson and Arabella represent the omnipotent parents who can never be successfully defied. They offer punishment, not love, to the returning child, humbled and broken. Sue's submission to Phillotson parallels Jude's submission to Arabella. Both Sue and Jude regress to infantile modes of behavior (one is creed-drunk, the other is gin-drunk) and obliterate themselves in a fatal union with hated love objects.

Object loss is a central theme in *Jude the Obscure,* and Freud's seminal essay, "Mourning and Melancholia" (1917), casts light on many of

the baffling psychological dynamics of Hardy's characters. Freud's definition of melancholia, which today is called depression, accurately
describes many of Sue's conflicts: "a profoundly painful dejection, cessa-
tion of interest in the outside world, loss of the capacity to love, inhibi-
tion of all activity, and a lowering of the self-regarding feelings to a
degree that finds utterance in self-reproaches and self-revilings, and
culminates in a delusional expectation of punishment" (14: 244). In depression, Freud continues, "dissatisfaction with the ego on moral
grounds is the most outstanding feature" (248), which is also true of
Sue's personality. Freud argues that the self-recriminations characteristic of depression are "reproaches against a loved object which have been
shifted away from it on to the patient's own ego" (248). Depression is
related to object loss in that the sadism directed initially against the object is converted to masochism. Mourning resembles depression, Freud
observes, in that the loss of an object deprives the individual of the love
necessary for growth and nurture. Unlike mourning, usually a temporary phenomenon, depression may last permanently, suggesting lifelong grief over lost objects. Freud viewed depression as arising from hostile feelings initially directed toward parents. These hostile feelings then
turn inward, producing feelings of guilt and unworthiness.[10]

Depression is widely regarded as one of the most common of psychiatric illnesses, and there is, predictably, sharp disagreement over its origin
and treatment. Since the publication of "Mourning and Melancholia,"
analysts have not hesitated to conceptualize distinctions between object-
related depression and narcissistic depression.[11] The sense of helpless-
ness and lowered self-esteem are common to both forms of depression;
but analysts conjecture that the depressive reactions originate from different sources. Object-related conflicts, which Freud had in mind, awak-
en virulent aggression toward the disappointing love object. Narcissistic
conflicts, by contrast, originate from keen disappointments in achieving
fantasized or idealized states. For object-related theorists like Otto Kernberg, depression represents the internalization of aggression originally
directed against the rejecting love object. The major conflicts in object-
related depression involve aggression—the fear of one's own destructive
rage and the fear of retaliation by the object. For theorists like Heinz
Kohut, on the other hand, depression represents the inability to merge
with the idealized object, which is experienced as a selfobject. The major
conflicts in narcissistic depression involve unrealistic or unobtainable
goals, such as the impossible pursuit of a perfect relationship.

Elements of both object-related depression and narcissistic depression appear in *Jude the Obscure*. The family backgrounds of Sue and Jude reflect a long history of parental neglect and abandonment. Both suffer object loss as children and parents. Their sadomasochistic relationship represents a defense against further object loss. That is, both the sadist and masochist "play out both sides of the pain-inducing/pain-suffering object relationship" (Avery 101). Masochism thus represents a bond to the early sadistic object. Contrary to the ending of the novel, in which Sue and Jude appear to go their own ways, remarried to former spouses, the cousins remain symbiotically bonded, like sadism and masochism, inextricably conjoined. Phillotson's remark that "They seem to be one person split in two!" contains more meaning than he realizes. The narcissistic element of their depression appears in their failure to merge with healthy, empathic selfobjects. Neither Jude nor Sue can sustain former ambitions, goals, ideals; both fall victim to virulent devaluation. Sue's movement from social rebellion to repressive conformity contrasts Jude's progress from unquestioning acceptance of life to embittered rejection.

Nowhere is Jude's shattered idealization more evident than in his desire to pursue a university education at Christminster. The novel opens with Phillotson telling Jude why a university degree is important. "It is the necessary hall-mark of a man who wants to do anything in teaching" (4). But Jude invests Christminster with mythical and mystical significance. Nothing less than his identity, self-esteem, and ambition are at stake in his devotion to university life. Jude transforms Christminster into a radiant city of light, a "heavenly Jerusalem" (18). Christminster, in short, is identified with the grandiose self. Additionally, Jude's infatuation with Christminster has erotic significance. "He was getting so romantically attached to Christminster that, like a young lover alluding to his mistress, he felt bashful at mentioning its name again" (22). Nor are we surprised that Jude's infatuation recalls the son's devotion to the mother. "Yes, Christminster shall be my Alma Mater; and I'll be her beloved son, in whom she shall be well pleased" (41). The eleven-year-old Jude associates the esteemed schoolteacher with the holy place, and he is understandably distressed by Phillotson's departure. Before leaving Jude, Phillotson invites him to Christminster, promising never to forget him. The promise is broken years later when Jude visits Phillotson and discovers that the teacher cannot remember him.

Jude's lofty idealization of Christminster becomes a deadly mirage, as elusive as Narcissus' reflection. Jude's idealization, we suspect, is defensive in nature, concealing his deep disappointment over parental abandonment. When he discovers the reality of university life, he is predictably dismayed by its hypocrisy, rigidity, and narrowmindedness. Jude suffers other setbacks: he is deceived by the quack Vilbert, who reneges on the promise to supply him with Greek and Latin grammars; disillusioned upon learning that Phillotson has given up his scheme to receive a university degree; and distressed upon receiving a letter from a Christminster professor advising him to renounce his intellectual aspirations. The reader strongly identifies with Jude's crushing rejection, and there is little doubt that he is right to feel outraged by the collapse of his hopes for a university education. And yet, given Jude's impossible idealization of Christminster, we sense that he would have been disillusioned by any university system.

Jude comes to perceive, with Hardy's approval, that "there is something wrong somewhere in our social formulas: what it is can only be discovered by men or women with greater insight than mine,—if, indeed, they ever discover it—at least in our time" (394). What Jude does not perceive, however, is the narcissistic meaning of his idealizing tendencies. As Kernberg and other analysts point out, defensive idealization conceals fundamentally ambivalent feelings toward the love object, feelings that arise in the early mother-child relationship. The repetitive and compulsive nature of idealization suggests the continual effort to deny the deep disappointment, aggression, and guilt associated with early object loss. Jude is eloquent in his social criticism and knowledge of literary and political history, but he is less convincing in his understanding of psychology. Wounded by early narcissistic injuries, Jude is rendered finally into a pining Echo, and his last words, *"Let the day perish wherein I was born"* (488), reflect the gloomy ending of his son.

We can now see more clearly the parallel between Father Time's infanticide and the defective nurturing Jude and Sue received as children. A shadowy bad parent haunts *Jude the Obscure*, linking three generations of Fawleys. Each generation executes a death sentence in the name of the parents. Sue interprets her children's deaths as a sign of divine punishment for her wickedness. "I see marriage differently now. My babies have been taken from me to show me this! Arabella's child killing mine was a judgment—the right slaying the wrong. What, *What* shall I do! I am such a vile creature—too worthless to mix with ordinary human beings!" (422–23). The reversal is astonishing. Sue now views Father Time, the murderer of her biological children, as morally good, while the two innocent children are evil, like herself. Sue seems close to psychotic here, lost in a terrible delusion. The violent self-hatred revealed in her speech to Phillotson conceals her infanticidal fantasies, now rationalized in the name of religious purification. "My children—are dead—and it is right that they should be! I am glad—almost. They were sin-begotten. They were sacrificed to teach me how to live!—their death was the first stage of my purification. That's why they have not died in vain! . . . You will take me back?" (439). By splitting the children into good and bad objects, Sue denies her ambivalence toward them, thus preserving her psychic life from massive extinction.

Jude and Sue fail to recognize the most terrifying insight of all, that their ambivalence has slain the children. Sue's key admission, that she is "glad—almost" of the children's deaths, intimates her unconscious wish for their deaths while they were still alive. This explains her complicity in Father Time's decision to annihilate the unwanted children of the world. The boy obediently carries out her wishes. Long before Sue brings children into the world, she has been relentlessly punishing herself for feelings of wickedness. The actual murders objectify her silent crimes. By colluding with Father Time's infanticidal fantasies, Sue reveals herself as the abandoning parent who must destroy the hated child within herself. But she is also the abandoned child who must now merge with the symbolic father. Although Jude, Sue, and Father Time refuse to name the bad parent, they create situations in which they punish themselves and the parental figures who have failed them. For the tragic protagonists of *Jude the Obscure*, the present repeats the nightmarish past. Hardy's symmetrical plot demonstrates that "What's done can't be undone" (70), suggesting a psychological determinism that cannot be overcome.

In short, *Jude the Obscure* portrays Nature as a deficient mother, the law as a repressive father, the two antagonists locked into a deadly, indissolvable marriage. "Radical disorder in the universe is finally matched by radical disorder in human personality," Heilman has remarked about the novel (10). Hardy's philosophical pessimism cannot be reduced to a single biographical determinant; yet the "General Principles" behind his artistic vision reflect the defective parenting, empathic failure, and object loss implicit in *Jude the Obscure*. In *The Life of Thomas Hardy*, ostensibly written by his second wife, Florence Emily Hardy, but largely ghost-written by the novelist himself, there is an important passage that evokes the spirit of the Fawleys:

General Principles. Law has produced in man a child who cannot but constantly reproach its parent for doing much and yet not all, and constantly say to such parent that it would have been better never to have begun doing than to have *over*done so indecisively; that is, than to have created so far beyond all apparent first intention (on the emotional side), without mending matters by a second intent and execution, to eliminate the evils of the blunder of overdoing. The emotions have no place in a world of defect, and it is a cruel injustice that they should have been developed in it. (149)[12]

Although it is unlikely that Hardy intended this passage either as a criticism of his own parents or as a commentary on *Jude the Obscure,* the novelist's world view reflects the philosophical pessimism in Father Time's farewell speech. It would be misleading, of course, to identify Hardy with a single fictional character, especially with a boy who ends his life before he has a chance to live it. Nevertheless, despite the narrator's claim of objectivity in *Jude the Obscure*—"The purpose of a chronicler of moods and deeds does not require him to express his personal views" (348)—he is deeply implicated in the characters' gloom and doom.[13] To give but one example, early in the novel the narrator asks why no one comes along to befriend the young Jude, already disillusioned by his hopeless struggle to master Greek and Latin. "But nobody did come, because nobody does; and under the crushing recognition of his gigantic error Jude continued to wish himself out of the world" (32). In *"I'd Have My Life Unbe"* (1984), Frank Giordano traces the striking pattern of self-destructive characters in Hardy's world, concluding that for the novelist, "the desire never to have been born was far more than a traditional poetic trope, while the wish to have his life 'unbe' seems to have recurred often and been very powerful at certain stages" (17).

We may now inquire into the biographical elements of Hardy's novel. Not surprisingly, Hardy insisted that "there is not a scrap of personal detail" in *Jude the Obscure* (*Life* 274, 392).[14] There is little in his biography to indicate overt object loss, certainly nothing like the early traumatic loss experienced by Jude and Sue. One fascinating detail emerges, however, about Hardy's entry into the world. When the infant was born, he was presumed dead and cast into a basket by the surgeon in order to attend the mother, herself in distress. "Dead! Stop a minute: he's alive enough, sure!" the midwife exclaimed (*Life* 14). The incident has a tragicomic quality entirely befitting Hardy's later vision of the world. As a child he was extremely delicate and sickly, often cared for by a neighbor. Hardy's biographers acknowledge his inauspicious beginning in life, suggesting a possible link between his early deprivation and lifelong bouts of depression. Robert Gittings speaks about an "early thread of perverse morbidity in Hardy, something near abnormality" (35), while Michael Millgate observes that Hardy's parents took little interest in him because they believed he would die in childhood (16). James W. Hamilton, a psychoanalyst, has suggested that the "actual circumstances of his birth burdened Hardy with profound guilt for having damaged and almost killed his mother," as revealed in his first poem, "Discouragement." Hamilton plausibly speculates that Tess's ambivalence toward her infant son, aptly named Sorrow (corresponding, perhaps, to the allegorical Father Time in *Jude the Obscure*), may well reflect Jemima Hardy's feelings toward her own child. "When the infant had taken its fill," Hardy writes in *Tess of the D'Urbervilles*, "the young mother sat it upright in her lap, and looking into the far distance dandled it with a gloomy indifference that was almost dislike; then all of a sudden she fell to violently kissing it some dozens of times, as if she could never leave off, the child crying at the vehemence of an onset which strangely combined passionateness with contempt" (76). Sorrow's death, like Father Time's, implicates both nature and nurture: "So passed away Sorrow the Undesired—that intrusive creature, that bastard gift of shameless Nature who respects not the social law" (*Tess* 81).

Hardy's acknowledgment that the fictional portrait of Mrs. Yeobright in *The Return of the Native* was closely based upon his own mother is also revealing. Closely resembling Mrs. Morel in Lawrence's *Sons and Lovers*, Mrs. Yeobright is an intimidating woman who alternates between moods of gentleness and anger. Like Paul Morel, Clym Yeobright is implicated in his mother's death. Michael Millgate points out in his biography that while Jemima Hardy always commanded the unquestioning devotion of her children, she could be "cold in her manner, intolerant in her views, and tyrannical in her governance" (21).

To what extent did Hardy suffer narcissistic injuries as a consequence of erratic maternal care? Giordano notes that Hardy was plagued by feelings of low self-esteem, referring to himself on his forty-seventh birthday as "Thomas the Unworthy" (*Life* 200). Although we do not usually think of Hardy as a mother-fixated novelist, as we do of D. H. Lawrence, Gittings points out that he repeatedly fell in love with women (in particular, with several maternal cousins) who reminded him of his mother. "More than most mother-fixed youths, Hardy was falling in love with his own mother over and over again, in a physical and consistent way that was a typical part of his almost literal-minded nature" (64). Hardy's attraction to his cousin, Tryphena Sparks, one of the chief sources of Sue Bridehead, has generated intense biographical interest and speculation.[15] Whatever actually happened between Hardy and his mysterious cousin, Jude and Sue reflect the novelist's fascination with not only incestuous love, but elusive, shadowy, and doomed love. Hardy's tragic heroes and heroines find themselves in Narcissus' situation, pursuing the unobtainable. Like Narcissus, they discover the bitter-sweet quality of infatuation, ending their lives defeated and broken, unable to recover lost primal unity.

Hardy's little-known novel, *The Well-Beloved* (1897), powerfully confirms the narcissistic infatuation to which his characters are particularly vulnerable. Subtitled "A Sketch of a Temperament," *The Well-Beloved* was written at about the same time Hardy was working on *Jude the Obscure*. Both novels explore spectral love. Critics generally agree that *The Well-Beloved* is perhaps Hardy's most autobiographical novel in its revelations into his unhappy love life. Jocelyn Pierston is a sculptor, not a writer, but like Hardy he is both blessed and cursed by a seemingly endless series of blinding infatuations that inevitably lead to bitter disillusionment. Pierston tires of his lovers as soon as he knows them well, and only one aspect of his life remains constant: the instability of his love. Unusually introspective, Pierston meticulously analyzes his infatuations, lamenting the havoc they wreak upon his life: "To see the creature who has hitherto been perfect, divine, lose under your very gaze the divinity which has informed her, grow commonplace, turn from flame to ashes, from a radiant vitality to a relic, is anything but a pleasure for any man, and has been nothing less than a racking spectacle to my sight. Each mournful emptied shape stands ever after like the nest of some beautiful bird from which the inhabitant has departed and left it to fill with snow" (38).

Pierston's pursuit of the Beloved One, as he calls his elusive love object, is clearly defensive idealization, concealing hostility toward women. "Each shape, or embodiment, has been a temporary residence only, which she has entered, lived in awhile, and made her exit from, leaving the substance, so far as I have been concerned, a corpse, worse luck!" (33). Like Narcissus, Pierston realizes that he is doomed to pursue phantoms who vanish upon close approach. Poetic justice catches up with him, and he finds himself infatuated hopelessly with a young woman (the daughter of the woman he rejected earlier) who, driven by the same psychology, tantalizes and finally spurns him. Pierston is in love with the idea of love, as Sue Bridehead is. Indeed, Sue's revealing admission, that sometimes her love of being loved gets the better of her conscience, causing her to treat a man cruelly, applies equally well to Pierston. Both Sue and Pierston fail in their reparative efforts to undo the harm they have caused others. Pierston does not undertake Sue's humiliating religious penances, but he does desire to make reparation to Avice Caro by attempting to marry her daughter and, when that fails, her granddaughter, both copies of the original love object.

In an illuminating article on *The Well-Beloved* that reveals as much about the creative source of his own fiction as it does about Hardy's, John Fowles has identified the real object of Pierston's hopeless quest. "The vanished young mother of infancy is quite as elusive as the Well-Beloved—indeed, she *is* the Well-Beloved, although the adult writer transmogrifies her according to the pleasures and fancies that have in the older man superseded the nameless ones of the child—most commonly into a young female sexual ideal of some kind, to be attained or pursued (or denied) by himself hiding behind some male character" ("Hardy" 33).[16] Intrigued by an interpretation of *The French Lieutenant's Woman* published by a Yale psychoanalyst, Gilbert Rose, Fowles posits in Hardy and other novelists an unconscious drive toward the unobtainable. Fowles accepts Rose's thesis that the wish to reestablish unity with the lost mother of infancy is an important motive behind the creative impulse.[17] Behind Tryphena Sparks and the other incarnations of the Well-Beloved, including Sue Bridehead and Tess, both of whom Fowles calls in *The French Lieutenant's Woman* "pure Tryphena in spirit" (216), lies the pre-Oedipal mother, the muse behind all creativity.

And yet the maternal muse was profoundly paradoxical for Hardy, the source of both creativity and destruction. *Jude the Obscure* remains his bleakest novel, arguably the bleakest in English literature. Of all Hardy's great tragic novels, *Jude the Obscure* alone lacks convincing affirmation. Despite Hardy's sympathy toward Jude and Sue, he casts them out to an indifferent world and then shows, in a novel at once beautiful and terrible, the tragedy of their self-extinction. "[H]ow cruel you are," Swinburne wrote to Hardy in an otherwise glowing review which the novelist cited in his biography, "Only the great and awful father of 'Pierrette' and 'L'Enfant Maudit' was ever so merciless to his children" (*Life* 270). Speaking like a disillusioned parent renouncing further children, Hardy observes in the "Postscript to the Preface" to *Jude the Obscure* that the experience of writing the book completely cured him of the wish to write additional novels. The novel provoked so much hostility, in fact, that he later referred to a book-burning incident in which the real object of the flames was the novelist himself. It may seem extravagant to compare Father Time's infanticide to Hardy's decision to create no more novels. The fact remains, however, that although Hardy published a voluminous amount of poetry in the remaining thirty-three years of his life, he repudiated the art of fiction, perhaps believing, like Father Time, that the world would be better off without him. In that decision lies the greatest loss of all.

Notes

1. One of the earliest comments on the double murder and suicide appears in Mrs. Oliphant's review of *Jude the Obscure* in 1896, when she sarcastically asks: "Does Mr. Hardy think this is really a good way of disposing of the unfortunate progeny of such connections? does he recommend it for general adoption?" See Page, *Jude the Obscure* 385. Quite apart from her outraged Victorian sensibility, Mrs. Oliphant raises an important question that more astute modern readers have ignored. "Mr. Hardy knows, no doubt as everybody does, that the children are a most serious part of the question of the abolition of marriage. Is this the way in which he considers it would be resolved best?" J. I. M. Stewart expresses the point more fairly in *Thomas Hardy: A Critical Biography:* "Little Father Time scarcely murders his siblings in the closet more effectively than his creator murders him with deadly prose" (189).

2. A complete bibliography of the criticism of *Jude the Obscure* is too long to cite here, but the psychologically oriented reader should consult the following books: J. Hillis Miller, *Thomas Hardy: Distance and Desire;* Perry Meisel, *Thomas Hardy: The Return of the Repressed;* Geoffrey Thurley, *The Psychology of Hardy's Novels: The Nervous and the Statuesque;* and Rosemary Sumner, *Thomas Hardy: Psychological Novelist.* The following articles are also of interest: Norman Holland, *"Jude the Obscure:* Hardy's Symbolic Indictment of Christianity"; Michael Steig, "Sue Bridehead"; George Trail, "The Consistency of Hardy's Sue"; and Carol and Duane Edwards, *"Jude the Obscure:* A Psycho-Analytic Study."

3. For additional feminist interpretations of *Jude the Obscure,* see Kate Millett, *Sexual Politics* and Penny Boumelha, *Thomas Hardy and Women.*

4. "Would it have been a lie," Robert Langbaum asks, "to tell the boy she loved him and to have withheld the information about the new baby? For all her beauty, intelligence and idealism, Sue emerges as a charming monster because she lacks instincts" (30).

5. Heinz Kohut's two major works are *The Analysis of the Self* and *The Restoration of the Self.* Despite his unwieldly definition of the mirror transference, Kohut has in mind the power of love:

The mirror transference is the therapeutic reinstatement of that normal phase of the development of the grandiose self in which the gleam in the mother's eye, which mirrors the child's exhibitionistic display, and other forms of maternal participation in and response to the child's narcissistic-exhibitionistic enjoyment confirm the child's self-esteem and, by a gradually increasing selectivity of these responses, begin to channel it into realistic direction. (*Analysis* 116)

Unlike orthodox Freudians, Kohut maintains that the proper analytic stance should not be strict detachment but introspective empathy.

6. As Freud shifted his attention away from the biological id to the defensive measures against forbidden drives, he began to investigate the ways in which the ego, now seen as a separate psychic structure, wards off intrapsychic anxiety. The two classic books are Freud's *The Ego and the Id* (1923), where he postulates the ego as a mediating agency between id and superego, and Anna Freud's *The Ego and the Mechanisms of Defense* (1936), an analysis of the role of defense mechanisms in the maintenance of health or illness. All references hereafter to Freud are to the *Standard Edition*.

7. See William R. Goetz, "The Felicity and Infelicity of Marriage in *Jude the Obscure*" (189–213).

8. See also J. Hillis Miller, "The Compulsion to Stop Repeating," in *Fiction and Repetition*.

9. According to object relations theory, internalized objects are created from the child's introjection of parental figures. These internalized objects may or may not correspond closely to external reality. They form a complex inner world of fantasy, shaping the individual's responses to the outer world. Good and bad objects in adult life relate to the earliest objects in childhood; a loss in later life reawakens the anxiety of losing the primary object. Hanna Segal's book, *Introduction to the Work of Melanie Klein*, provides a lucid introduction to object relations theory.

10. In two other important essays, " 'A Child Is Being Beaten': A Contribution to the Study of the Origin of Sexual Perversions" (1919) and "The Economic Problem of Masochism" (1924), Freud explores the relationship between masochism and Oedipal drives. He argues that the fantasy of being beaten, which may originate from the incestuous attachment to the father, allows the child to fulfill contradictory aims: to gratify the need for love and to punish himself for forbidden urges. Although Freud emphasized Oedipal over pre-Oedipal issues, contemporary analysts place greater stress on the primacy of the mother-child bond formed during the first year or two of life. The research of Margaret Mahler and others on the process of separation and individuation emphasizes the role of early object loss in the formation of mental illness. See Margaret Mahler, Fred Pine, and Anni Bergman, *The Psychological Birth of the Human Infant*.

11. See Michael W. Glazer, "Object-Related Vs. Narcissistic Depression: A Theoretical and Clinical Study" (323–37). The following distinctions between these two forms of depression come from Glazer's essay.

12. All references are to this edition, which combines *The Early Life of Thomas Hardy: 1840–1928* and *The Later Years of Thomas Hardy: 1892–1928*. Compare Hardy's "General Principles" to Jude's condemnation of nature: "And then he again uneasily saw, as he had latterly seen with more and more frequency, the scorn of Nature for man's finer emotions, and her lack of interest in his aspirations" (*Jude* 212).

13. For an opposing interpretation, see Dale Kramer, *Thomas Hardy: The Forms of Tragedy*.

14. For a discussion of the autobiographical elements in *Jude*, see F. B. Pinion, "*Jude the Obscure*: Origins in Life and Literature" (148–64).

15. See Lois Deacon, *Providence and Mr. Hardy*. For an incisive critique of Deacon's belief that Hardy actually had an affair with Tryphena Sparks, see Gittings (223–29).

16. For a discussion of Hardy's influence on Fowles, see Peter J. Casagrande, *Hardy's Influence on the Modern Novel*.

17. See Gilbert Rose, *"The French Lieutenant's Woman:* The Unconscious Significance of a Novel to its Author." For a psychoanalytic interpretation of *The Well-Beloved,* see David S. Werman and Theodore J. Jacobs, "Thomas Hardy's *'The Well-Beloved'* and the Nature of Infatuation."

Works Cited

Avery, Nicholas C. "Sadomasochism: A Defense Against Object Loss." *The Psychoanalytic Review* 64 (1977): 101–08.

Boumelha, Penny. *Thomas Hardy and Women.* Madison: U of Wisconsin P, 1972.

Bowlby, John. *Loss.* Vol. 3 of *Attachment and Loss.* New York: Basic Books, 1980.

Casagrande, Peter J. *Hardy's Influence on the Modern Novel.* London: Macmillan, 1987.

Deacon, Lois. *Providence and Mr. Hardy.* London: Hutchinson, 1966.

Edwards, Carol and Duane. *"Jude the Obscure:* A Psychoanalytic Study." *University of Hartford Studies in Literature* 13 (1981): 78–90.

Fowles, John. *The French Lieutenant's Woman.* 1969. New York: Signet, 1970.
———. "Hardy and the Hag." *Thomas Hardy After Fifty Years.* Ed. Lance St. John Butler. Totowa, N.J.: Rowman & Littlefield, 1977. 28–42.

Freud, Anna. *The Ego and the Mechanisms of Defense.* 1936. Rev. ed. New York: International UP, 1977.

Freud, Sigmund. *The Standard Edition of the Complete Psychological Works of Sigmund Freud.* 24 vols. Ed. and trans. James Strachey. London: Hogarth, 1953–74.

Giordano, Frank R. *"I'd Have My Life Unbe."* University: U of Alabama P, 1984.

Gittings, Robert. *Young Thomas Hardy.* Boston: Little, Brown, 1975.

Glazer, Michael Warren. "Object-Related Vs. Narcissistic Depression: A Theoretical and Clinical Study." *The Psychoanalytic Review* 66 (1979): 323–37.

Goetz, William R. "The Felicity and Infelicity of Marriage in *Jude the Obscure." Nineteenth-Century Fiction* 38 (1983): 189–213.

Gregor, Ian. *The Great Web: The Form of Hardy's Major Fiction.* Totowa, N.J.: Rowman & Littlefield, 1974.

Guerard, Albert J. *Thomas Hardy: The Novels and Stories.* Cambridge: Harvard UP, 1949.

Hamilton, James W. "The Effect of Early Trauma Upon Thomas Hardy's Literary Career." A Paper Presented Before the Wisconsin Psychoanalytic Study Group. Madison, Wis., April 1982.

Hardy, Florence. *The Life of Thomas Hardy: 1840–1928.* London: Macmillan, 1962.

Hardy, Thomas. *Jude the Obscure.* 1895. London: Macmillan, 1971.

———. *Tess of the D'Urbervilles.* 1891. New York: Norton Critical Edition, 1965.

———. *The Well-Beloved.* 1897. London: Macmillan, 1960.

Heilman, Robert B. Introduction. *Jude the Obscure.* By Thomas Hardy. New York: Harper & Row, 1966.

Holland, Norman N. "*Jude the Obscure:* Hardy's Symbolic Indictment of Christianity." *Nineteenth-Century Fiction* 9 (1954): 50-60.

Howe, Irving. *Thomas Hardy.* New York: Macmillan, 1967.

Jacobus, Mary. "Sue the Obscure." *Essays in Criticism* 25 (1975): 304-28.

Kohut, Heinz. *The Analysis of the Self.* New York: International UP, 1971.

———. *The Restoration of the Self.* New York: International UP, 1977.

Kramer, Dale. *Thomas Hardy: The Forms of Tragedy.* Detroit: Wayne State UP, 1975.

Langbaum, Robert. "Hardy and Lawrence." *Thomas Hardy Annual No. 3.* Ed. Norman Page. London: Macmillan, 1985.

Mahler, Margaret, Fred Pine and Anni Bergman. *The Psychological Birth of the Human Infant: Symbiosis and Individuation.* New York: Basic Books, 1975.

Meisel, Perry. *Thomas Hardy: The Return of the Repressed.* New Haven: Yale UP, 1972.

Miller, Alice. *Prisoners of Childhood.* Trans. Ruth Ward. New York: Basic Books, 1981.

Miller, J. Hillis. "The Compulsion to Stop Repeating." *Fiction and Repetition.* Cambridge: Harvard UP, 1982.

———. *Thomas Hardy: Distance and Desire.* Cambridge: Harvard UP, 1970.

Millett, Kate. *Sexual Politics.* 1970. New York: Ballantine, 1978.

Millgate, Michael. *Thomas Hardy.* New York: Random House, 1982.

Olinick, Stanley L., and Laura Tracy. "Transference Perspectives of Story Telling." *The Psychoanalytic Review* 74 (1987): 319-31.

Page, Norman, ed. *Jude the Obscure: An Authoritative Text, Background and Sources, Criticism.* New York: Norton, 1978.

Pinion, F. B. "*Jude the Obscure:* Origins in Life and Literature." *Thomas Hardy Annual No. 4.* Ed. Norman Page. London: Macmillan, 1986. 148-64.

Rose, Gilbert J. "*The French Lieutenant's Woman:* The Unconscious Significance of a Novel to Its Author." *American Imago* 29 (1972): 165-76.

Segal, Hanna. *Introduction to the Work of Melanie Klein.* 1964. New York: Basic Books, 1974.

Steig, Michael. "Sue Bridehead." *Novel* 1 (1968): 260-66.

Stewart, J. I. M. *Thomas Hardy: A Critical Biography.* London: Longman, 1971.

Stoller, Robert J. *Perversion.* New York: Dell, 1975.

Sumner, Rosemary. *Thomas Hardy: Psychological Novelist.* New York: St. Martin's P, 1981.

Thurley, Geoffrey. *The Psychology of Hardy's Novels: The Nervous and the Statuesque.* Queensland: U of Queensland P, 1975.

Trail, George Y. "The Consistency of Hardy's Sue: Bridehead Becomes Electra." *Literature and Psychology* 26 (1976): 61–68.

Werman, David S. and Theodore J. Jacobs. "Thomas Hardy's '*The Well-Beloved*' and the Nature of Infatuation." *International Review of Psycho-Analysis* 10 (1983): 447–57.

Rape, Writing, Hyperbole:
Shakespeare's *Lucrece*

David Willbern

In her paper on Lacan and Joyce in this collection, Ellie Ragland-Sullivan quotes Lacan's claim that "Joyce *is* his language," and that *Finnegans Wake* demonstrates all of language—in its plenitude and in its "fading out" of meaning. To balance the hyperbole, let us allow the claim. Let Joyce and Lacan be the morticians of meaning, presiding over its referential dislocations, celebrating its demise, writing its wake. For me, *Shakespeare* is language. That is, Shakespeare celebrates the genesis of modern poetic possibility in English: the birth of a Renaissance vernacular from the corpse of the classics.

But enough of my hyperbole. I want to discuss Shakespeare's, especially in his narrative poem, *Lucrece*. For those whose familiarity with this text has faded, I will briefly rehearse its narrative. One evening, at the siege of Ardea, the Romans hold an after-dinner discussion of wifely virtue. After all the husbands have praised their wives, they secretly return to Rome to spy on the women. All are discovered "dancing and revelling, or in several disports" (as Shakespeare puts it), except for Lucrece who is found chastely spinning. With Lucrece's husband, Collatine, the victor in this contest, the noblemen return to their tents. Prince Tarquin, however, is so aroused by Lucrece's beauty and probity that he returns to Rome later that night, where he is politely received by Lucrece. After he retires to his room, and after much internal debate, he creeps into Lucrece's chamber. Failing to seduce her by argument or compel her by threat, he overpowers and rapes her. He quickly departs, leaving Lucrece in vigorous lamentation. She blames Tarquin, then night, opportunity, and time; she studies a large depiction of the Sack of Troy hanging in the house; she then writes a brief note to Collatine, who quickly returns, accompanied by Lucrece's father and other Romans. Dressed in mourning, Lucrece makes them swear revenge, confesses her violation, and stabs herself. The men carry Lucrece's corpse through the streets, after which the Roman people rise up against the Tarquins, exile them, and institute government by consul.

As a dramatic poem, *Lucrece* enacts an elementary psychology: the sudden emergence of obsessive fantasy, its progression into action, and the consequences of action. In typical Shakespearean fashion (which is to say with astonishing wit and profundity) it explores primary issues of imaginative conception and linguistic creation, while simultaneously relating a classic story of violation and revenge. Constructed midway between poem and drama, its collocation within both genres makes it easier to "de-characterize," or to erase the superficial convention of dramatis personae and to treat "characters" who enact a paradramatic scene as linguistic representations of intellectual and emotional states: a dramatic narrative of self-division or fragmented self-representation. Such an interpretive perspective derives, of course, from much earlier conventions, such as medieval allegory, psychomachia, and contemporary Renaissance practice of extended allegory.[1]

I intend to treat the characters of Shakespeare's *Lucrece* as intrapsychic constructs and to describe the circulations of desire through the poem as independent of and prior to those nominal agents that momentarily represent them. Collapsing the poem's fictional agents into a circulating flux of desire displaces critical emphasis from character to event, and the event becomes not a narrative of rape, but a *fantasy of violation:* of ideals imagined and debased, wounds inflicted and suffered, taboos broken, thresholds crossed. Such an interpretation considers the poem as an intrapsychic debate, or a before-and-after design of a powerful desire followed from impulse to drive to fulfillment to reaction. "Tarquin" and "Lucrece" thus become reciprocal and inseparable aspects of the same trajectory of lust and guilt: they trace a hyperbolic curve, a rise and fall, of desire itself. (Although I shall maintain the convention of referring to "Tarquin" and "Lucrece" as dramatic characters, the names always carry invisible quotation marks.)

The illustration of this hyperbolic desire is the *hyperbola.* The ascending curve is occupied by "Tarquin," while "Lucrece" occupies the descending curve: the mirrored rise and fall of desire.

That the action of *Lucrece* occurs simultaneously on external and in-

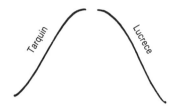

ternal planes is clear from the beginning, when Collatine's urge to idealize spurs Tarquin's lust to debase, and is reinforced by the language of
the poem, as when Lucrece's house retires, "every one to rest themselves . . . , / Save thieves and cares and troubled minds that wake"
(ll. 125-26). External agents (thieves) parallel internal events (cares and
troubled minds)—"As one of which doth Tarquin lie revolving" (127).
Tarquin here exists coequally as both (outer) agent and (inner) impulse.
A similar moment extends into allegory, when "pure thoughts are dead
and still, / While lust and murder wakes to stain and kill" (167-68). The
description reciprocally portrays both Lucrece and Tarquin, partially
allegorized into sleeping Purity and wakeful Lust, while it reflects the
psychology of dreaming and the release of repressed impulses.[2]

   A durable tradition of medieval psychomachia underlies Shakespeare's quasi-allegorical dynamic of passion, as when Tarquin is
"madly toss'd between desire and dread" (171), or when he is momentarily disabled by "disputation / 'Tween frozen conscience and hot burning
will" (246-47). Here the tradition of psychomachia blends with conventional Petrarchan conceits, vividly hyperbolized by Shakespeare. Yet
Shakespeare always does more than merely employ conventions: he explores them and ultimately exhausts them.

>Within his thought her heavenly image sits,
>And in the self-same seat sits Collatine.
>That eye which looks on her confounds his wits;
>That eye which him beholds, as more divine,
>Unto a view so false will not incline,
>   But with a pure appeal seeks to the heart,
>   Which once corrupted takes the worser part;
>
>And therein heartens up his servile powers,
>Who flatt'red by their leader's jocund show,
>Stuff up his lust, as minutes fill up hours;

> And as their captain, so their pride doth grow,
> Paying more slavish tribute than they owe.
> By reprobate desire thus madly led,
> The Roman lord marcheth to Lucrece' bed.
>
> (288–301)

The passage from idealization to violation is abrupt and linear, emerging from a con-fusion of self and other, Lucrece and Collatine, thought and object. Preceding his outward action, Tarquin looks within, where he discovers a version of Collatine's "sky of his delight" (12): the idealized Lucrece. She is already occupied, however, by Collatine. This highly sublimated primal scene seeks denial in "a pure appeal," but base eroticism is already released and quickly transforms mental images into physical arousal, as Tarquin's lust is "stuffed up" with blood in growing "pride."[3] Quick shifts from imagination to arousal to motion sketch the genesis of a basic drive that propels Tarquin along his linear course: "The locks between her chamber and his will, / Each one by him enforc'd" (302–03). Here is the rape played out in symbols both Shakespearean and Freudian; the device continues with the sexual tropes of glove and needle (316–22).

Shakespeare continues to play with standard poetic convention when he enlists Tarquin in the army of passions: "*Affection* is my captain, and he leadeth" (271; emphasis added). His march to Lucrece's chamber begins with the illusion of orderly direction, but soon the metaphor of martial leadership collapses into the bestial rush of compulsion: "But nothing can affection's course control, / Or stop the headlong fury of his speed" (500–501). No longer following an impulse, Tarquin is now impelled, driven. Like Macbeth, he is carried by his own intent (*Macbeth* 1.7.26); like Othello, he is swept up in the compulsive current of his rash desire (*Othello* 3.3.460–67). The model of "Affection" shifts from allegorical persona to psychological drive. Shakespeare later echoes this sense of affection in Leontes's violent and obscure ravings in *The Winter's Tale:*

> Affection! thy intention stabs the centre.
> Thou dost make possible things not so held,
> Communicat'st with dreams, (how can this be?), . . .
>
> (1.2.138ff)

At the source of Tarquin's affection, or the erotic compulsion culminating in the rape of Lucrece (the object of his affection), lies the idealization of her boastful husband, Collatine. Sublimely constellating Lucrece in the "sky of his delight," he "unlock'd the treasure of his happy state" in Tarquin's tent (12–15). As the narrator questions, " . . . why is Collatine the publisher / Of that rich jewel he should keep unknown / From thievish ears because it is his own?" (33–36). An answer to this question is that the impulse to idealistic display derives precisely from the pleasure of possession: as the proud owner of such a gem, Collatine cannot hide its virtue under a bushel. The contamination of virtue by possession is the first "rape of Lucrece," as she is seized (*rapire*, to seize) by Collatine's imagination and displayed for the admiration of others. His fantasy of ownership leads to the verbal exhibition that fires Tarquin's lust. Recently, feminist readers have focused on this point, calling Collatine's boasting "an act of excess that is a rhetorical analogue to Tarquin's sexual will" (Stimpson 58). "Rape," concludes Nancy Vickers, "is the price Lucrece pays for having been described" (Vickers 102). Collatine's boasting amid his comrades is an imaginative sharing of his wealth while arousing jealousy and envy. In effect, he offers his ideal possession to the potentially lewd admiration of his companions.

The point deserves stressing, because it enables us to take as a structural principle the narrator's opinion that Tarquin acts, literally, at Collatine's *suggestion*: "Perchance his boast of Lucrece' sov'reignty / Suggested this proud issue of a king" (36–37). In Shakespeare's Renaissance vocabulary the transitive verb, *suggest*, carried a stronger sense than it has today: it meant "urge," "prompt," "motivate," often to questionable acts (see Sonnet 144). From this perspective, the poem has a structure similar to *Measure for Measure*, where a presumably virtuous agent (the Duke) employs a lust-ridden substitute (Angelo) as a tool to debase an idealized woman (Isabella). Tarquin represents the displaced enactment of an unconscious *wish*, or "suggestion," proceeding from Collatine. The poem gestures toward this signification when Tarquin worries, "If Collatine dream of my intent . . . " (218–20). The rape enacts the trauma of debasement that shadows the dream of idealization. It is an axiom of psychoanalysis that idealization requires denial or repression, and that what is repressed will return, usually in another form. As the narrator of *Lucrece* asserts: "But no perfection is so absolute, / That some impurity doth not pollute" (853–54). The maxim carries both internal and external senses. It cautions that impurity endangers perfection from without, as the narrator warns: "What virtue breeds iniquity

devours" (872). And it implies that impurity already resides within perfection; that no ideal is unalloyed. Here is the ambivalent psychology of
idealization. It is just such a thought—that some impurity pollutes his
divine Desdemona—that maddens Othello and drives him to a murder
that is also a symbolic rape.

Within the intrapsychic circulations of unconscious desire configured
by the nominal agents of *Lucrece,* every external misdeed is an internal
trespass, and every violation is a self-violation. As soon as he "yields to
[Collatine's] suggestion," Tarquin finds his "single state of man" divided, so that "himself himself he must forsake" (*Macbeth* 1.3.134, 142;
Lucrece 156–60). He "pawn[s] his honour to obtain his lust," and at the
moment he commits the rape, "his soul's fair temple is defaced," becoming a "spotted princess" (719–23). These terms precisely prefigure Lucrece's response to her rape, when "her sacred temple [is] spotted,
spoil'd, corrupted" (1172). As Tarquin rapes Lucrece, he also rapes himself.[4] Beyond her typology of wifely virtue, Lucrece represents an *internal* figure, an icon of classical purity and integrity, a female imago of the
Christian soul. Psychoanalytically, she represents an internalized image
of maternal purity, whose vehement consecration to virtue is motivated
by the pressures of Oedipal desire. What *Lucrece* demonstrates is the
frailty and failure of the repression of such desires.

Tarquin's rape of Lucrece represents his self-violation on several levels. Reciprocally, Lucrece's responses to the rape demonstrate analogous
self-divisions, as she debates suicide and implicitly imagines the act as
self-rape: "To kill myself . . . alack what were it, / But with my body
my poor soul's pollution?" (1156–57). When she finally does kill herself,
her act formally reenacts the rape (and not merely through the sexual
symbolism of the dagger).[5] As she stabs herself, Lucrece exclaims, "He,
he, fair lords, 'tis he, / That guides this hand to give this wound to me"
(1721–22). Lucrece's climactic posture culminates in an exact identification with her rapist, in a poetic implication of the binary consanguinity
of victim and aggressor. The implicit coaction is a symbolic coitus that
leads to an actual and figurative commingling of bloods, as Lucrece's
blood, "bubbling from her breast," divides into two streams and encir-
cles her body like an island (1737–43).[6] Some blood is red (Lucrece's pure
blood) and some is black (defiled by Tarquin), but the two, red and
black, are not in separate streams (as some critics mistakenly read). The
emblem is not simply of division but also of confluence, not simply
opposition but also identity. "Lucrece," in the last half of the poem,

includes and encloses "Tarquin," who has vanished from the narrative. In terms of our geometric mnemonic, Lucrece takes over where Tarquin leaves off: her agency subsumes her shame and his guilt.

The inclusion of "Tarquin" by "Lucrece" effects changes in Lucrece after the climactic event. In a sense, rape opens her eyes. The poem initially presents an idealized, virtually virginal Lucrece who can neither discern nor imagine any duplicity in her sudden guest: she is an innocent reader, unable to gloss the "subtle shining secrecies" of Tarquin's false book (99–105). After the rape, her language reveals carnal contamination, as when she images Night as a demonic and bawdy ravisher who smothers the sun in poisonous mists "ere he arrive his weary noontide prick" (764–84), yet wishes that night would never end, in an ironic performance of the traditional lover's wish. After the rape, her eyes are opened to the ways of the world: she can now read signs of deceit in the Troy painting whose visages she scans—especially Sinon, the traitor who convinced the Trojans to admit the wooden horse. Her new knowledge positions her in an unfamiliar postsexual context: suffused by the complex of arousal and guilt, she becomes momentarily caught in a thick interchange of looks, thoughts, and blushes in her encounter with the "sour-fac'd groom" who provides contact with her husband: that is, the first agent to whom she entrusts her "confession." She urges him to hurry, and he obeys. Yet during their brief encounter she imagines that he perceives her guilt, and he, though ignorant of her stain, responds to her embarrassment with a blush, which she augments by reciprocation:

> His kindled duty kindled her mistrust,
> That two red fires in both their faces blazed;
> She thought he blush'd, as knowing Tarquin's lust,
> And blushing with him, wistly on him gazed;
> Her earnest eye did make him more amazed.
>   The more she saw the blood his cheeks replenish,
>   The more she thought he spied in her some blemish.
>   (1352–58)

Contrasted with her innocent inability to read Tarquin's libidinous look, this postsexual gaze combines guilt, self-suspicion, and projection. Violently, she is transported into a new register of erotic imagination: now possessed by *knowledge,* where before she was "unknown" (34). This brutal fracture of her conventionally virtuous relationship to

Collatine creates a sudden and poignant estrangement when they meet, at Lucrece's mysterious summons:

> He hath no power to ask her how she fares;
>   Both stood like old acquaintance in a trance,
>   Met far from home, wond'ring each other's chance.
> (1594-96)

The power of this alienation derives unconsciously from the sudden awareness of the other's sexual knowledge, the wish/fear that she *knows* and is *known*, the ambivalent recognition of Oedipal history.

> Being so caught up,
> So mastered by the brute blood of the air,
> Did she put on his knowledge with his power
> Before the indifferent beak could let her drop?
> (Yeats, "Leda and the Swan" 11-14)

The example of Yeats's modern revision of another classic rape resituates the event in terms of a Freudian epistemological trauma. For one way to describe the Oedipus complex is to say that "knowing" the mother sexually means to know that she has a sexual history, to recognize her as erotically experienced and available—to others and therefore potentially to oneself. Such a discovery or admission thus carries the awareness of rivalry (the knowledge of prior possession). When this recognition is coupled to fantasies of the primal scene, the sudden awareness of maternal sexuality becomes a kind of erotic epistemological assault—a rape. Or, we might say that shifting the image of the mother from a position of idealized and solitary possession to a position of debased and shared rivalry (with the father, with other men), can be felt as a violent disruption. Violently participating in this transition from what Lacan called the "Imaginary Register" to what he called the "Symbolic," the child in fantasy can simultaneously act out and enjoy sexual participation, while punishing this newly conceived image of the mother through assault and death—which can then also be avenged by rebelling against and casting out the father.

The dynamic of this postsexual knowledge is vividly portrayed in Lucrece's studied reading of the Troy painting. The rhetorical energies of this set piece simultaneously dilate outward from the formal debates of Tarquin and Lucrece into the large-scale scene of the Rape of Helen and the Sack of Troy, while they contract and distance events into the (apparently) static realm of pictorial representation. Whereas before Lucrece could read nothing beyond the bland civilities of Tarquin, now she perceives affect and motive in the pictured faces of the Greeks and Trojans, and especially "despairing Hecuba," who becomes a mirroring figure:

> In her the painter had anatomiz'd
> Time's ruin, beauty's wrack, and grim care's reign;
> Her cheeks with chops and wrinkles were disguis'd:
> Of what she was no semblance did remain.
> Her blue blood chang'd to black in every vein,
>   Wanting the spring that those shrunk pipes had fed,
>   Show'd life imprison'd in a body dead.
>   (1450–56)

Here the postsexual image of Lucrece is reflected in the ruined maternal figure of Hecuba. Lucrece identifies with Hecuba and speaks for her: " 'Poor instrument,' quoth she, 'without a sound, / I'll tune thy woes with my lamenting tongue' " (1464–65). This identification serves several functions: it provides Lucrece with a character or "type" she can imitate (beyond Penelope), and it offers her an option beyond lamentation—revenge. Immediately after her identification with victim and avenger, she turns her imagination to Helen:

> "Show me the strumpet that began this stir,
> That with my nails her beauty I may tear.
> Thy heat of lust, fond Paris, did incur
> This load of wrath that burning Troy doth bear. . . ."
>   (1471–74)

A metaphor of pregnancy expresses the genesis of Lucrece's own wrath from the "load of lust" that Tarquin left her. Yet insofar as the woman is blamed, an implicit identity of Lucrece, Helen, and Troy emerges. Helen becomes a debased image of Lucrece, a woman upon whose questionable virtue empires turn. When Lucrece transfers her "load of lust" to Troy's "load of wrath," she identifies with Troy, a city invaded and violated by male deceit. Next she identifies with Priam, as the master of Troy (1546–47). Lucrece's stream of confluent identifications (Hecuba, Helen, Troy, Priam) follows her previous relation to Night, whom she first blames but soon conjures and identifies with, as

"the silver-shining queen" who would also be raped by Tarquin, himself "Night's child," thereby becoming Lucrece's "co-partner" in victimage (785-89). The complexity of this particular confusion—Tarquin
would rape his own mother (Night), if he were her (Night)—produces
one of the most intense cross-identifications within the flux of shifting
representations in this poem. This design becomes even more complex
in the Troy painting.

For example, the figures of Sinon and Priam are manifest representations of Tarquin and Collatine: Sinon/Tarquin is the deceitful traitor
and Priam/Collatine is the master of the "sweet city" that is Troy/Lu-
crece. Just as Collatine's story inflames Tarquin to ruin Lucrece, so Sinon's narrative burns Troy:

> The well-skill'd workman this mild image drew
> For perjur'd Sinon, whose enchanting story
> The credulous old Priam after slew;
> Whose words like wildfire burnt the shining glory
> Of rich-built Ilion, that the skies were sorry,
>   And little stars shot from their fixed places,
>   When their glass fell, wherein they view'd their faces.
>   (1520-26)

The language echoes the initial rhetorical contest wherein Collatine's
praise of Lucrece inflamed (his agent) Tarquin to "bear the lightless
fire" that would pluck chaste Lucrece from the "sky of his delight"
(4-12). Since the inflammatory narrative belongs to Sinon and to Collatine, our reading of the Troy piece becomes knotted. Sinon clearly represents Tarquin, but he also represents Collatine. Just as Sinon talks the
giant Greek horse within the walls of Troy, so Collatine talks Tarquin
into Lucrece. In both cases, a deceitful male rhetorician introduces an
engine of ruin into a presumably well-fortified (feminine) city. The result is a violent debasement: the collapse of a pure constellation and the
fracture of the mirror of idealization.

The emblem of mute display that rouses others to voice and action
finds its ultimate locus in Lucrece's body. After Collatine, Lucretius (her
father), and Brutus have sworn upon the bloody knife just pulled from
Lucrece's body to avenge her shame and cleanse Rome of Tarquin kings,
they propose to carry the corpse into the streets, "To show her bleed-
ing body through Rome, / And so to publish Tarquin's foul offense"
(1851-52). On the statement of this intention, the poem abruptly ends.

The ritual vindictive gesture rests on a crude signification whereby *res ipsa*, the body, represents the crime done to it: Lucrece's corpse is simultaneously an icon of violation and of purity; her wound symbolizes both her suicide and Tarquin's offense—the rape objectified, both transitive and intransitive, suffered and inflicted. This public display of her wound is an ultimate seizure (a final rape) and display of her body within a masculine system of signification. It is the culminating *publication* of Collatine's "rich jewel he should keep unknown" (34), now known to all Rome. Ovid's phrase (which Shakespeare read), suggests a deeper, carnal meaning: *"vulnus inane patet"* (Ovid, *Fasti;* quoted in *Poems* 199). Literally, "the gaping wound lies open, is exposed." Thus reduced to passive display of her wound, her void or vacancy, Lucrece becomes a vaginal signifier, an "inanity" made sensible by the vigorous admirations, lewd or legitimate, of men who possess her.

One of the best examples of hyperbole in *Lucrece* is a stanza devoted to Lucrece asleep on her pillow:

> Her lily hand her rosy cheek lies under,
> Coz'ning the pillow of a lawful kiss;
> Who therefore angry seems to part in sunder,
> Swelling on either side to want his bliss:
> Between whose hills her head entombed is;
>   Where like a virtuous monument she lies,
>   To be admir'd of lewd unhallowed eyes.
>   (386–92)

Most critical evaluations of *Lucrece* disapprove of this sort of poetic excess. Yet the elaborate hyperbole of the pillow inscribes in miniature the complex motivations that prefigure the rape itself. The sleeping Lucrece, in all innocence, prevents her pillow from its "lawful kiss." Such deprivation results in anger, division, and swelling, as a response to the "want" (lack) of "bliss." Thus surrounded by an emblem of angry arousal, both erotic and violent, Lucrece is rhetorically murdered, transformed into a tomb, "a virtuous monument," while she is subject to the lewd admiration, not only of Tarquin (who is gazing on her at this moment), but also the reader, before whose eyes Shakespeare's highly eroticized rhetoric will exhibit all of fair Lucrece's charms: her hair, her breasts, "her azure veins, her alabaster skin, / Her coral lips, her snow-white dimpled chin" (400–420). The elaborate inventory of Lucrece's various beauties idealizes her while it simultaneously dehumanizes her; it is a rhetorical appropriation—a rape—analogous to Collatine's public exhibition of his pure jewel. As the pillow's swelling mimics Tar-

quin's arousal, it becomes a displaced expression of his "will," a symbol
of his erotic gaze: "But will is deaf . . . ; / Only he hath an eye to gaze
on beauty" (495-96). Here is lewd admiration reduced to its anatomical
organ: the phallic gaze, the monocular phallus.

The stanza enacts a model of the poem itself. It condenses a pattern of
denial and frustration that Joel Fineman discovers throughout the narrative, that "logic of 'let' that links Lucrece to Tarquin and that makes
Lucrece responsible for her rape by virtue of the energetic and energizing
resistance that she offers to it" (41). Although holding Lucrece responsible for her rape succumbs to the characterological temptation I am en-
deavoring to avoid, the dynamic of the poem does imply her culpability.
When Collatine arrives home, summoned by Lucrece's letter, her first
words allude to her own culpability: " 'Few words,' quoth she, 'shall fit
the trespass best, / Where no excuse can give the fault amending' "
(1613-14). She then proceeds to confess that " 'in the interest of thy bed /
A stranger came' " (1619-20). These at-best-ambiguous terms twist the
nature of her victimage, so that the crime is not initially rape, but
infidelity.

In her lament to Night, Lucrece earlier described her position as both
agent and victim:

> "Make me not object to the tell-tale Day:
> The light will show, character'd in my brow
> The story of sweet chastity's decay,
> The impious breach of holy wedlock vow;
> Yea, the illiterate that know not how
>   To cipher what is writ in learned books,
>   Will quote my loathsome trespass in my looks."
>   (806-12)

The ambiguous diction, through which such terms as *decay*, *breach*,
and *trespass* are both objective and subjective, active and passive, constructs a Lucrece whose rape is literally her "fault": it is a flaw, written in
her face and on her body. "Poor women's faces," the narrator opines,
"are their own faults' books" (1253). Lucrece's face is from the beginning an ambivalent ground of shame and arousal, demarcated by that
blatantly ambivalent physical sign, the blush.

> When virtue bragg'd, beauty would blush for shame;
>   When beauty boasted blushes, in despite
>   Virtue would stain that o'er with silver white.
>   (54-56)

This contest between heraldic signs of purity and beauty, that "silent war of lilies and of roses" (71), now transmutes into a darker image of the *stain* on a white surface: an implicit sign of *writing*.

> Her maid is gone, and she prepares to write,
> First hovering o'er the paper with her quill.
> Conceit and grief an eager combat fight,
> What wit sets down is blotted straight with will;
> This is too curious-good, this blunt and ill.
>   Much like a press of people at a door,
>   Throng her inventions, which shall go before.
>   (1296–1302)

Lucrece's writing posture emulates her rape. This stanza precisely delineates the process of the rape, both as endured event and as composed narrative. The image of Lucrece "hovering o'er the paper with her quill" exactly mirrors Tarquin "shak[ing] aloft his Roman blade . . . like a falcon tow'ring in the skies" (505–06) above the subject whose purity he means to stain, to "blot" with his "will." The pressure of invention at Lucrece's door reflects Tarquin's insistent drive to cross her threshold. These postures of rapist and victim replicate an original moment, I conjecture: the posture of Shakespeare at the instant of composition. Though deeply buried, linguistic associations further connect the rape with the process of writing: to silence her outcries, Tarquin wraps Lucrece's face in her bed-linen: "For with the nightly *linen* that she wears / He *pens* her piteous clamours in her head" (680–81; emphasis added). (Paper in Shakespeare's time was made primarily from linen; see *Othello*.) The effort of her tears to cleanse the stain of Tarquin's lust then becomes a wish to erase her shame from the historical record.

Precisely this intersection of rape and writing may return us to the figure of hyperbole and to the missing moment at the climax or apex. For the poem traditionally known as *The Rape of Lucrece* does not in fact describe that event.[7] The actual rape, insofar as it may be surmised or projected, occurs literally between stanzas, in lines 683–84. Our geometric figure draws a blank at this moment. Of course, issues of propriety and decorum pertain here, but they are not exhaustive explanations. *The Rape of Lucrece* is not about rape, but about the motivations and feelings that precede and succeed the event. It is a "before-and-after" design, pivoting on a central act that is not described (in this design it resembles *Macbeth*). I am interested not so much in the missing act, but in the nature of the division that marks "before" from "after": the gap or fault, intersection or union, violation or disjuncture, the moment of fusion that also forces separation, the illusory division between inside and outside, idealized and debased, sacred and taboo, the membrane that joins primary oppositions, that marks—like the use of walls, doors, and gloves in Shakespeare's poem—the fecund interval, the threshold of Oedipal sexuality.

My metaphor becomes transparent: it is the *hymen*, especially as elaborated by Derrida in his philosophical reverie out of Plato by Mallarmé, in which he analogizes crossing the threshold of the hymen to blotting the virginal blank page with writing. Mallarmé provides the fertile text:

> La scène n'illustre que l'idée, pas une action effective, dans un hymen (d'où procède le Rêve), vicieux mais sacré, entre le désir et l'accomplissement, la perpétration et son souvenir: ici devançant, là remémorant, au futur, au passé, *sous une apparence fausse de présent.* Tel opère le Mime, dont le jeu se borne à une allusion perpétuelle sans briser la glace: il installe, ainsi, un milieu, pur, de fiction. ("Mimique" xx, xxii)[8]

While the precise relevance of these symbolist meditations to Shakespeare's poem may be obscure, Mallarmé's rich confusions (idea and action, sacred and vicious) and his potent evocation of a medium, or space between, that separates yet connects desire and gratification, past and future, through an illusory present, apply to those images of motivation and of writing that Shakespeare explores in *Lucrece* and elsewhere, in terms of rape. From the grimly absurd scene in *Titus Andronicus* of the mutilated Lavinia writing *"stuprum"* ("rape") in the sand with her stumps, through the tragic melodrama of Othello's efforts to keep Desdemona's "most goodly book" free of the grimy term, *whore*, to the parody of rape and debased reputation via the Iachimo-in-the-box in *Cymbeline*, Shakespeare correlated the themes of despoiled innocence and inscription. *Lucrece* may be his most extended investigation of the hinge of this correlation: an elaborate study of the mediating moment between innocence and knowledge, purity and corruption, unity and disintegration. *Lucrece* is constructed on the principle of the climactic hinge, the sharp shift in direction from desire ("Tarquin") to response ("Lucrece"). Its pivotal point is literally absent (in terms of literary representation), yet crucially present as a structural principle. It is a moment of traumatic deprivation—for both Lucrece and Tarquin—and simultaneously a moment of sudden plentitude: desire is satisfied, delay terminated, the hyperbolic trajectory given final shape. Derrida's ornate and hyperbolic rhetoric suggests the power of this moment: "The hymen," he writes, "the consummation of differends, the continuity and confusion of the coitus, merges with what it seems to be derived from":

> the hymen as protective screen, the jewel box of virginity, the vaginal partition, the fine, invisible veil which, in front of the hystera, stands *between* the inside and the outside of a woman, and consequently between desire and fulfillment. It is neither desire nor pleasure but in between the two. Neither future nor present, but between the two. It is the hymen that desire dreams of piercing, of bursting, in an act of violence that is (at the same time or somewhere between) love and murder. (212-13)

Shakespeare's *Lucrece* is not merely about a classic rape, or about the hymeneal intervals between wish, deed, and response, but also about the process of writing—or of imaginatively conceiving a traumatic act and inscribing the conception on the page. Inscription leaves a permanent mark, or stain—unlike the vital yet ephemeral voices and gestures of a staged play. It is quintessentially emblematic that Shakespeare's two intended poetic publications conclude with images of stains and indelible memory: the blood-stained purple anemone in *Venus and Adonis* (1165-88) and the bloody corpse of Lucrece. Both are emblems of innocence re-marked by lust; both enter cultural mythology as images of victimized virtue, polluted yet consecrated, violently memorialized as monuments to chastity defiled.

I want to close with a concluding speculation. If Shakespeare imagined publication as leaving a permanent mark, and if his imagination of that mark was characterized by the sadomasochistic con-fusion of figure and disfigurement, love and violence—that is, by a fantasy of rape—then his conspicuous indifference to or ambivalence about publication acquires new significance. It may be that writing, for Shakespeare—when fixed in published form—did not represent a purely positive emblem of textual procreativity that would "bear his memory" through time (Sonnet 1). Shakespeare's is no mere erotics of poetry. His potent coupling of rape and remembrance suggests publication as a kind of violation: an arrest of the imagination, an insult to time, a blot on the stream of (dramatic) creativity. At creative core, he wrote for the stage, not the page. Ironically, of course, my notion about Shakespeare's resistance to publication derives from my intensive reading of his printed texts. Such speculation is a grand, indeed hyperbolic conjecture. That reading Shakespeare should tease us into such thoughts is a major motive for our continued reading of him.

Notes

1. The best Renaissance representative of this style of narrative psychodramatic allegory is Spenser. For an excellent description of the Spenserian background against which *Lucrece* is most profitably read, see Leonard Barkan, *Nature's Work of Art,* especially chapter 5, "*The Faerie Queene:* Allegory, Iconography, and the Human Body."

2. *Macbeth* is the richest parallel here, to the point of exact echoes. As Macbeth moves "with Tarquin's ravishing strides" toward the bloody business of regicide, he occupies the identical arena of dream and allegory, enacting Lust and "Murther" (*Macbeth* 2.1.49–56). M. C. Bradbrook calls Tarquin's soliloquies "a first cartoon for the study of *Macbeth*" (112). For an extensive mapping of the dreamscape of *Macbeth,* see my essay, "Phantasmagoric *Macbeth.*"

3. Shakespeare's language is manifestly bawdy here. "Pride" has frequent connotations of male arousal, and the physiology of tumescence is clear (see Angelo's erection in *Measure for Measure* [2.4.5–6] and Sonnet 151, where the signification is exact). "These terms darkly suggest," writes Saad El-Gabalawy, that Tarquin "is being led along by his own erect sexual organ" (80).

4. See Sam Hynes, "The Rape of Tarquin" (451–53). Hynes also notes the parallels of Tarquin's internal insurrection with Macbeth's. A. C. Hamilton notes that "Tarquin's desire for Lucrece turns into a desire to destroy himself through sin" (174).

5. The symbolism, frequently noted in current criticism, is hardly Freudian. Shakespeare takes pains to establish it in *Romeo and Juliet,* and it echoes through *Macbeth* and *Antony and Cleopatra.* For erotic depictions of Lucrece's suicide, see Ian Donaldson, *The Rapes of Lucretia.* Discussing Lucas Cranach's early sixteenth-century drawing of a naked and placid Lucrece pressing a long dagger into her abdomen, Donaldson quotes Michel Leiris's *L'Age d'homme* (1946): "Elle s'appretant à annuler l'effet du viol qu'elle a subi, par un geste pareil" (She prepares to annul the effect of the rape she has suffered by an identical gesture") (17 n. 36).

6. Renaissance physiologies of sex, derived from classical and medieval theories of "humours," held that procreation resulted from an actual commingling of "spirits" or bloods during coitus. For Shakespearean echoes, see Leontes's obsessions in *The Winter's Tale:* "Too hot, too hot! / To mingle friendship far is mingling bloods" (1.2.108–09).

7. The title during Shakespeare's lifetime was simply *Lucrece.* An editor augmented the title in the Quarto of 1616; tradition retains the emendation.

8. "The scene illustrates but the idea, not any actual action, in a hymen (out of which flows Dream), tainted with vice yet sacred, between desire and fulfillment, perpetration and remembrance: here anticipating, there recalling, in the future, in the past, *under the false appearance of a present.* This is how the Mime operates, whose act is confined to a perpetual allusion without breaking the ice or the mirror: he thus sets up a medium, a pure medium, of fiction" (Mallarmé, "Mimique"). For Derrida's elaborations, see 209–22.

Works Cited

Barkan, Leonard. *Nature's Work of Art: The Human Body as Image of the World.* New Haven, Conn.: Yale UP, 1975.

Bradbrook, M. C. *Shakespeare and Elizabethan Poetry.* London: Oxford UP, 1951.

Derrida, Jacques. *Dissemination*. Trans. Barbara Johnson. Chicago: U of Chicago P, 1981.

Donaldson, Ian. *The Rapes of Lucretia: A Myth and Its Transformations*. Oxford: Clarendon, 1982.

El-Gabalawy, Saad. "The Ethical Question of Lucrece: A Case of Rape." *Mosaic* 12 (1979): 80.

Fineman, Joel. *Shakespeare's Perjured Eye*. Berkeley: U of California P, 1986.

Hamilton, A. C. *The Early Shakespeare*. San Marino: Huntington Library, 1967.

Hynes, Sam. "The Rape of Tarquin." *Shakespeare Quarterly* 10 (1959): 451–53.

Mallarmé, Stéphane. "Mimique." Derrida xx–xxiii, 173–286.

Stimpson, Catherine. "Shakespeare and the Soil of Rape." *The Woman's Part: Feminist Criticism of Shakespeare*. Ed. Carolyn Lenz, Gayle Greene, Carol T. Neely. Urbana: U of Illinois P, 1980. 56–64.

Vickers, Nancy. " 'The Blazon of Sweet Beauty's Best': Shakespeare's *Lucrece*." *Shakespeare and the Question of Theory*. Ed. Patricia Parker and Geoffrey Hartman. New York: Methuen, 1985. 95–115.

Willbern, David. "Phantasmagoric *Macbeth*." *English Literary Renaissance* 16 (1986): 520–49.

Duel: Paranoid Style

Andrew Gordon

Steven Spielberg's **Duel** *was made* as a "Movie of the Week" for ABC television in 1971, but the acclaim it garnered after its release in Europe in 1973 permits it to be considered Spielberg's first theatrical film. *Duel* is a taut thriller in the Hitchcock tradition, considered one of the best movies ever made for television. One critic even ranks it with Clouzot's *The Wages of Fear* as "one of the most suspenseful films ever made" (Aldiss 173). *Duel* is a carefully calculated film. All the elements work together to involve the audience and allow us to identify with the hero, an ordinary man forced beyond his limits when he is terrorized by a huge truck in a highway duel to the death. Spielberg builds suspense gradually, momentarily slackens it, tricks us when we are off guard, and then screws the tension to an almost unbearable level in the climax. He plays with the audience, just as the truck toys with the hero.

The merits of the film are in the script by Richard Matheson (based on his story), meticulous storyboarding, crisp editing and pacing, fluid and dynamic camerawork, a tense and eerie musical score by Billy Goldenberg (reminiscent of Bernard Herrmann's music for Hitchcock's *Psycho*) (Larson 243),[1] and a gripping performance by Dennis Weaver as the protagonist David Mann. It is the film of a young man (twenty-four) who delights in showing what he can do with a camera to tell a story: for a car-chase movie, it has a rich variety of camera setups, angles, and lenses, as well as a sensuous menace in the lingering tracking shots along the sides of the huge moving truck or slow tilts down a truck driver's boots. It is an almost purely visual film. Spielberg wanted to make "a feature-

length silent movie" and cut most of the dialogue from the script, although the network executives made him restore some (Crawley 27). The
lack of dialogue emphasizes the hero's isolation in his paranoid world,
adding to the psychological power of the film. And it is as a psychological thriller, a kind of anxiety dream, and a study in paranoia, that I wish
to consider *Duel*.

Every thriller must be judged against Hitchcock's achievement, and
Duel, like *Jaws*, demonstrates that Spielberg is an apt disciple of the
master. The film follows many conventions of the Hitchcock formula—
I think of films like *The Thirty-Nine Steps, North by Northwest,* and
The Man Who Knew Too Much—although it is not a slavish imitation
of any particular Hitchcock film. Nevertheless, the elements are recognizable. The hero is an ordinary man who is suddenly plunged into
trouble by sheer happenstance. Chaos and violence erupt, totally dis-
rupting his complacent routine. Macabre and bizarre events take place
in broad daylight. The hero's life is in danger, he is chased by a malevolent force, and the climax is a plunge over a cliff. In other words, we get
the cinematic return of the repressed, a paranoid nightmare with a
happy ending. In *Duel,* as in the typical Hitchcock film, the hero is
stripped of his secure, everyday identity and must prove his manhood by
tapping hidden resources of endurance, resourcefulness, and courage.
Duel may be low-budget Hitchcock, lacking some of his complex human interplay, depth of theme and wit, but it is nonetheless a most effective thriller which successfully applies Hitchcock's essential method.

But whereas Hitchcock's thrillers (except *The Birds*) take place in the
real world, *Duel* borders on the fantastic, which makes it that much
more of an anxiety dream. A truck that large couldn't move that fast. The
hero's nemesis is a machine, not a man. The driver of the truck is a
shadowy presence, glimpsed only momentarily, in fragments: a hand on
the steering wheel, an arm signaling out the window, the bottom of
some jeans and boots. He is never viewed whole, nor is his face ever seen.
As a result, the truck remains apparently driverless, and the hero seems
pursued not by a human being but by a machine—a machine, moreover,
which embodies an irrational, demonic force. *Duel* fits Tzvetan Todorov's definition of the fantastic as a genre which involves the hesitation of
the protagonist and the reader between two possible explanations, one
natural and the other supernatural (33). Richard Matheson, the author
of the story and the script, is known primarily as a writer of science
fiction, fantasy, and horror, and particularly for his contributions to the

Rod Serling *Twilight Zone* television series. And the film has been discussed as science fiction (Aldiss 173) and as horror (King 163).

Critics have termed *Duel* the apotheosis of the car-chase movie, ninety minutes of pure highway pursuit (Aldiss 175). But beneath that elemental structure is a primal confrontation of man versus truck that, somewhat akin to the archetypal confrontation of man versus whale in *Moby Dick*, lends itself to many different interpretations. It can be read as Man versus Machine, Suburban Man versus Rural American, Bourgeois Man versus Capitalism, or simply Man versus Thing.

The duel between the man and the truck could first be seen, as Spielberg himself claims, as "an indictment of machines. And I determined very early on that everything about the film would be the complete disruption of our whole technological society. . . . And especially, where the truck was concerned, I wanted it to be the true, perfect, perpetual-motion machine" (Crawley 26). Like George Lucas's *THX 1138, Duel* expresses the mechanophobia of the late 1960s and early 1970s. But despite Spielberg's claim, *Duel* is not a clear indictment of machines; instead, it pits one giant machine run amok (the oil tanker) against a smaller machine (Mann's Plymouth Valiant). Spielberg criticizes not machines but the mechanization of life. He has also said, "Dennis Weaver's whole life is very much like the truck's. . . . [H]e's as regimented about his life style, about getting to work on time, as the truck is in waiting for people behind cul-de-sacs, ravines and canyons" (Crawley 26).

Spielberg also claims that *Duel* is an indictment of suburbia. "The hero of *Duel* is typical of that lower middle-class American who's insulated by suburban modernization. . . . And a man like that *never* expects to be challenged by anything more than his television set breaking down and having to call the repair man" (Crawley 26). If so, it is certainly a qualified indictment, for his suburban hero wins out in the end.

In a sociological sense, David Mann is suburban man—a white-collar businessman in suit and tie, emasculated, passive and harmless—challenged by a rural American, the truck driver—a blue-collar cowboy in boots and jeans, macho, aggressive, and deadly. When the truck first chases the Plymouth down the mountain, Mann's radio is tuned to a country music station. But the class conflict is posed in terms of the traditional codes of the American Western movie: the myth of the Easterner, a pale city fellow who lives by the rule of law, who becomes a man only after duelling a Westerner, a rugged individualist and outlaw bred by the anarchy of the frontier. The Easterner must adopt the ruthless methods of the Westerner to defeat him, as in John Ford's *The Man Who Shot Liberty Valance* (1962). According to some critics, before Mann's final confrontation with the truck, "he stalks toward it in the classic manner of a Western hero, and later snaps on his seat belt as though it were a six-shooter and gunbelt" (Pye and Myles 225). Spielberg says, "I felt very strongly that he should be a mild-mannered businessman of the hen-pecked variety, needing a major change in his life. His life needed changing, as they say in the Old West" (Crawley 26).

For that reason, Spielberg was reluctant to agree with Italian critics who wanted to interpret the film as a Marxist allegory: "Surely, his fiendish truck represented the all-crushing forces of the capitalist Establishment? He refused to rise to the bait. He saw the truck, almost inevitably, as a train without tracks. As for the film, why that was *Godzilla vs. Bambi* . . ." (Crawley 24). Spielberg is referring here to the animated cartoon short, *Bambi Meets Godzilla*, a brief parody in which Bambi the deer is seen peacefully grazing in the clearing in the woods until a giant foot enters the frame from above and squashes the animal flat, ending the film. Spielberg is being facetious, of course, but he points to the element of the fantastic in the film. Critics have also seen the influence of Chuck Jones's "Road Runner" cartoons in *Duel* (Mott and Saunders 20). As much as *Duel* follows the patterns of the thriller or the Western, it is also based on the classic fairy-tale scenario of little man versus giant monster. The "monster" of fantasy and horror—the truck in *Duel*—is a kind of floating signifier which one can interpret as wished.

Brian Aldiss emphasizes this multivalent nature of *Duel:* "The freedom it gives us—is that it is not, say, a Marxist tract, or a hymn of praise or hate about traffic on our roads. The ambiguities open up naturally when Mann moves from the safety and banality of the known to the challenge and beauty of the unknown" (178). Aldiss prefers to see the film as fantasy, "an archetypal confrontation between Man and Thing" (174), just as Thomas Lee Snyder sees the truck as Other, beast, or monster: "This fear of the Outside, or fear of the Unknown, serves as the basis for the archetypal image of the monster, the primary archetype in many horror films" (129).

Some critics of *Duel* hint at a psychological interpretation of the film but do not elaborate on this. Aldiss, for example, mentions that the film opens "with the car swinging out of one of those little suburban villas where The Family develops all its classic manias" (175). And Snyder claims vaguely that "the evil truck is really an attack from within, and David Mann's paranoia is really a fear of the savagery that lurks within us all" (131). David Pye and Lynda Myles write that "it would be amusing to read the film as a parable of a man denying his sexuality and its implacable force; perhaps even a man denying his homosexuality." But they admit that the hero's problems are not simply sexual:

> The whole giant weight of trivial problems is rolled together in one homicidal machine. We know Mann is anxious about a contract and worried about his job; we see the fragility of his relationship with his wife; there are hints of economic anxiety and overprotectiveness about possessions like his car. Under such pressure a man's identity becomes uncertain; he can be forgiven the paranoid fantasy that the truck represents. (225–26)

I want to concentrate on a psychological reading of the film, recognizing that there are multiple ways of viewing this primal confrontation of man and truck, and that the truck is a floating signifier as polysemous as the shark in *Jaws.* My reading is only one among numerous possible readings and may reflect my own psychological biases more than anything else. Nevertheless, an in-depth psychological reading of *Duel* is called for if only because, as Hitchcock taught us, any thriller that reaches us on more than a visceral level must have a psychological dimension.

All thrillers partake of "paranoid" elements, and both Snyder and Pye and Myles mention David Mann's paranoia. As Jerry Palmer says in *Thrillers,* "The world that the thriller portrays is a paranoid world . . . what it does is propose to the reader that he too should see the world through paranoid eyes" (86–87). *Duel* is not simply a chase story but also a psychological fable in the form of a paranoid nightmare for both hero and audience. The film begins like an anxiety dream in which you are prevented from getting to an important meeting by a series of frustrating delays. Then it turns into a real nightmare: the meeting is entirely forgotten, and you are fleeing for your life from some implacable and unstoppable evil. Through Mann's experiences, we can safely go crazy, participate vicariously in a paranoid state, confront the most monstrous evil imaginable, and emerge victorious. For those benefits, we are willing to undergo the director's controlled sadism.

"The thriller hero is always, intrinsically, isolated," writes Palmer (29). Throughout *Duel,* Mann becomes progressively more isolated in his battle with the truck. The roads are unnaturally empty of traffic, there are no police around, the one time he tries to phone for help, the truck rams the phone booth, and the driver he asks to call the police doesn't want to get involved. By the climax of the film, Mann finally realizes that he is on his own; no one is going to help him.

His most persistent difficulty is in persuading anyone that he is indeed being persecuted, that his life is in danger, that he is not, in fact, crazy. He even comes at times to doubt his own perceptions and wonders if he is losing his grip. An old farmer who sees Mann crash into a fence is skeptical and amused when Mann claims that a truck was pursuing him and tried to kill him. The crowd in a restaurant openly laughs at him, and when a man there whom he mistakenly believes to be the driver of the truck tells him, "You need help,"[2] Mann attacks him, is beaten, and is told to leave.

Impotence and humiliation seem to be the order of the day for Mann; the film is determined to give him (and us) the full treatment, enough to induce full-blown paranoia. He is first humiliated in front of an old man who watches him stagger into the restaurant and then in front of the crowd in the restaurant who witness his erratic behavior and enjoy his defeat in the fight. When Mann tries to push a stalled school bus, he is jeered by a crowd of children: "You can't do it!" one child mocks him. And he can't; for his pains, he gets his bumper stuck under the bus. He grows so hysterical when he sees the truck apparently approaching the children that one kid announces, "You must be outta your brain!" And when he tries to persuade the bus driver that the truck driver is crazy, the bus driver says, "If I had to vote on who's crazy around here, it would have to be you." To the outside world, Mann exhibits all the symptoms of a man suffering from classic delusions of persecution (Mott and Saunders 21). Their unease or laughter at him only increases his feelings of being persecuted or receiving no respect as a man.

Mann's seemingly crazy behavior is of course justified by the plot; the threat he faces is real. Yet on another level he *is* deluded and frequently acts on mistaken premises because he begins to sense threat everywhere: he attacks the wrong man in the restaurant, and he assumes the truck will harm the school bus when it actually turns around to help it! In a sense, the truck is merely symptomatic, a symbolic representation of the eruption of his deepest fears. Mann is predisposed to paranoia.

The most "paranoid" scene in the film is the unnerving episode in Chuck's Café. Mann goes to the men's room of this truck stop to recover after a narrow escape from his first pursuit by the truck. He reassures himself, "All right, boy, it was a nightmare, but it's over now. It's all over." Yet when he looks out the front window of the restaurant, the truck is parked outside, evidently awaiting him. The nightmare will continue. He tries to rationalize the presence of the truck to himself ("He probably eats here all the time"), but grows increasingly disturbed. The probing, subjective camera, the close-ups, and the eerie music emphasize his mental distress and heighten the suspense in the scene. Mann sits isolated in a booth, trying to hide his face behind a hand as he nervously scans a solid phalanx of the enemy: truck drivers seated at a counter, most wearing the boots and jeans that are the only identifying marks of the driver of the killer truck. That driver knows Mann's face, but Mann doesn't know his. Almost any man in the café could be his nemesis. All the faces seem to glare at him in hostile close-ups. This is elemental paranoia. The tension builds until Mann provokes an assault by the driver. But when the lethal truck suddenly pulls away, we realize that none of the men in the café could have been its driver. Spielberg has played a cruel and clever trick on both hero and audience, raising false expectations, enabling us to participate in Mann's unhinged state, and plunging us into the condition of paranoia where the ordinary becomes treacherous and we scan the environment for menacing clues. We become like Mann, victims of our own heightened awareness of danger, unable to trust our perceptions, subject to delusions.

Spielberg treats his hero and his audience with the same sadistic glee, subjecting us to such cruel teases at other points in the film: when the sleeping Mann is jolted awake by the blast of a horn which he (and we) take to be the truck's but proves instead to be a train's, or when Mann, with the truck in hot pursuit, pulls off to the side of the road toward what looks like a police car but turns out to be a company car painted black and white. Once the director induces paranoia in the hero and audience, he can play such tricks at will.

Of the many psychoanalytic explanations of paranoia, the best-known (though by no means universally accepted) theory is Freud's, for whom paranoia represented a defense against a homosexual wish fantasy. By means of projection and denial, claimed Freud, "I (a male) love him" is transformed into "I do not love him—I *hate* him, because HE PERSECUTES ME" (33). Freud theorized that an external threat was easier to cope with than an internal one.

As mentioned before, Pye and Myles speculate that Mann may be "denying his homosexuality, since truckers, boots, and cruel game-playing have a disproportionate importance in the commercial American gay culture" (225). And the scene in Chuck's Café, when Mann sidles up nervously to a trucker, could be read as either confrontation or come-on. There is also an unexplained detail in that scene: while Mann is eyeing the truckers, a man in a blue workshirt is playing pool with a buxom blonde in a short red dress. We see the woman in some other shots, too: she seems to be a loose woman associated with the truckers. We could read the male pool player symbolically as Mann's antagonist, and the woman, because of her red dress, becomes associated with Mann's red car (the color red is used very sparingly in the film; when it is used, we notice it) and with Mann himself. The pool game may represent another kind of duel, a sexual combat underlying Mann's confrontation with the truckers.

Positing an unacknowledged homosexual conflict is one way to explain the symbolism of the film, in which a red Plymouth Valiant is pursued over the California highways by a giant oil tanker bent on ramming it from behind. Mann continually scans the mirror, afraid of an imminent assault from the rear. He even expresses a perverse admiration for the truck and its driver, exclaiming once (albeit sarcastically), "O boy, you're beautiful!" And when the truck plunges over the cliff along with the little car at the climax of the film, it is a true *liebestod*, a "death-locked embrace" (Crawley 27).

But even if we posit an unconscious homosexual component to Mann's paranoia, the opening of the film suggests that his problems lie elsewhere and are rooted in a fear and hatred of women. It is not so much that he is attracted to men but that he feels less than a man because he is dominated by women.

The film opens in darkness, with the sound of a car starting up, and then we see a garage and the street and realize that we are folowing a character's point of view as he drives. The subjective camera at the beginning helps us merge with Mann's viewpoint, and it continues throughout the opening credits. Aldiss calls the hero's home a "nursery middle-class environment" (175); we can, if we wish, interpret the opening as Mann's leaving the womb and entering the world. But it is a dangerous world; as Pye and Myles note, "The first shot that is not from the driver's viewpoint is framed, menacingly, by strands of barbed wire" (224).

After the first close-ups of the driver, the soundtrack on the radio also changes. Up to this point, it consisted of traffic reports and commercials, emphasizing the routine and the mundane ("Things seem to be pretty normal on our southbound freeways"). This is a standard Spielberg tactic: making the fantastic more believable by first grounding it in the everyday. Now we hear a talk show and the first suggestion of the abnormal. A beleaguered middle-aged man with a fruity voice calls in, wondering if he can honestly check the box on the government census form identifying himself as "head of the family." He says he hates "getting involved in the rat race," so his wife works and he stays home and does the housework. He dresses at home in a housedress and slippers and worries that the neighbors will find out; "it's so embarrassing." His ambiguous gender status bothers him: "I'm not really the head of the family, and yet I'm the man of the family, although there are people in the neighborhood who would question that. . . . " Then he launches into a misogynistic tirade against his feared and hated wife, the longest stretch of dialogue in the film:

> "Well, quite frankly, the day I married that woman, that, unfortunately, I've been married to for the last twenty-five years. . . . Well, it's true, I lost the position as head of the family. . . . You know how women are before you marry them. They're so nice. Suddenly, they become so aggressive. I mean, she became so *aggressive* after. Just took over everything. I'm afraid of her. I've been wanting to divorce her. . . . She doesn't know I'm calling. But that woman just *drives me* up the wall and over the other side." (Emphasis added.)

Later we realize that Mann resembles this unintentionally comic, pathetic, disturbed character; he, too, has problems containing his anger at his wife and at himself. So the duel could become a way to release safely his violence against an object which becomes the incarnation of pure evil.

As the radio caller's complaint concludes, we first glimpse the aggressive oil truck that will become Mann's antagonist. Spielberg and Matheson's tactic here is unmistakable: the protagonist, who is not so much driver as driven, becomes identified with the henpecked man and the truck with his wife—or, by the logic of misogyny, with women in general. So the truck cannot simply be equated with a persecuting phallus; in some ways, it is also a smothering breast.

Duel does not appear to support Freud's theory of paranoia so much as it does Melanie Klein's. Where Freud spoke of the persecuting homosexual love object (symbolically, the patient's father), Klein talks of paranoid persecution having its basis in infantile imagos of both parents: "These two dangerous objects—the bad breast and the bad penis—are the prototypes of internal and external persecutors" (*Envy* 32). It is not surprising that the internalized images of the "bad parents" should be conflated into a single image. As Karl Abraham mentions about paranoia, "Another point to be noted in regard to the part of the body that has been introjected is that the penis is regularly assimilated to the female breast'' (490). Metaphorically, then, we might say that the problem of the hero of *Duel* is the uncertainty of his gender role identity, and that the figure who pursues him (the truck) is also sexually ambivalent, since it is his own projection. The truck combines both "bad penis" and "bad breast," the internalized persecuting imagoes of both sexes and both parents.

The point that Mann's difficulties are with both male and female authority figures (though more with women than with men) is reemphasized in an early gas station scene. As Mann pulls up to a pump, the trucks pulls in also, vastly overshadowing his car. The truck looms there ominously throughout the scene, twice impatiently blatting its horn for service. We are not allowed to ignore its presence, since many of the shots favor the truck. The attendant, by contrast, is unthreatening: a servile, short, skinny man who lisps and limps, perhaps a reflection of the hero's shrunken self-image. Mann tells him, "Fill it with ethyl," and the attendant replies with a tired pun, "If Ethel don't mind." He tells Mann, "You're the boss," but Mann replies with unexpected bitterness, "Not in my house, I'm not." Mann is under a woman's heel and can only do things "if Ethel don't mind." Meanwhile, we see shots of the trucker's boots and jeans as he paces behind the truck; here is a man accustomed to being the boss.

When Mann next goes into a laundromat to phone his wife, his anxiety and anger are further revealed. He starts to apologize to her "about last night," but her replies quickly anger him:

"You think I should go out and call Steve Henderson and challenge him to a fist fight or something?"

"No, of course not. But, honey, I think you could have at least said something to the man last night. I mean, after all, . . . practically trying to rape me in front of that whole party."

She drops the subject, only to start badgering him about getting home on time, to which he replies:

"If Forbes lets me go in time."

"Is it that important that you see him?"

"Huh! He's leaving for Hawaii in the morning. The way he's been griping to the front office, if I don't reach him today, I could lose the account."

She persists in browbeating him about being home for dinner: "It's your mother. God knows she's not coming to see me." He has to repeat twice that "there probably won't be a problem," but he is obviously irritated, and when she hangs up, he looks whipped and unsettled. The call, which began as his apology, has only worsened things.

Throughout this scene, Mann is also diminished and entrapped by the camera setup. We see him in a long shot, framed in a narrow space between the telephone on the wall and a table in the laundromat. He props his leg against the table but must remove it to let a fat lady pass to get her clothes from a dryer in the foreground. For much of this shot, Mann is further framed within the circle of the open dryer window, which makes him look like a specimen under glass (Mott and Saunders 20). In the background looms the truck, and in the foreground the arm of the fat lady intrudes into the shot as she extracts her clothes, coinciding with the line, "It's your mother." Dialogue and images combine to emphasize how trapped Mann is by the domestic. The fat lady and the dryer, the wife on the phone, the mother coming to visit: these make up the world of women who imprison him. And looming above it all is the image of the truck. According to one psychoanalytic commentator, "One finds in certain paranoids that the father . . . has paradoxically posed less of a threat to the patient's integrity in childhood than the first source of woe—a mother intensely intrusive, suffocating, destructive of her child's bid for autonomy and independence" (Greenberg 76). That certainly seems true of the protagonist here.

The conversation with his wife suggests that Mann's encounter with the truck takes the place of his encounters with the various figures, both male and female, who are plaguing him on this particular day: the nagging wife, the unwelcome mother, the "rapist" Steve Henderson, and the complaining Forbes. The duel with the truck replaces the fist fight with Henderson, the meeting with Forbes, and the dinner with wife and mother, all of which he is unable to carry out. The truck, in fact, is as overbearing, griping, and demanding as his wife and Forbes, as intrusive as his mother, as phallically aggressive as Henderson, and as oppressive yet elusive as Forbes. The enormousness of the truck—emphasized by slow and low travelling shots of its bulk, shots with it filling the screen or driving aggressively toward us, or numerous shots where it dwarfs the car—suggests the size of the threat Mann is avoiding.

The situation in the laundromat is repeated later in the restaurant when Mann meets a kindly, gray-haired waitress old enough to be his mother. She seems maternally sympathetic when he requests an aspirin: "Oh, your head aches." But aurally and visually she is presented as threatening. We hear her before we see her, through the noisy rattle of silverware flung onto the table, which startles both the nervous, distracted Mann and the viewer. He sits as she stands and looks down at him. He seems indecisive as she awaits his order. In one shot, her arm dangles into the right-hand side of the frame, reminding us of the fat lady in the laundromat. And in another shot, we see the truck through the window, in the background behind her; the waitress is yet another woman or mother figure associated with the malevolent truck.

Another ambiguous woman in the film is the "snake lady," an old woman who runs a gas station and "Snakearama" by the roadside where Mann stops to telephone the police. Like the waitress, she is gray-haired and friendly, and we even pity her when the truck smashes her snake tanks. Nevertheless, the scene is touched with macabre humor. Mann brushes a tarantula off his pants, and we last see the lady with a snake in her hands. The image is a parody of a distraught mother holding a sick child. Snyder interprets these snakes, like the leaking radiator hose in Mann's car, as "phallic metaphors" symbolizing "Mann's loss of masculinity and fear of castration," and he mentions that they prefigure the snakes in *Raiders of the Lost Ark* (131). But we could also see this "snake mother," who seems to combine the bad breast with the bad penis, as yet another representative of the undercurrent of sexual ambivalence in the film, with its feminized males and aggressive women.

The final woman Mann encounters is the worst of all, the culmination of the film's misogyny. Mann flags down an old car driven by an old man and his wife and asks them to call the police for help. They look like archetypal kindly grandparents, but the man is weak and reluctant to get involved. As Mann grows increasingly desperate in his plea, the woman becomes frightened and orders her husband not to help. This couple repeats the pattern of the film: the weak man and the domineering woman. They resemble Mann and his wife; on another level, however, they are the bad parents who refuse to help him.

Their refusal emphasizes Mann's physical and psychological isolation in his paranoid nightmare. Once they leave, he realizes that no one is going to rescue him, and he heads back to his car for the final showdown.

One interesting aspect of his duel with the truck is that he seems to wish it. First, he deliberately provokes the truck by responding to its dangerous highway games and playing stupid passing games of his own. Next, at many points in the day, he could have stopped his journey, driven to a police station, or simply reversed direction and gone home. His efforts to seek help are belated and halfhearted. He doesn't have to accept the truck's challenge, but he really seems to welcome it. All this reinforces the notion that the truck represents his own psychic projection, and that the threat it symbolizes has a peculiar personal urgency for Mann.

Up to now, I have suggested that the truck can be seen as functioning, on one level, as a symbol of the persecuting parents, a projection based on internalized imagoes. It can also be considered simultaneously as an embodiment of the hero's own hostile and sadistic impulses against love objects turned back against himself; that is one way to preserve the objects and disavow one's aggressive or ambivalent feelings about them. But the possible unconscious significance of the persecuting force in paranoia does not end there. Psychoanalysts such as Karl Abraham, Otto Fenichel, and Melanie Klein agree that the symbolism of the persecuting object is strongly colored by the "anal sadistic" phase of development: "to a paranoiac . . . the love object is equivalent to feces which he cannot get rid of" (Abraham 490); "among the organs projected onto the persecutor, feces and buttocks play a predominant role" (Fenichel 429); and Klein believed that in the unconscious, the bad penis was "equated with these dangerous feces" (*Love* 412). The persecuting object, in other words, represents whatever the person disavows or rejects in himself— such as homosexual or aggressive impulses—so unconsciously it is associated with the body's own waste products.

Mann himself shows certain traits that might be labeled "anal": he is worried about being on time for his appointment or for dinner at home, and he is fastidious about his dress (he wears a tie even in the car) and his car. Before the day is over, however, he will be reduced to a sweaty, bloodstained wreck, and his car will be dirtied, bashed, scratched, pounded, dented, and finally totally demolished. When he first encounters the truck, it offends him: he is stuck in his clean, shiny car right behind a large, dirty tanker spewing out exhaust fumes from its stack (Mott and Saunders 19). The smoke invades his car and makes him cough, and he mutters to himself, "Talk about pollution!" Later he can't escape the truck, try as he might; it keeps hounding him from the rear. Thus, when the truck topples over a cliff at the end, the revenge is psychologically appropriate. One might say that he has eliminated the persecuting object by excreting it.

Aside from the possible sexual or anal symbolism associated with the truck, it is also figuratively a savage beast and thus not so far removed from the shark in *Jaws*. Nightmares and phobias are closely connected to paranoid states. According to one psychoanalyst, the content of night-mare experience is regressive: "Generally, the introjects prior to the age of two are represented as threatening aspects of other persons or as menacing machines and animals" (Meissner 592). The menacing machine in *Duel* requires no commentary, but it is interesting that many critics have seen the truck as a wild animal such as a wolf, shark, or dinosaur (Pye and Myles 223; Aldiss 174; Snyder 130). It stalks Mann like a wolf tracking its prey, and it charges like a bull or rhino. Its horn sounds like the cry of an enraged bull elephant, and it spouts smoke like a fire-breathing dragon. As the truck plunges over the cliff in a fall prolonged by slow motion, we hear its "death cry," which Stephen King aptly describes as "a series of chilling Jurassic roars . . . the sound, we think, a tyranno-saurus rex would make going slowly down into a tar pit" (163).

We can therefore see the truck alternately or even simultaneously as homosexual persecutor, the image of the bad parents, Mann's own sadis-tic aggression turned against himself, a projection of his buttocks or feces, or a savage beast. All this possible unconscious symbolism is not contradictory so much as mutually reinforcing; it enriches the symbolic suggestiveness of the truck through layers of overdetermined meaning. The movie itself may be carefully programmed, but it provides us with a great deal of imaginative latitude. We project onto the truck our own nightmare fears and thus battle alongside Mann against our worst pri-vate demons. The film may be misogynistic on the surface, but its terrors are so free-floating that any viewer can translate them into the terms he or she most fears and desires. *Duel* offers the pleasures of suspense and of mastering anxiety. We root for Mann to stop being a wimp, for in his assertion of manhood lies our only hope to defeat our own personal demons.

Duel is a paranoid fantasy posing as reality, a nightmare assaulting us in broad daylight. Spielberg may not be as intellectually challenging a filmmaker as Hitchcock, but he is an extremely skilled craftsman who knows which buttons to push to engage the audience on a primal level. He must be well acquainted with the territory of phobias, nightmares, and paranoid anxiety to have made a film as riveting as *Duel*.

Notes

1. See Larson's discussion in *Musique Fantastique* where he mentions the "wild,

Herrmannesque swirling strings," the "apprehensive, ominous chords" of the truck stop scene, and the use of "strings and piano tones to build a tense mood as the truck waits in the tunnel for the salesman to help the stranded school bus" (243).

2. All quotations from *Duel* refer to the ninety-minute version of the film available on VHS videotape.

Works Cited

Abraham, Karl. *Selected Papers of Karl Abraham*. 1979. New York: Brunner/Mazel, 1927.

Aldiss, Brian. "Spielberg: When the Mundane Breaks Down." *This World and Nearer Ones: Essays Exploring the Familiar*. Kent, Ohio: Kent State UP, 1979. 173–80.

Crawley, Tony. *The Steven Spielberg Story*. New York: Quill, 1983.

Duel. Dir. Steven Spielberg. Screenplay: Richard Matheson. Cast: Dennis Weaver (David Mann), Jacqueline Scott (Mrs. Mann). Music: Billy Goldenberg. Universal, 1973. Running time: 90 minutes.

Fenichel, Otto. *The Psychoanalytic Theory of Neurosis*. New York: Norton, 1945.

Freud, Sigmund. "On the Mechanism of Paranoia." *General Psychological Theory: Papers on Metapsychology*. 1911. Ed. Philip Rieff. New York: Collier, 1963.

Greenberg, Harvey R., M.D. *The Movies on Your Mind*. New York: Dutton, 1975.

King, Stephen. *Danse Macabre*. New York: Everest House, 1981.

Klein, Melanie. *Envy and Gratitude and Other Works, 1946–1963*. New York: Delacorte, 1975.

———. *Love, Guilt and Reparation and Other Works, 1921–1945*. New York: Delacorte, 1975.

Larson, Randall D. *Musique Fantastique: A Survey of Film Music in the Fantastic Cinema*. Metuchen, N.J.: Scarecrow Press, 1985.

Meissner, W. W. *The Paranoid Process*. New York: Jason Aronson, 1978.

Mott, Donald R., and Cheryl McAllister Saunders. *Steven Spielberg*. Boston: Twayne, 1986.

Palmer, Jerry. *Thrillers: Genesis and Structure of a Popular Genre*. New York: St. Martin's, 1979.

Pye, Michael, and Lynda Myles. *The Movie Brats: How the Film Generation Took Over Hollywood*. New York: Holt, 1979.

Snyder, Thomas Lee. "Sacred Encounters: The Myth of the Hero in the Horror, Science Fiction, Fantasy Films of George Lucas and Steven Spielberg." Diss. Northwestern U, 1984.

Todorov, Tzvetan. *The Fantastic: A Structural Approach to a Literary Genre*. Ithaca, N.Y.: Cornell UP, 1975.

"A Child Is Being Eaten":
Political Repressions, Alien Invasions

Terrence Holt

In The Political Unconscious, Fredric Jameson, arguing "the priority of the political interpretation of literary texts," writes that he "conceives of the political perspective not as some supplementary method, not as an optional auxiliary to other interpretive methods current today—the psychoanalytic or the myth-critical, the stylistic, the ethical, the structural—but rather as *the absolute horizon of all reading and interpretation"* (17; emphasis added).[1] Such a claim invites a response from psychoanalytic critics, and not least by its figure for an absolute perspective. A "horizon" is a curious trope for a totalizing vision of the world, for it necessarily implies a hemisphere beyond its bounds; invoking this figure, Jameson calls into doubt the absolute scope of his historicist political perspective. Although Jameson claims that his concept of a political unconscious retains the theoretical power of the psychoanalytic while purging it of its ahistoricism,[2] others have pointed out a crucial flaw in his construction of the unconscious, especially its denial of the countertransference (see Culler 370–71). As Jameson constructs it, the political unconscious ignores the full implications of the Freudian unconscious, along with the mechanism of repression that sustains it. But Jameson's attempt to repress psychoanalysis suffers the fate of all such repressions: the repressed returns. In his metaphor of the horizon, Jameson chooses a figure that gestures beyond the scope of his absolute perspective, toward the unconscious.

I would like to consider the role of repression in politics: the ways in which repression of unconscious material can subvert conscious political motivations, and what that drama of the political will and its undoing has to tell us about the wish for total knowledge that Jameson's claim expresses. It is important to be explicit on this point: it is not with Marxian analytics, but with the totalizing scope of Jameson's claim that I differ here. Although the tools I use in this essay are primarily those of the skeptical hermeneutics that have emerged from France in recent years, as well as certain fundamental principles of Freudian psychoanalysis, I make no claim for the totality of this perspective; beyond the horizon of this essay lies a world of textual problematics to which Marxian and other materialist discourses provide invaluable points of entry. My aim in the present case is not to repeat the history of American academic criticism in which Marxists have for so long been an excluded minority, but only to question the Marxian response to this repression as articulated by Jameson, in which the methods of the oppressor are simply co-opted by the victim. One of the points of this essay is the futility of such gestures, the way in which they simply reinscribe the subject in power relations.

Jameson anticipates the charge of totalization and is careful to assign total systems of knowledge a place within his critique. There are two forms of totalization, he finds, an improper and a proper. Totalization errs whenever it posits a mystified, pre-Hegelian absolute. When given its proper form, however, by Lukacs, as a methodological standard, Jameson holds (through a dazzling series of transformations that reaches its conclusion only in a discursive footnote) that totalization is not only permissible, but a political imperative: "the only realistic perspective in which a genuine Left would come into being" in the United States (*Political* 52–54n). There are several problems with this attempt to evade the onus of totalization while making use of it at the same time. First, it works primarily through a strategy of binary division and supplementation, making totalization (in its deficient, idealist form) the other guy's problem. While absolving Lukacs, Marx, and Hegel (and of course himself) from the charge of idealist totalization, Jameson, in *The Political Unconscious*, implicates Deleuze, Derrida (53), Weber, and Foucault (90n) in the raising of false absolutes.

Such a strategy trades on the false-consciousness model of ideology (despite his attempt to make other, unspecified misreaders of Lukacs bear this burden [52]), as yet another series of transformations reveals: the proper understanding of ideology, Jameson concludes, building on Marx's *Eighteenth Brumaire* and Lukacs's *History and Class Consciousness*, "posits ideology in terms of *strategies of containment*"

(52–53; original emphasis). This model of ideology, corresponding to Jameson's relative horizons, establishes Marxism as the absolute horizon and gives to Marxian analytics the heroic task of "unmasking" these containing strategies, a task that requires "a method whereby the 'false' and the ideological" (53) are equated—and the true and the Marxist take up a position as the ultimate, totalizing container. The real aporetic moment in this argument, however, is Jameson's description of Lukacs's achievement: the understanding that such strategies of containment "can be unmasked only by confrontation with the ideal of totality which they at once imply and repress" (53). In this essay I propose to apply this method to Jameson himself, confronting his own containing horizon with its implied, repressed ideal of perfection in power and knowledge.

The texts I will consider are drawn from science fiction, a genre that has also been excluded from the literary mainstream, and as a consequence has been in recent years very much a Marxist critical domain.[3] Narratives of invasions by alien creatures, H. G. Wells's *War of the Worlds,* Robert Heinlein's *The Puppet Masters,* and the recent motion pictures *Alien* and its sequel *Aliens* deal with a particular kind of political struggle, one with powerful resonances within the colonial-imperial politics of the twentieth century, as well as offering a metaphor for class and sexual politics. All of these texts adopt an overt political stance, but in each case that stance is subverted by repressed sexual anxieties which stem ultimately from a fear of our own construction within ahistorical systems of power and knowledge beyond our capacity to master.[4]

This subversion of the overt, class-oriented political suggests the particular difficulty Marxian analytics has in digesting all aspects of a particular text, but such difficulty is not entirely unanticipated by Jameson, who discusses the sexual material on which psychoanalysis is to a great extent founded, and dismisses it with the claim that

> The psychoanalytic demonstration of the sexual dimensions of overtly nonsexual conscious experience and behavior is possible only when the sexual "dispositif" or apparatus has by a process of isolation, autonomization, specialization, developed into an independent sign system or symbolic dimension in its own right; as long as sexuality remains as integrated into social life in general as, say, eating, its possibilities of symbolic extension are to that degree limited, and the sexual retains its status as a banal inner-worldly event and bodily function. (*Political* 64).

This claim situates the Freudian sexual as another aspect of the problem

Jameson finds fundamental to Freudianism, its partaking of the increasing "rationalization" (or "reification") of life in the capitalist era, a process in which

> the traditional or "natural" unities, social forms, human relations, cultural events, even religious systems, are systematically broken up in order to be reconstructed more efficiently, in the form of new post-natural processes or mechanisms; but in which, at the same time, these now-isolated broken bits and pieces of the older unities acquire a certain autonomy of their own, a semi-autonomous coherence which . . . in some measure serves to compensate for the dehumanization of experience reification brings with it, and to rectify the otherwise intolerable effects of the new process. (*Political* 63)

Like so many of Jameson's anticipations of possible objections to his argument, his argument here trades on our prior acceptance of the Marxian hermeneutic—here, most tellingly, on its teleology.

Jameson explains the significance of rationalization and contains its tendency to "acquire a certain autonomy" by emphasizing "the Utopian vocation of the newly reified sense" (63), its urge to restore a lost unity of perception—in other words, by naturalizing it within the Marxian scheme of history, wherein all alienated subjects yearn for their natural communal condition. But for readers who do not already share Jameson's faith in that vocation, the tendency of the rationalized fragments of our intellectual life to take on a life of their own could just as plausibly demonstrate the drift of the signifier as any tendency to return to a unitary origin. This passage also, it is worth pointing out, describes the totalizing narrative of history that Marx constructed out of the shattered and materialized biblical system of history.[5] It suggests that the utopian vision of Marxism, in its totalizing, teleological sweep as invoked everywhere by Jameson, is itself a "symbolic experience of libidinal gratification" (63) rather than an entry into the register Lacan has termed the "Real."[6] At the very least, the circularities involved in Jameson's argument on the relations between history and Freudian theories of sexuality point to a problem in Marxian analytics in its attempt to digest phenomena whose historical behavior may work itself out on time-scales greater than that originally envisioned by Marx.

The question that should engage our attention at this juncture, however, is not one of choosing between hermeneutics: to respond to Jameson's claim that everything is political with the counterclaim that everything is sexual is simply to invert and repeat his totalizing gesture. The more useful line of investigation might treat the reasons behind the need to totalize, an investigation that, as Jameson offers the issue to us, bears on the problem of repression. What might readings of political struggles tell us about Jameson's need to repress the sexual, about his (and our) own nostalgic, utopian vocation? And what might such readings tell us about the difficulties lying in the way of Jameson's—or our own—achievement of a totalizing theoretical position?

Considering science fiction stories of alien invasion from a psycho-analytic perspective offers one set of answers to these questions. In these fantasies of invasion, the structures of authority are displacements of the structures of the Oedipal sexual hierarchy. The sign of power resolves continually into the phallus: the invading alien threatens an expropria-tive castration in which the phallus is absorbed into the body of a female Other; its phallus co-opted, the powerless body of the male subject is physically invaded. The female alien cloaks the authority of the Oedipal father in the guise of the phallic mother,[7] who functions as a scapegoat for the real threat of the Oedipal father. This scapegoat (or, as Julia Kristeva has termed it, a figure of abjection), when expelled, allows the subject to retain a fantasy of independence or integrity by cloaking a repressed desire to capitulate to the father.

The desire to submit to authority and the repression of that desire are described by Freud in "A Child Is Being Beaten" (17: 177–204). The essay is interesting for the dual role repression plays, not only in the cases themselves, but also in Freud's account of them. One repression of patients is their inability to characterize a persistent fantasy in any more detail than the phrase, "a child is being beaten." Under analysis, more detail emerges: another child, not the patient, is being beaten. But the picture refuses to resolve; the identity of the one administering the beat-ing remains hidden. Freud can only infer, by a process his account never fully explains, that the one beating is the subject's father, and the beat-ing stands for sexual intercourse. The subject's inability to identify the victim or the aggressor allows the patient to indulge a fantasy otherwise forbidden; the fantasy is plainly a pleasurable one. But Freud himself colludes in this repression: his essay never reveals the full content of his patients' fantasies, or the process by which he infers it. Evidently an element of countertransference is involved: the fantasy is plainly an ex-pression of the patients' transferential desire for Freud, and this accounts both for the cloaking of the aggressor's identity *and* Freud's collusion in that repression.[8] Freud, customarily the revealer of the repressed, in his account aligns himself with the agencies of repression, concealing from the reader his own forbidden desires just as his patients concealed their desire from him. Freud's essay, treating as it does both the use of force and the adjustment of behavior, touches on the political and demonstrates one way in which the repression of the sexual can overturn political agenda.[9]

The exemplary case of such subversion in the context of alien invasion is H. G. Wells's *War of the Worlds*. Although ostensibly a critique of imperialism and class struggle,[10] Wells's story succumbs to a sexual hysteria figured in the form of the Martian invaders. With their malign oversight, multiple tentacles, and predatory habits, Wells's Martians are terrifying images of the phallic mother as castrating avenger. Their vaguely defined features are dominated by those tentacles and "a pair of very large dark-colored eyes, and just beneath this a kind of fleshy beak" (139). A caricature of the female body, this description focuses our attention on the castration anxiety generated by the sight of female genitals: the fleshy beak—both vagina and mouth—is a fantasy of the *vagina dentata*.

The Martian mouth is the central horror in *The War of the Worlds* because it not only threatens castration, but it also figures intercourse as a vampirism in which men are helpless victims. As the narrator describes it, this process begins with the Martians gripping "a *man* . . . a man of considerable consequence" (151–52). This figure is of considerable consequence not least because (as the authorial emphasis insists) he shares the narrator's gender. To feed, the Martians

took the fresh living blood of other creatures and *injected* it into their own veins. . . . [S]queamish as I may seem, I cannot bring myself to describe what I could not endure even to continue watching. Let it suffice to say that blood obtained from a still living animal, in most cases from a human being, was run directly by means of a little pipette into the recipient canal. . . . (141; original emphasis and ellipsis)

The description both represses and underscores a process conflating copulation and consumption. The means of that injection, the "little pipette" which figures the man's phallus, is diminished by both the adjective and the suffix. The site of the injection, "the recipient canal . . . ," is not only euphemized, but the description also trails off in an ellipsis, a double verbal blankness that stands for an anatomical absence. Wells's invasion, then, depicts men as victims of creatures imagined as phallic women, into whose recipient canals men insert their fragile pipettes—and die.

The War of the Worlds is, however, finally apotropaic—as such fantasies usually are. (See again Freud on the Medusa's head.) The invasion is repulsed, and the prevailing hierarchies are reestablished with a vengeance: if mere microbes can vanquish the invaders, a man of consequence—or, anyway, of a little pipette—need have no fear. But the counterphobic need to squash the threat of the invaders has derailed the novel's political train: it is microbes that vanquish the rulers of the Earth, not the proletarian artilleryman; class struggle has been subsumed in a sexual one.

In the work of an avowedly conservative author, Robert Heinlein, the same overreaction occurs, with the same subversive political effects. Over his life's work Heinlein has figured himself as a foe of authority in all its guises. Yet in his 1947 novel, *The Puppet Masters*, the threat of alien domination provides an occasion for indulging a desire to be dominated sexually. The novel offers itself as a story of armed battle against totalitarian authority, over the course of which a young man grows up to supplant his father. Again, the threat figured by the alien invaders is castration, and the challenge confronting the narrator is to prevent a feared inversion of a sexual order. In the story's catastrophe, however, that inversion occurs; even while supplanting the father, the young man capitulates to him sexually, and satisfies a repressed desire to be dominated by the very authority against which he seems to be waging war.

The invaders in *The Puppet Masters* seem a typical product of the postwar Red Scare.[11] Parasites who control their human hosts' minds, they are not easily detected. In historical context, the novel's political moral is obvious (the narrator tells us, for instance, that the invaders feel most at home in the Soviet Union). But the novel's overt politics are only a blind; the power struggle that drives the plot is plainly Oedipal. Investigating the alien landing, for instance, the narrator Elihu, who is a secret agent, works undercover with his boss, called throughout the novel "The Old Man," and a female agent, Mary. They pose as a family group. The Old Man, naturally, acts the part of the father, Elihu his son, and Mary his daughter. Elihu's sexual overtures toward Mary are squashed by The Old Man, with the warning that The Old Man values Mary more, and that Elihu is expendable. This Old Man functions, as Old Men generally do, as the Oedipal father, thwarting the son's sexual desires for the women in the family, threatening death for disobedience. But Heinlein makes the Oedipal scenario explicit, for this Old Man actually is Elihu's father. (We learn this only in chapter 11, in a scene that also reveals that Mary is "a great deal like" Elihu's mother [122].)

The female component of the family triangle, Mary, is another figure for the phallic mother. Described as a "walking arsenal" who would "as soon shoot as shake hands," when searched for weapons, on two occasions she produces four or more handguns. The surplus of phallic symbols helps to identify her with the phallic mother, but the key to her role is her talent for detecting humans under control of the alien invaders. She identifies victims by detecting a peculiar lack. "I *know*," she tells Elihu. "I always know. Something was wrong with them. They were dead inside. Harem guards, if you know what I mean" (14). To be captured by these aliens (or "hagridden," as the novel calls it) is to be castrated, and Mary, the woman with all the guns, is the one who detects the lack.

Mary's talent reveals that the aliens, from Saturn's moon Titan,[12] figure a threat of castration, but the source of that threat in *The Puppet Masters* is ultimately the Oedipal father. At the novel's climax, The Old Man is himself possessed by a Titan and takes Elihu prisoner; The Old Man's parasite starts to divide, preparing a second for Elihu. Elihu realizes "with rigid terror, I had no more than five minutes of individual life left to me. My new master was being born and would be ready to mount me" (339).[13] The active participle that ends the passage gives the game away. We have had hints previously, but nothing that makes so very plain that what Elihu has to fear from the invaders is anal rape—rape by the Oedipal father. Worse, he fears his complicity in it. Earlier in the novel, when The Old Man coerces Elihu into hosting a captured Titan so that it can be interrogated,[14] Elihu reports "a dark and certain thought that if I were alone with it, I would be able to do nothing, that I would freeze while it crawled up me and settled . . . between my shoulder blades, searched out my spinal column, took possession of my brain and my very self" (94). This "dark and certain thought" suggests that The Old Man has no need to coerce: it is not only fear, but also *desire* that stiffens Elihu as his Old Man now prepared a second "master" to mount him.

This desire has a political implication as well as a sexual one. Here, as with Wells, it undoes the novel's overt political concerns, figuring a capitulation to the totalitarian invaders Elihu fights desperately to repel. Over the course of the novel, Elihu has managed to supplant The Old Man as chief of his intelligence agency, and singlehandedly developed a strategy to repel the alien invasion. But at the climax of the novel, the one invasion he cannot repel is the one that has been determining, like a puppet master, all the others: his father's invasion of Elihu's anatomy.

Elihu struggles to forestall this outcome, but he succeeds only in sustaining its repression. He saves The Old Man, the world, and himself, in one sexually charged convulsive gesture, a gesture that refers to a sexual coupling between father and son, but dissipates its threat by keeping it figurative. Elihu achieves this deliverance (not incidentally) by firing off all the rockets of the airship in which his father is holding him. This explosive thrust slams The Old Man back in his seat, squashing his parasite: "Dad was caught in that terrible total reflex, that spasm of every muscle that I had seen three times before. He bounced forward against the wheel, face contorted, fingers writhing" (340). In the silence after the crash, Elihu recalls, "I lay face to face with him, almost cheek to cheek," crying, "Don't die. I can't get along without you" (342, 343). Elihu receives in reward his father's blessing: the gravely injured—or orgasmically winded—Old Man gasps, "Your mother—said to tell you—she was—proud of you," and collapses (343). The Old Man is freed from his identification with the Titan and ceases to stand between Elihu and his mother, freeing Elihu to confess his need for The Old Man; the sexual threat realized in The Old Man's spasm is dispelled with the parasite's death. A new order of things is achieved, but that order is a wishful sexual one, not political. The novel's attention to the political scene has come to concentrate primarily on the passage of a law requiring all Americans to strip naked, a political victory that seems to have more to do with a fantasy of uninhibited sexual access than anything else.[15]

The 1979 film *Alien* and its 1986 sequel *Aliens* also begin by offering an explicit political context. The overt political concern of these films is colonialist exploitation, but once encoded into a creature that colonizes human beings, this concern is sexualized, and a progressive critique of colonial politics embraces conservative sexual politics. The films portray Warrant Officer Ripley in her struggles to maintain her position within male power structures, but repressed anxiety about gender continually undermines her position.

The gender anxiety in *Alien* concentrates first on childbirth. The film begins by raising a conventional political issue that punningly tropes that anxiety, labor unrest among the crew of the spaceship *Nostromo*. But the issue is set aside when a distress signal lures the ship to an abandoned, alien vessel. There one of the *Nostromo*'s crew is colonized by a parasite whose reproductive life cycle causes it to burst from the distended belly of its human host in a terrifying—and fatal—parody of labor. The emergence of the alien, converting fears of labor unrest to fears of what it means to go into labor, acts out the emergence of sexual fears from beneath the mask of political issues. The fear that inhabits this film is of what it means to be a woman in a world dominated by men; it is terrified about the implications of female sexuality. *Alien*, along with its sequel *Aliens*, pursues these implications in a variety of ways, all of which tend to portray women as monstrosities—terrifyingly Other,[16] and ultimately powerless in a world wherein gender is constructed solely in terms of the phallus. This is the issue repressed behind the films' apparent concern with mothers and mothering, and it undoes all of their explicit or implicit political thematics.

The sexual politics of both films are ostensibly feminist. The heroine, Warrant Officer Ripley, is a strong woman: the only survivor in *Alien*, she defeats the invader singlehandedly at the film's climax; in *Aliens*, along with the orphan girl Newt, she defeats an entire nest of the monsters. She is equally alone and similarly threatened in her relations to a male-dominated human world. As the only woman on the crew of the *Nostromo*, her accession to command on the death of its captain is greeted by a murderous attack from a male android (an attack that consists of attempting to force a rolled up skin magazine down her throat). In *Aliens*, she is cashiered by a predominantly male board of inquiry, then blackmailed by a male representative of the colonist Company: the price of her being permitted to return to her old job is that she return to the planet where the *Nostromo* was colonized, to aid in the investigation of a loss of signal from the human colony the Company has established on that world.

The weakness of Ripley's position is attributed to a biological essentialism. On her voyage out, Ripley travels with a platoon of marines, a group that includes women, but women so muscular as to invite doubtful jokes about their gender from their male comrades (the film reinforces these doubts by equipping one of these women with a cannon mounted on a belt slung low across her hips). In the company of these marines, Ripley feels useless. When they laughingly rebuff her offer to help in loading munitions on their landing craft, Ripley counters by demonstrating her skill with a loading machine. The demonstration impresses the marines, primarily because of the nature of that loader. It is in the shape of an enormous man: to operate it, Ripley climbs inside it, puts it on like a suit of armor. Wearing it, the motions of her limbs are strengthened; she becomes as powerful—as useful to the marines—as a man.

Ripley's use of andromorphic mechanical aids to gain power prefigures later metamorphoses. As she stalks through the alien nest, armed with machine gun, grenade launcher, *and* flame-thrower, her armaments identify her with a familiar figure, the phallic mother. Here, she is both phallic and mothering: she stalks the nest in order to rescue the orphan Newt, who has been captured by the aliens. Her nemesis, the queen of the alien nest, is yet another phallic mother. The queen's angular, spiky foreparts, modeled apparently after a praying mantis, are attached to an enormous, bulbous, pulsating ovary the size of a dirigible, from the end of which emerges a series of slime-covered eggs.[17] The battle between the two is actually a contest between specular opposites and is therefore no contest.

Detaching her phallic foreparts from her female posterior, the queen becomes pure marauding phallus, demonstrating the fear underlying the fear of motherhood that has informed both *Alien* and *Aliens*. This detachment, revealing the phallus that was cloaked in female guise, acts out the real logic of the film: within every phallic mother is just another phallus. And the function of that phallus is to threaten castration: from within her toothy mouth, the alien queen projects a long, barbed tongue: a *penis dentatus*. This strange organ raises yet another fear: a penis that bites, it conflates an image of the phallic with one of castration. The fear is that behind every phallus there may be no phallus at all: that women, even the phallic mother, are merely castrated men.[18]

In these films the super-powerful, murderous alien conflates absolute power with the phallic; within an order that figures power as phallic, to be castrated is to be powerless. Within this definition of perfection, anyone constructed as castrated will always be lacking, always doomed to go down in defeat before the unbeatable, perfect organism. And in *Aliens*, as in culture in general, women are the abject figures of castration. As Ripley does battle with this monster for Newt, she demonstrates a doomed, apotropaic response to her fear of her own construction, one that is doomed because it only confirms the film's construction of both power and woman. In her battle with the alien queen, Ripley is bested at every turn, until she climbs into the man-shaped loader. It is this mechanical contrivance that gives her the strength to face and ultimately defeat the queen. But the victory is pyrrhic: her tactics have lost her the real battle before it was begun. By adopting a man-shaped contrivance to fight off the phallic mother, Ripley accepts a phallocentric culture's judgment of the female body as deficient, ultimately as monstrous as the queen itself. (In fact, in her angular armor, she demonstrates her essential similarity with the queen: they are both made murderously capable only by assuming the form of men.) And in Ripley's case, this armor is only a temporary refuge: in her battle with the queen, she loses it, and it is expelled out the ship's airlock with the alien. The film acknowledges her change of status immediately, as Newt clings to her, calling her (to Ripley's evident relief and joy) "Mommy." The phallic has been expelled, and what remains is the mother—hardly the "new woman" Ripley seemed at first to represent.

I would like to turn now to consider the implications of that alien infestation in its apparently absolute power as a reflection on Jameson's claim for the absolute power of the political. "Always historicize," Jameson writes (*Political* 9). What he seems to mean, however—what *Aliens* in its inscription of power under the sign of the phallus suggests he means—is "always phallicize."[19] If the phallus functions, as Lacan writes, ambiguously as a sign of the loss of our integrity as selves, and as a dream of what that integrity might be, I would like to suggest that *The Political Unconscious* invokes history for the same reason *Aliens* invokes the phallus—as a consoling fantasy of totalizing power and knowledge, one that places both texts outside of and in control of forces within which they are actually constructed themselves. One of these forces is, as I have been arguing, a biological one, a force that is as much a part of historical processes as it is determined by them.

The emphasis on the phallus in *Aliens* is ultimately a consoling one. That this should be so has been partially concealed by my collusion with the films in their central repression—their claim that, in figuring their protagonist as a woman, they are ultimately female texts. This is, of course, an impossibility: the "horizon" of these films (and, as Luce Irigaray and other feminist critics have argued, of all acts of representation) is male.[20] Within a male text, the notion that the phallus is omnipotent and capable of reproducing itself endlessly and without female help is profoundly consoling. The universality of castration anxiety demonstrated in the texts we have been reading suggests why such a consolation would be needed. But this fantasy also says something about the nature of totalization itself, and the message it gives us speaks past the confines of science fiction to Jameson's wish for a totalizing explanation of human history.

Alien makes that statement during an interview with the decapitated head of an android, Ash. Ash, the ship's science officer,[21] loses his head while attempting to murder Ripley. When the crew revives his dismembered head and interrogates it,[22] it is not Ash who replies, but a part of his body that has been removed; his voice is that of the body's absent member. Ash represents a fantasy of the phallus speaking past castration, of the subject speaking outside of its own disintegration: it is an

oracular voice, speaking from an unattainable place beyond all horizons, the seat of total knowledge, speaking in what Lacan has called the
Name of the Father (179–221). And the message it brings is of a self-
reflexive worship of totalization. Ash's head admires the phallic alien, it
says, because it is "perfect," and goes on to tell how it is perfect in terms
that describe its decapitated self as well.

Ash admires the alien precisely for its lack of a body and the unruly
emotions that a body inevitably generates. "I admire its purity," he tells
the crew. It is "a survivor, unclouded by conscience, remorse, or delusions of morality." Here is a fantasy of perfection in the agencies of
power and knowledge, one that is equally consoling, equally impossible, as the fantasy of the immortal phallus. The source of that perfection,
Ash's head proclaims, is that the alien, like this imaginary phallus, is
completely integrated, free of discontinuity, perfectly rationalized.[23]
The perfect detachment with which Ash speaks is the detachment one
seeks in any theoretical stance that places one outside of and in control of
forces one fears because they imply the subject's own contingency and
construction with them. This fantasy, to the extent that it is an apotropaic response to the insufficiency of the subject, reflects a fear, the same
fear that Jameson attempts to scare away with his totalizing system, a
system that denies the influence of the body and the sexual members
attached to it, within our reconnaissance of the historical process.

One conclusion such fantasies bring us to is that our reconnaissance
of history should return to the body. Fredric Jameson himself unconsciously suggests something similar, through another set of figures that
emerges within his political narrative. Arguing the inescapability of
"allegorical master narratives" such as his own, Jameson makes an intriguing characterization of the affect of the historical: such allegories,
he writes, correspond to

> those cobwebs of topical allusion which the ahistorical and formalizing reader
> attempts desperately to brush away—that dry and intolerable chitinous mur-
> mur of footnotes reminding us of the implied references to long-dead contem-
> porary events and political situations in Milton and Swift, in Spenser or Haw-
> thorne; if the modern reader is bored or scandalized by the roots such texts send
> down into the contingent circumstances of their own historical time, this is
> surely testimony as to his resistance to his own political unconscious and to
> his denial . . . of the reading and the writing of the text of history within
> himself. (*Political* 34)

The rhetoric in this passage deploys two complementary tactics. First, it projects repression onto a deficient, imaginary Other, as if repression were a problem of false consciousness, avoidable from a proper perspective. That "ahistorical and formalizing reader," so "desperately" attempting to brush aside "cobwebs of topical allusion," "bored and scandalized" by the "long-dead historical: who is this reader? The figure is unmistakably a straw man, a scapegoat. What is being scapegoated here? Perhaps a better question might be, what is being abjected? For the "cobwebs" and the "chitin" that cling to Jameson's rhetoric point to the crucial intersection between *Aliens* and *The Political Unconscious:* both use excrement and armor, the slime and exoskeletons of insects, to figure both a threat and its apotropaic repression. The slime and webbing of the alien—the monstrous Other which Jameson identifies with the historical—point us to the threat that always inhabits the abject: the "long-dead" figures of the past, of our biology and its concomitant mortality, announcing our contingency within history.[24]

For the history that haunts Jameson's narrative of the political—that which he desperately brushes aside, against which he armors himself within his own master narrative, the Marxian organism that subsumes the threat of history within itself—is not, ultimately, political history. It is biological history which binds us in time between slime and chitinous whispers, between birth and death, boundaries that are the only absolute horizon the world knows. These boundaries do not totalize: they announce our prevenient and ultimate disintegration. And what both Jameson and *Aliens* offer as consolation for this is only armor: the terrifying chitinous carapace of the alien queen, the clanging machinery of Ripley's loader, or the totalizing embrace of Jameson's own master narrative, which repels all fragmenting, skeptical hermeneutics, subsumes them, "at once canceling and preserving" them (*Political* 10)—seals them up, like the colonized colonists, and expropriates their hollow bodies to reproduce itself eternally, world without end.

Although I argue with Jameson's privileging of one interpretive mode, on his most important point I agree with him: the political *is* the crucial realm of human behavior today and will continue to be so long as political acts can hold the human race in jeopardy. We need a proper understanding of the political now more than ever and should reject no insight that offers hope of furthering our knowledge in this area. What we must do now is expand our horizons in a construction of the political in all its manifestations, of which the Marxian paradigm of class struggle is only one.

The first place to do this would be to reopen the question: How do we define the political? The burden of this question is on the implications of *define*—a term that, by drawing boundaries, must always exclude. The persistent invasions that we've been tracking here of the overt political by the repressed sexual suggest that the political involves more than we think—that it is literally more than we *can* think. Repression, like ideology, is more than false consciousness: it is an inescapable aspect of our lives, and this is as true of us as political beings as in any other phase of our existence. These texts show us some of the ways by which repression serves authority, by blinding us to the ways in which *we* construct authority, colluding in our own oppression. The things we choose to leave out of our definitions of the political are the ones most likely to confine us, precisely because we wish to believe ourselves immune to them.

The crucial fact about power, as Foucault has taught us,[26] is our own contributions to it, and these contributions have as at least one of their sources our unconscious fears about our nature as individuals, our bodies and their sexuality. The important feature of these constructions, however, is that they never remain within the unconscious, nor do they keep themselves safely within the boundaries of the Imaginary. Transcoded onto the social, they operate as agencies of authority. Our fears about authority, the kinds of powers that we attribute to it, lead us to grant it power it might not otherwise have.

The authorities we create in our imaginations are, like the authority constructed by Marx, expropriative: but what they take from us is not our labor, but, through our repression of our own involvement in them, our political autonomy.[27] So long as we are capable of calling figures of authority into being, of altering our behavior at the behest of projections of our own unconscious—which is to say, always—we ourselves are complicit in the expropriation of our freedoms, are always a part of the system of relations within which our freedoms are both circumscribed and inscribed. To recognize our complicity with those systems is the necessary precondition to taking action to limit our subjection, to taking back, to whatever limited extent is possible, what we otherwise too willingly, too blindly give away.

Notes

1. For responses to Fredric Jameson from a variety of perspectives, see Geoff Bennington's "Not Yet"; Alice N. Benston's untitled review in *Sub-stance;* Jonathan Culler's

"Textual Self-Consciousness and the Textual Unconscious"; Jerry A. Flieger's "The Prison-House of Ideology"; and Michael Ryan's "The Marxian-Deconstruction Debate."

2. For Jameson's most extensive treatment of the relationship between Marxism and psychoanalysis, see his "Imaginary and Symbolic in Lacan: Marxism, Psychoanalytic Criticism, and the Problem of Subject." In this essay, Jameson resists the tendency toward totalization that overtakes *The Political Unconscious*, insisting on the discontinuity between the areas of sexuality and class dynamics, arguing that the "local interrelationships" between the two fields cannot "properly furnish a model of the relationship of sexuality to class consciousness as a whole" (385-86). It is in fact his respect for the Foucauldean concept of discontinuity (see, e.g., his statement on "the limits of meaning," p. 390) that preserves this earlier essay from the absolutism of *The Political Unconscious*.

3. In addition to H. Bruce Franklin's *Future Perfect*, Robert Scholes's *Structural Fabulation*, Darko Suvin's *Metamorphoses*, and Patrick Parrinder's *Science Fiction*, all of them leading figures in science fiction criticism who use, explicitly or implicity, Marxian analysis, Jameson himself (in "Generic Discontinuities in SF" and "World-Reduction in Le Guin") has worked in this genre. One reason for Marxian interest in science fiction might be the one implied by Franklin's title. Science fiction critics repeat the original gesture of Marx in moving historical study into a realm where anything is possible—even the achievement of the goals of a grand historical plan. (The long-standing legitimacy of the genre in the Soviet Union points to such an interest; see Suvin's *Russian Science Fiction* for an indication of Russian interest in the field—an interest that grows, interestingly, from prerevolutionary utopianism.) Other reasons might have to do with resistance to Marx within the critical mainstream, which has forced Marxists to marginal genres. (Although both Marx and science fiction have been brought somewhat within the mainstream in recent years, neither camp is entirely confident of their welcome there.) Finally, the status of science fiction as a "popular" literature makes it a natural subject for Marxian analyses.

4. The language of mastery is, of course, Jameson's, who offers the Marxian teleology as the "master code" (*Political* 10) against which he measures all other interpretive modes.

5. M. H. Abrams makes this parallel in *Natural Supernaturalism* (313-16).

6. For discussion of the "Real" in relation to the "Imaginary" and "Symbolic," see Jacques Lacan, *Ecrits: A Selection* 179-225.

7. The phallic mother appears in several guises in psychoanalytic literature. She possesses the phallus in accordance with what Freud in "Medusa's Head" calls "the technical rule according to which multiplication of penis symbols signifies castration" (18:273-75); having not one phallus but many, she functions as a sign of castration, or appears as a potential castrator. Common symbolic representations of the phallic mother include spiders and octopuses, whose multiple legs are multiplied penises and whose feeding habits displace the common infantile anxiety about being eaten by the mother (which can itself be seen as a displacement of castration anxiety). For a political reading of this aspect of the castration complex, see Neil Hertz's article, "Medusa's Head: Male Hysteria."

8. That repression is a strategy deployed in the agency of power has become a truism in the study of power relations. See Michel Foucault, *History of Sexuality, I* 15-50. One point that Foucault's discussion of the juridical demonstrates is that relations between analyst and analysand, writer and reader are also relations of power, especially when the relationship revolves, as it does here, around the extraction or withholding of information.

9. For discussion of the role of violence in the political, see Foucault, *Discipline and*

Punish (esp. 3–72). Also, in "The Subject and Power," Foucault identifies violence as power's "primitive form, its permanent secret, and its last resource," but maintains that the essence of power relations is that it acts upon the actions of others so as to shape them to its ends (789).

10. In *Science Fiction: A Critical Guide,* both Patrick Parrinder and John Huntington acknowledge the novel's interest in imperialism and dialectical conflict, as does Jameson himself in "Generic Discontinuities." See also Bernard Bergonzi, *The Early H. G. Wells* 123–69.

11. H. Bruce Franklin, in *Robert A. Heinlein* (98–101), notes that anti-Communist agenda of *The Puppet Masters,* contextualizing it in terms of the post-World War II Red Scare.

12. The name given these creatures is, of course, evocative of the original Oedipal castration myth. The epithet persistently attached to their predations—"hagriding"—also associates them with a typically female figure of the abject, the witch, the nightmare, the incubus/succubus, figures of horror cast out because they suggest the subject's own lack of integrity. Lacan's theory of the creation of the subject in castration and Kristeva's concept of the abject intersect nicely in the two names given the castrating authority figures in this novel.

13. That Elihu watches "with rigid terror" suggests some of the apotropaic functions of this fantasy. As Freud outlines in "The Medusa's Head," the stiffening in men petrified by the sight of phallic women is a consoling reminder of sexual potency. In this context, however, it also expresses the victim's desire.

14. It is interesting to note that this interrogation, like another scene in which The Old Man confronts Mary with her own history as victim of the parasites so as to elicit information from her, echoes the relationship between analyst and analysand in Freud's "A Child Is Being Beaten." The Old Man's effort to extract withheld information in these scenes indicates the structural similarities, in terms of power relations, between the Freudian therapeutic relationship and the Foucauldean juridical.

15. In his study of Heinlein, Franklin also notes, without comment, the prominent role of this curious fantasy of the law (100).

16. For a feminist reading of *Alien,* which places the film within a larger context of the abjection of the mother in science fiction horror film, see Barbara Creed's "Horror and the Monstrous-Feminine."

17. This sexual chimera, phallus on top, grossly distorted mother below, echoes the form of the *Nostromo* in *Alien,* which is angularly mechanical above, but on its smooth hull sports six rounded, dark-tipped projections, unmistakably breasts. For viewers who miss this brief shot, the film also provides a clue in naming the ship's master computer "Mother." The crew's encounters with the ship are all conversations with "Mother" in which missions are (or are not) "aborted," "umbilicals" detach, etc.

18. Whether this image is more frightening than that of the *vagina dentata* or is apotropaic, as Freud describes in "Medusa's Head," is a matter of perspective. Whereas Freud would call it apotropaic, reminding his (male) audience that they still possess the phallus, Lacan would see such an image as phobic, reminding the (gendered) audience of their construction within castration (see *Ecrits* 281–92, as well as Jane Gallop's *Reading Lacan*). Perhaps the best explanation of the affect of the alien queen is Julia Kristeva's theory of abjection as set out in *Powers of Horror* (5–6, 56–89), in which she argues that the mother's power of reproduction, calling into question the integrity of the subject, makes her a figure of particular loathing.

19. As does, as well, Jameson's persistent rhetorical tic: the use of the epithet "master" to signify the totalizing power of history (e.g., p. 33, where the Marxian philosophy of history appears as "a master narrative in its own right"). A Lacanian reading of the historicist (especially the new historicist) reverence for the historical datum reinforces this identification: the spectacle of historical fact turns history into Lacan's *objet petit a*, a gaze at a fetishized part-object that stands, in a perversely consoling relationship, for the missing phallus.

20. See Luce Irigaray, *Speculum of the Other Woman*, for a discussion of the essentially male nature of representation.

21. This rank owes something to the character Spock in *Star Trek*, an association underscored by Ash's rejection of emotion. The detachment of science from emotion (a detachment Ash's decapitated head figures neatly) is a rarely questioned dogma in culture generally, one often echoed in the assertion that Marxism offers a "scientific" analysis of culture. For a suggestive feminist critique of this dogma, see Mary Jacobus, *Reading Woman*, in which she argues that science is no more immune to sexualization than any other discourse.

22. Here, too, the interrogated subject speaks of the totality of power in a context that reveals a frequent misprision of Foucault: power may not actually *be* total, but that totality is the wish of the subject within power relations. Ash speaks to the subject's desire that there be such totality: the audience's *frisson* at this scene is the essence of Lacanian *jouissance*, the mixture of ecstasy and despair with which we contemplate the imaginary, unattainable objects of our desire. Here, that desire is for a totalizing matrix of power.

23. *Discontinuity*, the crucial term in Foucault's definition of the discursive, points (like Lacan's castration and Derrida's *différence*), to the inaccessibility of total knowledge. Rationalization, or *reification*, is also a key term in Jameson's critique of Freud (*Political* 58-67).

24. Another term for which might be Lacan's Name-of-the Father, which is, as Lacan reminds us, always the dead father, and through which we are constructed in terms of our insufficiency as subjects, an insufficiency dictating our interminable cure from the nightmare of history, the inescapability of repression, our eternal exile from the real in which that dead father might have lived.

25. A fascinating prefiguration of this identification between the alien queen-mother and the master narrative of *The Political Unconscious* appears in Jameson's earlier piece, "Imaginary and Symbolic in Lacan," where, discussing the origins of Lacan's imaginary in the work of Melanie Klein, Jameson describes the "logic specific to Imaginary space, whose dominant category proves to be the opposition of container and contained, the fundamental relationship of inside to outside, which clearly enough originates in the infant's fantasies about the maternal body as the receptacle of part-objects (confusion between childbirth and evacuation, etc.)" (356). Identifying mothers (mothers who implicitly eat part-objects) with containers, Jameson points toward an inevitable conflation of totalizations: the all-encompassing container of Marxian theory with the all-embracing mother, the logical ultimate step in a historical discourse that seeks to naturalize itself in the material. Jameson's note to this passage makes the connection even closer: in it, he characterizes a science fiction story (Philip José Farmer's "Mother") as "the archetypal realization of these fantasies" of the containing mother (356n).

26. On the subject of repression, Foucault has also raised some enormously generative questions, aimed generally at interrogating the possible uses to which repression might be put within power relations. In *History of Sexuality, I* (15-49), he observes that some spe-

cies of repression may be no repression at all but a ruse, deployed in order to mystify and ultimately call attention to the agencies by which the subject is known, ordered, and disciplined. Although by defining repression too broadly (or more broadly than Freud's usage would admit) it is possible to read this claim as a refutation of psychoanalysis, such a refutation is easily dismissed and finally irrelevant. No matter what the agency that deploys repression, for whatever purpose, the fact remains that a gesture we recognize as repression does occur, our recognition of it as repression indicates that it is not effective, and from that point a double drama of concealment and revelation ensues, which results not only in the articulation of whatever agency initiates the repression, but also, through the transference and the countertransference, in the implication of the subject and the normalizing analyst in that agency. Whether we call such a process *psychoanalysis* or *power relations* seems beside the point, especially in light of the political ramifications of such a choice: the use of the Foucauldean paradigm can be every bit as normalizing (at least insofar as it serves as an apology for the use and abuse of power) as the Freudian (which can, in the hands of a feminist like Gallop, unsettle phallocentrist structures of authority).

27. Whatever autonomy we possess (even locally) is, of course, always under question to the same extent and for the same reasons that our individual existence as subjects is, but Foucault himself, in "The Subject and Power," does not deny the efficacy of local action against power. To question that autonomy is, in fact, simply another way of participating in the expropriation of our independence, and reveals not only our own responsibility for giving it up, but our desire to give it up to an imaginary authority, whether we call it the father or the phallus, historical process, politics, or power. Certainly, autonomy and independence are impossible ideals, but so long as humans in community tend to exert power to self-destructive ends (and the history of the world, as well as the present geopolitical situation, suggests that this tendency is strong), these are ideals that we would do well to cultivate or at least keep in reserve.

Works Cited

Abrams, M. H. *Natural Supernaturalism*. New York: Norton, 1973.

Alien. Dir. Ridley Scott. Prod. Gordon Carroll, David Giler, Walter Hill. Writ. Dan O'Bannon. With Sigourney Weaver, Tom Skerritt. Twentieth Century Fox, 1979.

Aliens. Dir. and writ. James Cameron. Prod. Gale Hurd. With Sigourney Weaver and Michael Bilhn. Twentieth Century Fox, 1986.

Bennington, Geoff. "Not Yet." *Diacritics* 12 (1982): 23–32.

Benston, Alice N. Untitled review. *Sub-stance* 41 (1983): 97–103.

Bergonzi, Bernard. *The Early H. G. Wells*. Toronto: U of Toronto P, 1961.

Creed, Barbara. "Horror and the Monstrous-Feminine: An Imaginary Abjection." *Screen* 27 (1986): 44–70.

Culler, Jonathan. "Textual Self-Consciousness and the Textual Unconscious." *Style* 18.3 (1984): 369–76.

Flieger, Jerry A. "The Prison-House of Ideology: Critic as Inmate." *Diacritics* 12 (1982): 47–56.

Foucault, Michel. *Discipline and Punish: The Birth of the Prison*. Trans. Alan Sheridan. New York: Penguin, 1979.

———. *The History of Sexuality, I*. Trans. Robert Hurley. New York: Random, 1980.

———. "The Subject and Power." *Critical Inquiry* 8 (Summer 1982): 777-93.

Franklin, H. Bruce. *Future Perfect: American Science Fiction of the Nineteenth Century*. New York: Oxford UP, 1966.

———. *Robert A. Heinlein: America as Science Fiction*. New York: Oxford UP, 1980.

Freud, Sigmund. "A Child Is Being Beaten." *Standard Edition* 17:177-204.

———. "Medusa's Head." *Standard Edition* 18:273-75.

———. *The Standard Edition of the Complete Psychological Works of Sigmund Freud*. Ed. and trans. James Strachey. London: Hogarth, 1953-74.

Gallop, Jane. *Reading Lacan*. Ithaca, N.Y.: Cornell UP, 1985.

Heinlein, Robert A. *The Puppet Masters*. New York: New English Library, 1986.

Hertz, Neil. "Medusa's Head: Male Hysteria under Political Pressure." *Representations* 4 (Fall 1983): 27-54.

Huntington, John. "The Science Fiction of H. G. Wells." *Science Fiction: A Critical Guide*. Ed. Patrick Parrinder. New York: Longman, 1979. 34-50.

Irigaray, Luce. *Speculum of the Other Woman*. Trans. Gillian C. Gill. Ithaca, N.Y.: Cornell UP, 1985.

Jacobus, Mary, ed. *Reading Woman: Essays in Feminist Criticism*. New York: Columbia UP, 1986.

Jameson, Fredric. "Generic Discontinuities in SF: Aldiss' *Starship*." *Science Fiction Studies: Selected Articles on Science Fiction, 1973-75*. Ed. R. D. Mullen and Darko Suvin. Boston: Gregg Press, 1976. 28-39.

———. "Imaginary and Symbolic in Lacan: Marxism, Psychoanalytic Criticism, and the Problem of the Subject." *Yale French Studies* 55/56 (1977): 338-95.

———. *The Political Unconscious: Narrative as a Socially Symbolic Act*. Ithaca, N.Y.: Cornell UP, 1981.

———. "World-Reduction in Le Guin: The Emergence of Utopian Narrative." *Science Fiction Studies: Selected Articles on Science Fiction, 1973-75*. Ed. R. D. Mullen and Darko Suvin. Boston: Gregg Press, 1976. 251-60.

Kristeva, Julia. *Powers of Horror*. Trans. Leon S. Roudiez. New York: Columbia UP, 1982.

Lacan, Jacques. *Ecrits: A Selection*. Ed. and trans. Alan Sheridan. New York: Norton, 1977.

Parrinder, Patrick, ed. *Science Fiction: A Critical Guide*. New York: Longman, 1979.

———. *Science Fiction: Its Criticism and Teaching*. New York: Methuen, 1980.

Ryan, Michael. "The Marxian-Deconstruction Debate in Literary Theory." *NOR* 11.1 (1984): 29-35.

Scholes, Robert. *Structural Fabulation*. Notre Dame, Ind.: U of Notre Dame P, 1975.

Suvin, Darko. *Metamorphoses of Science Fiction*. New Haven, Conn.: Yale UP, 1979.

————. *Russian Science Fiction, 1956–1974: A Bibliography*. Elizabethantown, N.Y.: Dragon Press, 1976.

Wells, H. G. *The War of the Worlds*. New York: Signet, 1986.

A Brainy Afterword

Norman N. Holland

I feel quite superfluous at this juncture. Our book, like the conference from which it sprang, has been a rich one, full of ferment and excitement, to which I can add little. Freud invented psychoanalytic literary criticism ninety years before our conference, and we can see in a collection like this the great energy with which we still combine psychoanalytic psychology with the study of literature.

Our discipline's present seems large, but its future is immense. Perhaps the most useful thing I can do in this afterword is look around the corner at what I think that unknown tomorrow will bring. I want to tell you some things about the brain, because I think that's where the future of psychoanalysis and psychology lies. It is also where I've been writing recently, and it gives me a chance to plug my last two books, *The I* (1985), which tries to open up this new territory, and *The Brain of Robert Frost* (1988), which goes still further along the same lines.

The brain is where Freud began in his pre-psychoanalytic days. Today, we have a new science of the brain, and we literature-and-psychology people can find two things in this new knowledge: a confirmation of some psychoanalytic ideas and new directions for our enterprise.

For example, consider one of the axioms of psychoanalytic theory from almost its earliest days. As Milton put it in *Paradise Regained*, "The childhood shows the man, / As morning shows the day." Psychoanalytic metapsychology calls this the "developmental" or the "genetic" hypothesis: the experiences of infancy determine the character of the adult. Recently, very recently in fact—the first major conference in this field was held in the summer of 1986—neuroscientists have given us a new way of thinking about this principle of human development.

Research in the last few years has evolved the picture of a changing brain that first grows and then ungrows (Purves and Lichtman 153, 359–63). In one researcher's image, nature is like a sculptor of the brain. Nature first applies plaster (brain-stuff) to an armature provided by genetics, applying more than is needed but in roughly the shape that is desired. Then nature chips the excess away until the adult brain appears (Blakeslee).

All of the higher mammals that have been studied show this brain growth and ungrowth. The bigger the animal is and the longer it takes to develop from infant to adult, the greater is this growth and ungrowth relative to the rest of the brain. We humans, big as mammals go and with the longest period of dependency, are the best example of the rule (Purves and Hadley 404–06).

The human infant is born with all the neurons it is going to have, but few of the synapses. Then, in a spurt of dendritic and synaptic elaboration the number of connections increases by a factor of twenty, so that the infant's neurons acquire their full complement of synapses by age one year. The child's brain develops virtually all its potentially useful neural interconnections by the age of two, and then goes on to develop many more.

Moreover, the brains of children from three to eleven use much more energy (relatively) than adults' brains. Specifically, in the first year of life, the metabolic rate of the baby's brain (established by PET scan) is about two-thirds that of an adult brain. By the age of two, while the neurons have been branching and interconnecting, the child's brain metabolizes at the same rate as an adult's. Then, by three or four, the metabolic rate becomes twice that of an adult's. By the age of six or seven, a child's brain equals an adult's in weight and volume, but it uses twice as much energy, and it has twice the number of synaptic connections.

The human child's brain stays "supercharged" until early adolescence. Then, from eleven to fourteen, probably because of those famous (or infamous) hormones of "the awkward age," the metabolic rate begins to fall until it subsides to the adult level. Similarly, there are twice as many synaptic connections in the cortex of a child's brain as in an adult's. Then that number falls by half in early adolescence. Young children experience twice as much deep sleep as adults, and then from eleven to fourteen years of age, children move into adult sleep patterns.

Further, as is well known, a child's style of thinking differs from an adolescent's or an adult's. Young children can often propose brilliant concepts, but they cannot take them further. They cannot concentrate for long. They daydream, perhaps (these researchers suggest) because too many neural connections interfere with sustained logical thought. Possibly the adolescent changes in the brain explain why previously well-adjusted children can become schizophrenic in adolescence, or why children between four and ten can learn languages or musical instruments so much more easily than adults. The latency child has what has been called a "baseball averages" kind of learning, procedural learning, but (as Piaget found) it is only in adolescence that we learn to solve complex, abstract problems. A brain-injured child of three or four can recover speech pathways, but a similarly brain-damaged adolescent cannot (Blakeslee), because the period of growing and ungrowing is over, and the brain has much less capacity to make up its deficits.

What has happened by late adolescence, then, is that nature has grown a supercharged child's brain and then ungrown it to adult size. Nature first made the brain branch out into vast numbers of dendrites and synapses and then pruned them away in the course of bringing the human mammal from infancy to adulthood. What happened in that ungrowing process?

It is activity—experience, if you will—that determines both what will grow and what will ungrow. It is well known that a lack of activity in animals deprived of sensory input leads to a lack of development of connections in the brain. Conversely, "well-used neurons and synaptic connections seemed to release nerve growth factors, substances that help insure their survival." When a kitten's motor activity is blocked, its eye cells develop differently. In the same way, activity by the heart or by hormones can change the kind of chemical transmitter a given neuron is programmed to emit, as, for example, muscular activity promotes the growth of neurons in the spine (Henderson).

We grow the neural circuits we need to support our activities and experiences. Then once the neural circuits have grown, those that get more use generate substances that help them to survive. Neural circuits that get little or no use are sacrificed, probably in the interests of stabilizing the brain itself and reducing the energy consumption that the supercharged childhood brain had required (Barnes 155–56). Within the supercharged brain, there is a Darwinian competition among neurons and synapses.

In effect, to survive, nerves compete for a limited supply of such things as NGF (nerve growth factor). This competition went on all through the growing and ungrowing, so that when the brain was growing up to its supercharged level, those synapses that were used were favored and grew. Then in the ungrowing, the competition became even more intense: the synapses that were not used disappeared. Since those cells that survive are those we use the most, the effect of the competition is that we grow brains suited to the environment in which this particular human being has to survive. In this mechanism lies the extraordinary ability of the human animal to develop skills and habits so as to thrive in environments as different as the ice floe and the jungle, Wall Street and an English department (Easter 507–11).

Hence, in the nature-nurture, heredity-environment controversy, these researches prove that nurture, as well as nature, determines the *physiology* of the brain. In the earlier view, experience provided only the software, the programming, for the brain's already determined hardware (or, more properly, "wetware"). In principle, software could be easily changed, like any computer program. By contrast, the genes inalterably set the physical layout of the brain and the routes of synaptic contact.

In fact, the human brain has one hundred million million synapses. There are not enough genes, however, in our complement of genes, our genome, to account for this much complexity. The new discoveries resolve this inconsistency by a newer model that does not contradict the earlier, but radically complicates it. Genes determine overall aspects of brain architecture and wiring patterns, but factors outside the genome must change the details in the basic organization.

We need to think of three elements in any given action (such as the making and appreciating of literature): heredity, environment (culture), and personal activity. Brains are a genetic given, but they change because of life experiences, which in turn depend upon how the individual chooses among the various activities his or her environment (including culture) offers and demands. Brain functions do occupy sites, but the sites and the architecture of each brain may differ.

Childhood experience is the outside factor that shapes the final architecture of the individual brain. Evidently, then, as such psychoanalysts as Jonathan Winson and Morton Reiser are showing, this early growing and ungrowing is the "critical period" when (in an older terminology) the "infantile unconscious" is established or, in a newer terminology, both the conscious and unconscious, habitual processes of character or identity, come into being.

Experience causes the neural circuits that are used in childhood and latency to be strengthened, and then, in adolescence, experience causes the unused ones to be eliminated. Thereafter, all the rest of our lives, experience alters the brain, growing some connections and letting others die off, but slightly, not to the extraordinary degree experience does during the growing and ungrowing of the brain in childhood.

Since this changing the physiology of the brain takes place all through life, whatever you learn or experience changes the brain. It changes therefore what you bring to the next experience. As the great Soviet neuroscientist Aleksandr Luria bluntly wrote: "The principle of feedback is universal in the operation of the central nervous system" (40). That is, we have to take seriously the cybernetic model of human functioning in which physiology or past experience sets standards and hypotheses that we try out against the world. We get a return, compare it to our standard, and we modify our hypotheses and our behavior accordingly. This is the way we experience things: not, as a stimulus-response model would have it, directly from outside stimulus to inside response; rather, from the brain outward and only in reaction from the outside in.

Interestingly, for psychiatry departments, these new discoveries about the growing and ungrowing of the brain mean that the current split between pharmacological therapy and "the talking cure" is a split only if we focus entirely on the tactics of therapy. If we focus on the aim of the two therapies, there is no split, because the ultimate aim is the same in both: alteration of the brain. Chemicals change the brain quickly, willy-nilly, and massively, en bloc, not in particular details. Insight works in a different way, at a different rate, with a different efficacy and a different precision from medications, but it too changes the chemistry and functioning of the brain.

But what about those of us in literature-and-psychology? What does this new understanding of brain development mean to us?

Early experience leads to later personality. Well, we knew that, didn't we? But now we are seeing it in a much stronger way. We are learning about the inscribing of individuality on the brain. What we believed from reading Freud or Winnicott or Lichtenstein or Daniel Stern (perhaps even Lacan's "individual myth of the neurotic") now rests on an altogether different kind of evidence from that of couch or clinic. Now we have a body of physiological and neuroscientific evidence that buttresses our discipline. We can use psychoanalysis to interpret the details of a literary transaction. We can use this new knowledge about the brain to model the process of having an experience.

Literary scholars have long liked to insist on the importance of culture and particularly literary and linguistic culture to the making and recreation of literature. (A recent example is the "New Historicism"; an older one the old "literary history.") Now, again, we have a new way of understanding the importance of culture in literary experience: as shaping the early experiences that in turn shape the individual brain.

This presence of culture in the brain may imply that different cultures have different brains. For example, the Japanese have both a syllabic writing that is processed in the left half of the brain and a pictographic writing that is processed in the right. For the Japanese, then, verbal information comes in both halves, while for us it comes in only through the left brain. That may be why the Japanese can find meaning in sounds that are just noise to us, sounds like the chirping of a cricket or the dripping of water. Perhaps that is why Japanese art is so different from Western.

The neuroscientists are describing, quite literally, the "inscribing" of culture in the personality, the inscribing of language in our brains and even of what the ego-psychologists used to call the "average expectable environment." What we learn is that the presence of culture in our brains does not mean we are not there (as in current theoretical rhetoric about "the disappearance of the subject" or "the death of the author"). It means that culture takes its place in our minds, functioning through a physiological base (which is much the same for all individuals) but used in the service of conscious and unconscious desires that are unique for each individual. Japanese culture may differ from American, but within that large grouping, each individual Japanese differs from every other, because each has had different infantile (and later) experiences.

For that reason, I think the discovery of the growing and ungrowing of the synapses not only gives a new "visibility" to culture in our brains, but also radically reemphasizes the importance of the individual in literary and other experiences. Because brain structure depends on experience, no two brains are identical. Moreover—shades of Heraclitus!—any one brain is not the same from moment to moment, not quite the same, anyway. Theories of reading that talk about "the" meaning or texts as "generating meaning" or "the free play of language" or the "sliding of the signifier" or even plain "signifying" simply ignore the individuality and the activity of the mind that is doing the reading. They fly in the face of what we know about the functioning of the human brain, particularly the way our brains deal with language through feedback processes. The brain physiologists are confirming the account of reading given by psycholinguists and by psychologists of reading, which is altogether different from the idea of signifying which current literary theory takes from Saussure or the old New Criticism. Literary scholars, by clinging to the formalist idea of texts delivering fixed meanings or the Saussurean idea of signifying, may be creating a new scholasticism, like the old, out of touch with the science of its day.

All this goes to say that I think that because of these new discoveries, something exciting is happening to psychoanalysis and therefore to literary criticism based on psychoanalytic and other psychologies. All in all, it seems to me, literature-and-psychology can look forward to a fourth stage.

I have suggested in the past that literature-and-psychology, along with psychoanalysis, has progressed through three stages.[1] We can identify them by the terms each stage uses for explanation. The first psychoanalytic explanations came in terms of "the" conscious versus "the" unconscious, and this was the period of classical psychoanalysis. Next came ego-psychology and explanations in terms of the ego and its taskmasters. At the moment we are in a third stage, in which we explain mental events in terms of self and non-self, as in object relations theory, identity theory, Lacan's version of psychoanalysis, or the new American theories of narcissism. Now, I think, we are moving into a fourth stage of psychoanalytic thinking and necessarily, therefore, in literature-and-psychology. We are beginning to be able to place the insights of psychoanalysis in a much larger scientific context.

I know literary people do not go for scientific theories. (Wow, do I know that!) There is such great potential here, though, that I hope you will not let the scienticity of it all intimidate you. There are some thoroughly readable popular accounts of the new developments.[2] When you look at them, I think you will conclude, as I have, that over the next ten or fifteen years we will see psychoanalytic psychology enter a tremendously exciting new phase. Partly we are seeing a return to the biological and organic base that Freud sought, but with (of course) great differences. We will be able to trace psychological concepts as physiological things: anxiety or aggression as neurotransmitters; repetition compulsion as the sum of our well-worn neural pathways; cultural codes and identity as structures in the brain. If you will permit the pun, this is heady stuff.

More importantly, however, we are beginning to see psychoanalysis no longer isolated, but a contributing member of a whole cluster of other sciences: psychology, linguistics, psycholinguistics, artificial intelligence, systems theory, cybernetics, and neurophysiology. These are

"harder" sciences. They provide stronger evidence than the always
shaky clinical claims of psychoanalysis. These other sciences describe
vision, anatomy, ways of knowing, memory, processes of perception and
cognition. They will apply to people in general. Psychoanalysis will
supply, as it always has, holistic methods of interpreting behavior, concepts of unconscious functioning, and especially a way of talking about
the individual. Together these various disciplines will—to some extent,
have already begun to—yield a general science of the mind. I hope that,
at our next International, we from literature-and-psychology will have
joined the colloquy.

Notes

1. See my discussions in "Literary Interpretations and Three Phases of Psychoanalysis"
221–33, and *The I* 331–63.

2. See Howard Gardner's *The Mind's New Science* and Richard M. Restak's *The Brain*,
the picture book that accompanied the recent educational television series. For psychoanalysts and others with medical training, I would recommend Jay E. Harris, *Clinical Neuroscience: From Neuroanatomy to Psychodynamics.*

Works Cited

Barnes, Deborah M. "Brain Architecture: Beyond Genes." *Science* 253 (11 July
    1986): 155–56.

Blakeslee, Sandra. "Rapid Changes Seen in Young Brain." *New York Times* 24
    June 1986: C1, C10.

Easter, S. S., Jr., et al. "The Changing View of Neural Specificity." *Science* 230
    (1 Nov. 1985): 507–11.

Gardner, Howard. *The Mind's New Science: A History of the Cognitive Revolu-
    tion.* New York: Basic, 1985.

Harris, Jay E. *Clinical Neuroscience: From Neuroanatomy to Psychodynamics.*
    New York: Human Sciences, 1986.

Henderson, Christopher E., et al. "Increase of Neurite-Promoting Activity for
    Spinal Neurons in Muscles of 'Paralysé' Mice and Tenotomised Rats." *De-
    velopmental Brain Research* 25 (1986): 65–70.

Holland, Norman N. *The I.* New Haven: Yale UP, 1985.

———. "Literary Interpretation and Three Phases of Psychoanalysis." *Critical
    Inquiry* 3 (1976): 221–33.

Luria, Aleksandr Romanovich. *Higher Cortical Functions in Man.* 2nd ed.
    Trans. Basi Haigh. New York: Basic, 1980.

Purves, Dale, and Robert D. Hadley. "Changes in the Dendritic Branching of
    Adult Mammalian Neurons." *Nature* 315 (30 May 1985): 404–06.

Purves, Dale, and Jeff W. Lichtman. *Principles of Neural Development.* Sunderland, Mass.: Sinauer Associates, 1985.

Reiser, Morton F. *Mind, Brain, Body: Toward a Convergence of Psychoanalysis and Neurobiology.* New York: Basic, 1984.

Restak, Richard M. *The Brain.* New York: Basic, 1984.

———. *The Infant Mind.* Garden City, N.Y.: Doubleday, 1987.

Winson, Jonathan. *Brain and Psyche: The Biology of the Unconscious.* Garden City, N.Y.: Anchor Press/Doubleday, 1985.

Contributors

Vera J. Camden is Assistant Professor of English at Kent State University where she is also Associate Director of the Center for Literature and Psychoanalysis. She is a candidate at the Cleveland Psychoanalytic Institute and has published on Crashaw, Bunyan and Puritan women's autobiography.

Robert Silhol is Professor of American Literature at the University of Paris VII where he also directs research on psychoanalysis. He is the author of *Les Tyrans tragiques, Le Texte du désir*, and a novel, *Autobiographie d'une étoile égoïste*.

Peter L. Rudnytsky is Assistant Professor of English and Comparative Literature at Columbia University and a Fulbright Western European Regional Scholar (1988–89). He is the author of *Freud and Oedipus* and has served as guest editor of *American Imago* and *The Psychoanalytic Review*.

Frederick Wyatt is Professor Emeritus of Psychology at the University of Michigan and Professor (h.c.) at Freiburg University in West Germany. He is a Training and Supervising Analyst in the German Psychoanalytic Association, Fellow of the American Psychological Association, and a member of the International Psychoanalytic Association. He has numerous publications on psychoanalysis and literature, psychoanalysis and history, the theory of ego-psychology, the history of the psycho-analytic movement, and related topics.

Jan Ackerman is Lecturer in English at Pennsylvania State University where she is also editor for the *Bulletin* of the Center for Psychoanalytic Studies.

Ellie Ragland-Sullivan, Professor of English at the University of Florida, is the author of *Rabelais and Panurge: A Psychological Approach to Literary Character* and *Jacques Lacan and the Philosophy of Psychoanalysis.* She is also founder and editor-in-chief of *The Newsletter of the Freudian Field.*

Diane Richard-Allerdyce is a doctoral candidate at the University of Florida, completing her dissertation on Anaïs Nin.

Virginia Blum, doctoral candidate at Brown University, is completing her dissertation on the "fictional child" in literature. She has published on Edith Wharton.

Carol Mossman is Assistant Professor of French at the University of Maryland. She is the author of *The Narrative Matrix: A Study of Stendhal's 'Le Rouge et le Noir'.*

Nancy Blake is Professor of Literature at the University of Montpellier (France) and a psychotherapist. Coeditor of the literary journal *Delta* and of the psychoanalytical journal *Dires,* she is also author of *Ezra Pound et l'imagisme* and *Henry James: écriture et absence.*

Elise Miller is a Lecturer in English at the University of California at Berkeley where she is also finishing a master's degree in clinical psychology. She has published on Sarah Orne Jewett and Henry James.

Jeffrey Berman, Associate Professor of English at SUNY Albany, is trained as a Research Scholar at the Training Institute of the National Psychological Association for Psychoanalysis. He is the author of *The Talking Cure: Literary Representation of Psychoanalysis* and *Joseph Conrad: Writing as Rescue.* His essay in this volume will be included in a forthcoming book, *Narcissism and the Novel.*

David Willbern is Associate Professor of English at SUNY Buffalo where he was Director of the Center for the Psychological Study of the Arts and is currently Associate Dean of the Faculty of Arts and Letters. He has numerous publications on Shakespeare, Renaissance drama, and psychoanalytic theory.

Andrew Gordon is Associate Professor of English at the University of Florida where he is also Associate Chairman of the Institute for the Psychological Study of the Arts. He is the author of *An American Dreamer: A Psychoanalytic Study of the Fiction of Norman Mailer.*

Terrence E. Holt, Assistant Professor of English at Rutgers University, is author of the novel *The Universe Next Door* as well as short stories and articles on science fiction and myth.

Norman Holland is Milbaur Professor of English at the University of Florida where he is also the Director of the Institute for the Psychological Study of the Arts. His most recent books include *Five Readers' Reading, Laughing: A Psychology of Humor,* and *The I.*

Index